Migration, Mobility, and Sojourning in Cross-Cultural Films

Migration, Mobility, and Sojourning in Cross-Cultural Films

Interculturing Cinema

Ishani Mukherjee
Maggie Griffith Williams

LEXINGTON BOOKS
Lanham • Boulder • New York • London

Published by Lexington Books
An imprint of The Rowman & Littlefield Publishing Group, Inc.
4501 Forbes Boulevard, Suite 200, Lanham, Maryland 20706
www.rowman.com

6 Tinworth Street, London SE11 5AL, United Kingdom

Copyright © 2021 by The Rowman & Littlefield Publishing Group, Inc.

All rights reserved. No part of this book may be reproduced in any form or by any electronic or mechanical means, including information storage and retrieval systems, without written permission from the publisher, except by a reviewer who may quote passages in a review.

British Library Cataloguing in Publication Information Available

Library of Congress Cataloging-in-Publication Data

Names: Mukherjee, Ishani, 1979– author. | Williams, Maggie Griffith, 1980– author.
Title: Migration, mobility, and sojourning in cross-cultural films : interculturing cinema / Ishani Mukherjee, Maggie Griffith Williams.
Description: Lanham : Lexington Books, 2021. | Includes bibliographical references and index. | Summary: "This book uses an intercultural communication lens to analyze six cross-cultural films and their depictions of migration, mobility, and the resulting intercultural communications. It argues that the results of these complex and stressful moments of conflict include personal growth, oppression, familial or social separation, and loss of identity."—Provided by publisher.
Identifiers: LCCN 2020036277 (print) | LCCN 2020036278 (ebook) | ISBN 9781498587686 (cloth) | ISBN 9781498587709 (pbk)
 ISBN 9781498587693 (ebook)
Subjects: LCSH: Intercultural communication in motion pictures. | Emigration and immigration in motion pictures. | Migration, Internal, in motion pictures. | Culture in motion pictures.
Classification: LCC PN1995.9.I55 M85 2021 (print) | LCC PN1995.9.I55 (ebook) | DDC 791.43/655—dc23
LC record available at https://lccn.loc.gov/2020036277
LC ebook record available at https://lccn.loc.gov/2020036278

Contents

Acknowledgments   vii

1   Introduction   1

PART I: MIGRATION: GLOBALIZATION, CULTURAL ADAPTATION, AND VALUE ORIENTATION   7

2   The African Doctor: Migration, Medicine, and Racialization in a French Village   9

3   A Better Life: Immigration Industrial Complex, Conflict Styles, and Facework in a Mexican-American Family   31

PART II: MOVEMENTS: COLONIALISM, POSTCOLONIALISM, AND CONFLICT   55

4   Rabbit Proof Fence: Kidnapping, Colonization, and Segregation of Australian Aboriginals   57

5   A Borrowed Identity: Religious and Ethnic Relationships in an Israeli High School   73

PART III: SOJOURNING: NON/VERBAL COMMUNICATION, CULTURAL DIMENSIONS, AND INTERCULTURAL BARRIERS   93

6   Outsourced: Holi, Kali, and Capitalism in an Indian American Call Center   95

7	Front Cover: Fashion and Fluid Sexualities in an Intra-Asian Relationship	119
8	Afterword	141

References	145
Index	159
About the Authors	165

Acknowledgments

While this book was written by the two authors, it was a community effort with support and guidance along the way. We would like to take this opportunity to thank our partners, Sandeep and Jermaine, for their unwavering support as we embarked on this project. Their encouragement for our professional goals has been significant in making our book idea a reality. We would be remiss if we did not thank our boys, Siddharth, Jackson, and Malcolm for keeping us grounded, driving us a little crazy, climbing on our laps, interrupting our FaceTime meetings, yet being troopers that let their mommies get enough work time to complete this book!

We would like to thank Steve Jones (University of Illinois at Chicago), Zizi Papacharissi (University of Illinois at Chicago), Rebecca Lind (University of Illinois at Chicago), Roy Christopher (Savannah College of Art and Design), Dale Herbeck (Northeastern University), and Thomas K. Nakayama (Northeastern University) for their advice and guidance on book publishing. We are also thankful to the respected scholars who have offered their endorsements of our book. Their support has been very meaningful to us. Moreover, we are deeply grateful to our many friends, both personal and professional, and our parents and families for their positivity and encouragement.

Finally, the editorial team at Lexington also deserves many thanks for their patience and support, including Nicolette Amstutz and Jessica Tepper. We appreciate and value the reviewers' feedback and we are grateful for their critical comments and suggestions.

Chapter 1

Introduction

APPROACHING INTERCULTURAL COMMUNICATION THROUGH FILM

The United States is an increasingly diverse nation. What keeps adding to its diversity is the constant ebb and flow of people across its borders—people who bring in, or take their own cultures, experiences, struggles, and identities to new physical and ideological places. The country is historically majority-white, but by 2044 it is projected to become a majority–minority nation, and as early as 2020 for the child population (Colby & Ortman, 2015). Despite the growing diversity and the fact that across the globe people increasingly live in densely populated urban areas ("World's population," 2014), American communities are notoriously segregated (Rothstein, 2017). Work and travel may be where people encounter the most diversity (Martin & Nakayama, 2013), but knowing how to navigate those spaces and relationships is difficult. With limited opportunities, resources or skills to interact with people who are culturally different in our communities, and the simple fact that many of us are not able to travel around the world, media becomes an important avenue for learning about other cultures. Moreover, in the midst of the COVID-19 global pandemic, even those with the resources to travel are restricted from doing so and spending time at home with media is among the few ways that we can engage with different cultures.

Cinema that depicts cross-cultural interplay can be of tremendous help here—it can help individuals learn how to handle intercultural communication as a result of mobility, migration, and globalization. But, how are these kinds of relationships, experiences, and movements depicted in popular cinema? What are films teaching audiences about how to communicate, behave, or relate to culturally different individuals in moments that are stressful, confusing, oppressive, and/or ambiguous?

These are some pressing questions that we want to address, if not answer, in this book. In this book, we analyze a collection of six cross-cultural films that serve as sites where selected intercultural communication theories and constructs intersect. Specifically, this book examines how popular cross-cultural films present migration, mobility, and intercultural relationships, uncovering patterns and trends in the way that these topics are portrayed. For instance, white savior narratives appear in some of the films we analyze, and migratory spaces as sites of cultural, ethnic, social, racial, and gender conflicts are also a common pattern found across these media texts. To encode into larger themes, the myriad patterns of mobility and migration, we decoded select cross-cultural films and then divided this book into three parts. Each part is dedicated to two films, or two case studies, that explore how intercultural communication functions in storytelling and in the movement or stasis of the characters' relationships. Using intercultural communication as the conceptual paradigm, we visit and revisit key concepts including cultural adaptation, value orientations, non/verbal communication, cross-cultural barriers, post/colonialism, conflict and social justice, and how they intersect within contexts of migration, mobility, and sojourning. In the process, we cut up and critique these cross-cultural artifacts and identity movements for how they inform audiences about real life patterns and experiences.

THE THREE THEMES

Global movements, within and across borders, is an oft-explored theme in popular films from Hollywood and beyond. We have paid homage to this cinematic trend by selecting and locating six cross-cultural films within three key themes that tie into global movements, their complexities, and implications. While a few chosen films focus on migrants' experiences of culture shock, cultural assimilation, and/or integration, other films focus on cultural identities that are in transition within contexts of social mobility and movements. Some of the selected films explore the short-term intercultural impact that sojourners experience in unfamiliar cultural spaces and in different social positions. In the films we analyzed for this title, migration and mobility, and their resulting intercultural communications are depicted as complex and stressful moments of conflict, with mixed outcomes ranging from productive personal growth to endless oppression, familial or social separation, and loss of identity.

Part I of this book follows the theme of 'Migration,' and charts how globalization, cultural adaptations, and diverse value orientations within intercultural communication are presented in the cross-cultural films, *The African Doctor* (2016) and *A Better Life* (2011). Chapter 2 examines racism, othering, culture shock, and complex migration experiences through the lens of the French-Congolese comedy-drama, *The African Doctor* (2016), cowritten by famous French rapper Kamini Zantoko and directed by Julien Rambaldi. It tells the story of the Zantoko family arriving in a French village in 1975 from a politically unstable Zaire, their struggles to adjust to rural life, and their frustrations on being rejected by locals. The film addresses issues of the racialization and othering of migrants in French society. While the Zantokos try to find a new home in France moving from phases of culture shock to cultural adjustment, the film presents immigration as stressful and filled with conflict, but also as an experience that can produce positive outcomes for both migrants and hosts.

Chapter 3 unpacks the American drama *A Better Life* (2011), based on Roger L. Simon's story and directed by Chris Weitz. It charts the Galindo family's migration challenges with Carlos, the father, an unauthorized laborer from Mexico and his teenage son Luis, who is a U.S. citizen, as they try to build a better life in Los Angeles. The film shows us the impact of situational factors (Sorrells, 2016), such as the desperation of poverty and unauthorized status, and the negotiation of culturally different conflict styles and facework. Underlying the story about a father–son relationship is also a story about the repercussions of the immigration industrial complex (Golash-Boza, 2009) that becomes like an additional character in the film affecting all relationships. In this film, migration-related conflict, stress, oppression, and familial separation are reflective of the current climate of legal uncertainty and anxiety that exists among the unauthorized in the United States.

Part II of this book examines the theme of 'Movements,' and explores how the mobilities of colonialism, postcolonialism, and conflict in intercultural communication are apparent in the cross-cultural films, *Rabbit-Proof Fence* (2002) and *A Borrowed Identity* (2014). Chapter 4 pays homage to a true story inspired Australian drama *Rabbit-Proof Fence* (2002), based on Doris Pilkington Garimara's book, *Follow the Rabbit-Proof Fence* (1996), and directed by Phillip Noyce. Set in the 1930s, the film follows the escape of three half-caste Aboriginal girls, part of the 'Stolen Generation,' and their arduous journey across the West Australian desert after they were forcefully taken from their families to a Christian school that would teach them to assimilate into white society as domestic workers. The film's symbolic use of the fence and the movement of children belonging to the 'Stolen Generation' marked a cultural breach and countermobility against the colonial discourses of racial segregation (Sorrells, 2016; Tilbrook, 2007). The movements shown in the film are multilayered, and across geophysical planes, generational spaces, racial labels, and colonial realities, as three half-caste Aboriginal girls move in search of their lost cultural identities despite oppression and familial separation.

Chapter 5 examines conflict, compromise, and constant movements of cultural identities along interreligious and interethnic lines in the Israeli drama *A Borrowed Identity* (2002), based on Sayed Kashua's book, *Dancing Arabs* (2002) and directed by Eran Riklis. The story of the film centers on a gifted, Palestinian-Muslim boy, Eyad, who is brought up in a small Israeli town—othered because of his minority ethnicity and religion. Palestine has long been the subject of geopolitical conflict, and its mobile identity as an autonomous nation within the Arab states has been historically questioned and subject to religious fundamentalisms (Sorrells, 2016), much like the identity movements of the protagonist in the film. This film text surfaces as a site of conflict, oppressive situations, familial and social separations, and religious anxiety for the protagonist, whose identity is continuously moving, changing, rejecting, and adapting to intercultural challenges.

Part III of our book takes up the theme of 'Sojourning,' revisiting cultural dimensions and adaptations, and addressing how non/verbal communication and intercultural communication barriers are evidenced in the cross-cultural films, *Outsourced* (2006) and *Front Cover* (2015).

Chapter 6 explores global capitalism, U-curve model of adaptation, and de/stabilization of interethnic stereotypes in the Indo-American comedy-drama *Outsourced* (2006), directed by John Jeffcoat. The film tells the story of Todd, an American business sojourner, who is sent to his company's Indian call center to train local employees in ways commensurate with U.S. corporate culture, but who eventually gets acclimated to the Indians he befriends and their lived insights on India. The film shows how economic globalization has pushed multinational corporations to outsource services to nations where labor is less expensive, but has also intensified the necessity of intercultural awareness and understanding in business contexts. *Outsourced* (2006) touts familiar South Asian and American stereotypes, but also challenges and changes cross-cultural assumptions for most characters and their relationships within a diverse workplace and beyond.

Chapter 7 reflects on movements of contested sexualities, ethnic stereotyping, and identity ascription within Asian cultures (Sorrells, 2016; Chavez, 2013) in the Asian American romance-drama *Front Cover* (2015), written and directed by Ray Yeung. It tells the story of a gay Chinese American male, Ryan, who works with and embarks on a romantic relationship with Ning, a Chinese actor who is sojourning in New York. As both deal with relational complexities, Ryan and Ning's sexualities seem rooted in the former's rejection and latter's acceptance of their Chinese heritage, suggesting that "intercultural relationships are often sites where notions of sexuality and sexual identities intersect, collide and coalesce with ethnic, racial, religious, and national cultural differences" (Sorrells, 2016, p. 105). In presenting intercultural dynamics around sexuality, the film concurrently reinforces and challenges ethnic othering, stereotypes, and cultural assumptions in the context of sojourning and tourism.

WHY THIS BOOK, AND WHY NOW?

In an age of growing social, cultural, and political uncertainties, this book provides readers and audiences a way to engage with timely topics and communication contexts that are controversial, complex, or divisive. Rather than using examples from current news, social media or historical events that may be subjective, scattered, or alienating, films provide an ideal narrative distance for audiences to connect with similar contexts but in more academic, objective, and coherent ways. A compelling reason that we selected the media genre of popular cinema to represent migration, mobility, and intercultural contact is the power of relatable topics and visual storytelling that helps readers and audiences better understand and apply complex concepts.

Using films to explore and explain intercultural communication is also an effective strategy for engaging students and scholars (e.g., Martin & Davis, 2001; Park & Finch, 2016). Learning about intercultural complexities, migration, and/or media frames is not only important for students of communication and film, but also those studying international relations, international business, history, and sociology, among other disciplines. We encourage an intersectional and dialectical reading of the cross-cultural films featured in this book, and to do that we have addressed pertinent intercultural communication constructs using interpretive and critical lenses to frame each chapter. We suggest that readers first watch the six films and then use this book as a theory and critical analysis guide to engage with the films in a deeper way. For example, an educator could include these six films in their course syllabus and have students read the corresponding chapters after having watched the films, which would also aid in more interactive and in-depth class discussions. We hope this book will prove seminal for exploring the fields of intercultural and interpersonal communication, visual and mobility studies, culture and media studies, as well as related areas in the liberal arts, humanities, and social sciences.

As coauthors of this book, we selected the films through a combination of our pedagogical experiences of viewing and analyzing them, as well as searching for additional films that present a range of cultures and intercultural dynamics. To help our students comprehend and be critical of various scholarly concepts and theories, we regularly use cross-cultural films as texts in the different communication courses we teach. In our experience, students often become invested in the characters and narrative threads of the film, but we hope the critical analyses provided in the following chapters will focus readers' attention on the complex and sometimes subtle ways that certain intercultural communication situations arise in people's lives and through the process of their global movements. In addition, our research agenda for the last decade has frequently crossed paths and led us to collaborate on topics covering popular media and intercultural communication, visual cultures, mobility, and social change, as well as marginalized groups, migrations, and media activism. Having studied, researched, and taught intercultural communication and film/media studies for over a decade, both in the United States and abroad, we are excited to share our critical-cultural scholarship with you.

Accessing the films was itself a study in mobility and movement in that we viewed them on a variety of streaming platforms, at times finding that a film was no longer accessible on one platform and needing to locate it elsewhere. If instructors want to make these films available to students, they can work with their institutional libraries, or use institution-supported online services like Kanopy to provide streaming access for selected films. It is also common practice for college students to use streaming services like Netflix, Amazon Prime, and YouTube to consume media of their choice (Maruca, 2019). Watching films and media in mobile ways has, in fact, taken on a new meaning in the midst of the COVID-19 pandemic, offering viewers access to content via low subscription costs, free and paid streaming platforms, and sometimes the ability "to download content for later use without wifi" (Maruca, 2019), in case of connectivity problems. Notwithstanding internet accessibility issues, the 'mobile' aspect of streaming services (anywhere and anytime) lends itself well to the book's goal and focus.

For educators, finding films that are compelling and inspiring to student audiences is crucial and the films analyzed here meet that need. These films and our corresponding analyses establish the value and relevance of film for opening discussions of real-world issues. The films selected as case studies for this book, and their accompanying intercultural communication frames, are by no means exhaustive or inclusive of all film genres or conceptual categories that explore global cultural issues. Rather, the chosen films are intended to function as an illustrative microcosm of the types of popular culture or cinematic artifacts that audiences are exposed to and invite analysis, criticism, and/or corroboration of the messages contained therein.

Part I

MIGRATION

GLOBALIZATION, CULTURAL ADAPTATION, AND VALUE ORIENTATION

Chapter 2

The African Doctor
Migration, Medicine, and Racialization in a French Village

As Seyolo Zantoko drives his children to their first day at their new school in rural France, he reminds them about how he grew up in Zaire as an orphan and worked hard to become a medical doctor. He insists that they must also be successful in school—bad grades will result in punishment, he explains [12:34]. Seyolo then says: "Only education matters. Especially when you're Black." His young son, Kamini, responds by asking, "Why is it harder when you're Black?" After a knowing glance is exchanged between Seyolo, and his wife Anne in the front seat, the school bell rings and Seyolo rushes the children to school before he can answer. Kamini and his sister, Sivi, enter the schoolyard and are met with stares, racist insults, and laughter from the other children. They may not yet understand why, but they quickly experience how, at least in rural France at the time, things are "harder when you're Black."

The 2016 comedy-drama, *The African Doctor*, cowritten by French rapper Kamini Zantoko and directed by Julien Rambaldi, tells the story of Kamini's family arriving in the rural French village of Marly-Gomont in 1975, from what was then Zaire, and the struggles they faced in becoming accepted. In the film the characters mostly speak in French, with few spoken instances of Lingala, a regional language of the Democratic Republic of Congo (Zaire). To clarify, the dialogues quoted in this chapter have been taken from the film's English subtitles. Dr. Seyolo Zantoko (Kamini's father) turns down a prominent position in Zaire, fearing the political corruption and economic turmoil in his country under the absolute dictatorship of President Mobutu Sésé Seko. He accepts a position as the village doctor in Marly-Gomont in hopes of gaining French citizenship and providing a better future for his children in France. Locals in Marly-Gomont are afraid, having never met Black people before, and are unwilling to accept Dr. Zantoko as their physician. The film addresses issues of racism, racialization of migrants in French society, and "construction of the 'Other'" (Sorrells, 2016, p. 61). The villagers mark the Zantoko family as 'Other,' placing themselves as superior, and preferring to travel long distances to visit a white, French doctor rather than see Dr. Zantoko who is close to home.

In the film, migration is depicted as stressful and filled with conflict, but a life-altering experience nonetheless that can produce positive outcomes for both migrants and hosts. Particularly from an intercultural communication perspective, the film reveals micro-level theories of migration at work, as the Zantoko family experience different levels of the U-curve theory of adaptation (Lysgaard, 1955), including anticipation and culture shock upon arriving in Marly-Gomont, and adjustment toward the end. In terms of meso-level theories of intercultural adaptation, the challenge that the family faces can be attributed to their lack of a supportive migrant network in their host country (Sorrells, 2016). Eventually, the Zantoko family are accepted by locals, and achieve intercultural transformation (Sorrells, 2016), while balancing their complex cultural identities.

In this chapter, we begin with a brief historical overview of the political situations in Zaire and France in the 1970s and explain how cultural adaptation works in long-term migration situations, after which we move into our case study analysis of the film using the aforementioned conceptual framework.

ZAIRE IN THE 1970s: AUTHENTICITY AND NATIONALISM

Migrant mobilities in *The African Doctor* (2016) are obliquely framed within a macro-context of intercultural conflicts and nationalist politics that governed Zaire in the 1970s. The film's backstory also connects to the policies of racialization and integration that were dominant in French society at the time the Zantoko family moved to Marly-Gomont. The present Democratic Republic of Congo was called Zaire (officially, the Republic of Zaire) from 1971 to 1997. President Joseph Désiré Mobutu of the Popular Movement of the Revolution party (*Mouvement Populaire de la Révolution*) took over as a totalitarian leader in 1965 following a peaceful coup d'état. He renamed the country to signify a postcolonial shift from an Afro-Belgian identity to its native Central African roots. The coup d'état was a part of the Congo Crisis, a chaotic period of "regional secessions, intervention by several foreign countries and extended domestic turmoil" that Congo faced after gaining independence from Belgium in 1960, up until Mobutu came to power in 1965 (Gibbs, 1991, p. 77). Military and civil unrest, ethnic wars, Congo's role as a sub-Saharan ally to America during the Cold War, and a vehicle of Belgium's neocolonial agenda that preferred race-based hierarchies in Congolese administration and trade resulted in it being labeled the "first 'failed state'" (Reno, 2006, p. 44; Gibbs, 1991).

In pre-Mobutu Congo, advances in industrialization and modernization had been made under Belgian colonial rule, but without Congolese participation (Reno, 2006). This became a cause for concern for Congolese nationalists. Before gaining independence in 1960, nonwhite professionals in Congo were few and far between, with "only 16 university graduates among the country's indigenous population" (Reno, 2006, p. 45). Nationalists in newly independent Congo, among whom President Mobutu was a forerunner, saw the potential to "take over a Western-dominated economy and redirect these resources" to create a modern and indigenous African nation (Reno, 2006, p. 45). From some perspectives the indigenous movement within Congolese society, and Mobutu's absolutist politics, were seen as largely effective. His party's mobilization of indigenous authenticity was considered a call to "cultural nationalism and nativism . . . to combat the sense of cultural inferiority that was inculcated by colonial domination" (Kannyo, 1979, p. 61).

During the Mobutu era Zaire moved rapidly toward modernization that lasted until the 1970s (Reno, 2006). At the time Mobutu advocated a return to *Zairianization*, or a move to authentic Zairian nationalism. He denounced regional and tribal differences through his authenticity policy that stressed the need for Zaire's citizens to be proud of their precolonial cultural identity (Kisangani & Scott Bobb, 2010). This was accompanied by the Africanization of names of Zaire's people and places, including its president who adopted the name Mobutu Sésé Seko and authorized a nationalist rhetoric for Zaire combining "patronage politics with more formal state-building projects" (Reno, 2006, p. 43). Political theorist Edward Kannyo (1979) analyzes this authentic Zairian nationalism as Mobutu's intended movement toward "the 'indigenization' of the political and economic structures of Zaire without altering them to provide for a more egalitarian and democratic socioeconomic system" (p. 61)

However, during the 1980s the same progressive ruler of Zaire had become corrupt and the state was in decline (Reno, 2006). It was during this time of governmental tyranny and "spiralling economic decline in the mid-1970s because of economic and political mismanagement" that many Congolese-Zairian families and professionals migrated to Europe, including to France and Belgium in search of different opportunities (MacGaffey, 2005, p. 552), much like the protagonists in the film.

FRANCE IN THE 1970s: RACIALIZATION AND INTEGRATION

Like many other countries, France allowed migrant workers to enter the country in order to fill gaps in labor needs throughout the latter half of the

1800s and early 1900s. In fact, immigration was a key factor in the evolution of France's economy through the mid-1900s, with labor migration being perceived as essential to post-Second World War economic recovery (Ogden, 1991). Simultaneously, a significant change in France's economic system involved the shift during the twentieth century from a rural to largely urban society, and this shift is depicted in *The African Doctor* (2016) right from the beginning. In an opening scene, Seyolo's classmates notice the mayor of Marly-Gomont (which a graduate describes as, "some god-forsaken town") come yet again to recruit "a sucker to bury out there." In other words, rural villages such as Marly-Gomont, as opposed to urban centers such as Paris, are perceived as backward and hopeless where a young professional goes to see their career die. Anne Zantoko herself adheres to this preference for urban over rural life throughout the film as well. This shift in economic and social structures, along with changes in immigration policies, sets the stage for the Zantoko family's arrival in France.

French immigration policy, especially postwar policy, focused on recruitment of migrants who were perceived as "assimilable" to French culture, with a particular preference for Italians (Ogden, 1991, p. 298). During the 1950s and 1960s, with waves of independence movements in former colonies, migrants from African nations became more frequent, especially those from Algeria, a former French colony (Hamilton, Simon & Veniard, 2004). By the mid-1970s, however, France (along with many other Western European countries) began efforts to stop immigration into the country. In fact, since that time, the country's immigration policies have mostly been focused on discouraging migration (Guiraudon, 2001). Additionally, changes in the French economy combined with high unemployment during the latter part of the 1900s resulted in French employers not needing to rely on foreign workers, and "high unemployment [feeding] xenophobic sentiments in public opinion" (Guiraudon, 2001). In the film, the Zantoko family migrates to Marly-Gomont in 1975—right in the midst of these political and economic changes.

Integration of migrants in France is not always an easy thing. In recent decades, there was the so-called headscarf (and other overt religious garb) ban of 2004 and in 2011 France was the first country to ban full face veils ("The Islamic veil," 2018). Such policies and other actions by the state have led some to describe the country as "a 'laboratory' for discriminatory laws targeting minorities, particularly Muslims" (Hussain, 2019). When the host country seems unwelcome to migrants, it is more difficult for those migrants to integrate or assimilate.

Integration and how social boundaries are drawn is a key focus of Onasch's (2017) analysis of a French civic integration program. Racialization and othering through assumptions about everything from dress to gender relations that bubble under the surface of the program Onasch (2017) analyzed ultimately undermine its purpose of integrating non-European migrants into European, specifically French, culture. The author argues that the very existence of programs such as the one analyzed are "premised, in part, on the idea that many migrants possess cultures that are incompatible with those of many European nation-states and must be shed before they can integrate successfully" (Onasch, 2017, p. 578).

The boundaries around who is considered French, and who is not, form the basis of such integration programs, and these boundaries may be related to institutions (e.g., citizenship) and they can also be symbolic. These kinds of more opaque, symbolic boundaries impact to what extent a migrant is able to integrate into the host nation (Onasch, 2017). The non-European migrants who are typically the focus of integration programs come from countries in the Global South and "while racial formations . . . shift over time and space . . . the over-all relationship between European and non-European remains and provides a set of anchoring poles" (Onasch, 2017, p. 579). The basic assumption of these racial formations is hierarchical with Europeans being superior to non-Europeans (Onasch, 2017)—a type of *othering*.

Othering is the process of reinforcing and reproducing "distinctions, dominance, and subordination against those without power" and it appears when "one group emphasizes a commonality, while belittling the lack of that commonality in the other" (Williams & Korn, 2017, p. 23; Al-Saji, 2010; Johnson et al., 2004; Said, 1978). Othering can happen on the basis of gender, race, religion, and any number of identities. Racialization is a type of othering centered around presumptions of race that is often tied to physical traits such as skin color, attire, accents, and "it normalizes unfair treatment of the othered group" (Williams & Korn, 2017, p. 24). It is important to note that racialization is not solely a type of othering on the basis of skin color—rather it can "essentialize cultural and religious attributes" as well (Onasch, 2017, p. 579).

In the case of the Zantoko family, however, the racism and othering they experience is largely centered on skin color and presumptions of cultural differences. Seyolo and his family are Christian like most of the villagers in the film. That is, while France has a fraught history with the integration of non-Christians into the culture, the fact of the Zantoko's shared religious identity, not to mention their shared love of soccer, becomes a thread that the characters use to begin weaving together intercultural relationships.

INTERCULTURAL ADAPTATION IN MIGRANT MOVEMENTS

Movement of migrants across the globe and the intercultural adaptation processes that they undergo, as we find the Zantoko family experience in differing degrees, can be charted across three levels: macro (large), micro (individual), meso (intermediate) levels. *Intercultural adaptation*, or *acculturation*, can be defined as the process by which migrants adapt to life in the host society, both by "maintaining one's own cultural identity" and by "maintaining relationships with other groups in one's new culture" (Jandt, 2016, p. 303; Berry, Kim & Bosky, 1987). In this chapter we look at selective micro- and meso-level processes of cultural adaptation that long-term migrants like the Zantokos encounter in host countries.

Kathryn Sorrells advocates a multilevel analysis of migration patterns to make better sense of the "structural inequities and sociocultural networks that circumscribe migrants' process of cultural adaptation" (2016, p. 134). Micro-level theories study the role of interpersonal and individual dimensions of intercultural adaptation. A commonly adopted micro-level theory is the *U-curve model of adaptation*, which we approach here in the context of long-term migration. The U-curve model, developed by Sverre Lysgaard in 1955, which posits that migrants experience relatively predictable phases of adjustment to the new society, a pattern which resembles the letter 'U.' The three phases of Lysgaard's (1955) U-curve model are as follows: (1) *anticipation*, characterized by excitement, apprehension, and perhaps a sense of adventure about spending time in the new culture; (2) *culture shock* (bottom of the curve), characterized by disorientation, loneliness, and a sense of unhappiness; and (3) *adjustment*, characterized by greater satisfaction and a sense of ease. *Culture shock* was coined by anthropologist Kalvero Oberg (1954, 1960) who labeled this phenomenon of cultural disorientation as an ailment that manifested not just socially and emotionally, but physically too. Later, theorists like Adler (1987) and Pedersen (1995) identified the process as one of many complex transitions that result in "growth, learning and personal change" in the affected individual (Jandt, 2016, p. 278).

Culture shock is particularly salient for those who feel socially distanced from the traditions and expectations of the foreign land they are inhabiting, and anxious that "one's familiar ways of behaving are no longer appropriate or functional" (Jandt, 2016, p. 278). Honing in on culture shock specifically, most scholars have theorized it as a four-step process comprising (i) *incubation* or *fascination*, (ii) *crisis* or *hostility*, (iii) *recovery* or *adjustment*, and (iv) *acculturation* or *biculturalism* (Oberg, 1954; Smalley, 1963; Kealey, 1978; Richardson, 1974). Others have charted it as a five-step process (Adler, 1987; Pedersen, 1995; Jandt, 2016), with the first step being a "honeymoon" period where the migrant approaches a new environment as an excited tourist who is still deeply connected to their home culture. The second step in the five-step process leads to the migrant feeling isolated and/or distant toward dissimilar experiences faced within the host culture. This sentiment becomes more complex in the third or reintegration stage, with the individual experiencing culture shock in two separate ways: first, becoming more acclimated to the new culture, and second, feeling discontent toward the host space for "'being different'" (Jandt, 2016, p. 279). The fourth or adjustment phase leads to a more balanced outlook toward the host and home cultures, as the individual starts feeling like more of a cultural insider. In the final phase of the five-step model, also known as the *acculturation* or *reciprocal independence* phase, the individual has finally found a way to accept the similarities and differences of both host and home cultures, or has become adept at *biculturalism* (Jandt, 2016, p. 279; Neuliep, 2015). Both the four- and five-step models cover all relevant phases of culture shock and can be used to theorize this phenomenon interchangeably.

Globalization has made more complex the dynamics of movement across borders for people who are now very adept at moving fluidly between home and host spaces. While home denotes the migrant's "own culture within their country of origin," their "country of resettlement" is the host culture representing a destination where immigrants "live, work, develop affinities, and build community in the global context" (Sorrells, 2016, p. 137). At the same time, the labels 'home' and 'host' do not always take into account challenges, struggles, ambiguities, and/or technology-facilitated connections that migrant communities experience as members of both cultures. How easily an immigrant or their family can adapt to a host culture depends largely on the nature of the relationship between them and members of the host society. Berry (1992) and Sorrells (2016) cite four ways in which migrant–host relationships can function, particularly for long-term immigrants in a foreign land: assimilation, separation, marginalization, and integration.

In *assimilation*, migrants fully adapt to life in the host culture, while forfeiting their own traditions and values. The history of early twentieth-century European migration to the United States is one that fits into the assimilation model of migrant–host relations. In *separation* or *segregation* the immigrant has a "strong sense of ethnic identity" and stays largely uninvolved with the host society (Jandt, 2016, p. 305). Separation can be voluntary for migrants who willingly decide to separate their cultural practices from those of the dominant host society, or involuntary where groups are legally and spatially separated from the host culture (Sorrells, 2016). A *marginalized* migrant feels socially distant with the host culture, while also losing a sense of belonging with their own cultural identity. In *integration* or *biculturalism* the migrant learns to equally value home and host cultures, balancing the expectations and traditions of both identities, thus guaranteeing a more fluid "continuity of culture" (Jandt, 2016, p. 305).

Migrant–host relations rely closely on the acceptance of, and attitudes toward migrants by the host society. From their immigration rules, civic policies, reception of migrant and ethnic communities within the dominant culture, and the emotional makeup of migrant individuals, Kim (2001) points to the importance of cross-cultural communication in migrant–host relationships using the integrative theory of cultural adaptation. Kim's (2001) theory postulates that in the process of acculturation migrants can experience "stress, adaptation and growth" as they adjust to different behavioral expectations of the host culture, and partly go through *deculturation* or the "unlearning of some aspects of their culture of origin" (Sorrells, 2016, p. 138). In this readjustment process, the migrant can undergo what Kim (2001) calls *intercultural transformation* in three distinct steps, including (a) the migrant's ability to function more successfully in the host society, (b) increased cognitive and emotional wellbeing of the migrant within dominant cultural spaces, and (c) the move toward a bicultural or interculturally adept identity that allows the migrant to comfortably network with their own and other cultural groups.

Migrant networks play a critical role in facilitating human movements across borders and in acculturation. Massey et al. (1993) have defined migrant networks as groups of "interpersonal ties that connect migrants . . . in origin and destination areas through ties of kinship, friendship and shared community origin" (p. 448). These networks act as informational (living, employment, medical, transportation, etc.) and communication bridges (social and emotional ties) for new immigrants as they try to navigate the systemic aspects of global immigration, and the individual struggles they face as cultural outsiders (Sorrells, 2016). Such networks also provide social and cultural capital to support migrants' transitions to new cultures. In this chapter, we examine from multiple levels, *how* one migrant family and members of one village get to know each other to build intercultural bonds.

FILM ANALYSIS

We organize our analysis of the film by following the Zantoko family's movements along the U-curve of cultural adaptation and their negotiation of different migrant–host relations. These movements reflect key intercultural communication problems addressed in the film as this migrant family sets up their new home in 1970s rural France amid racism, prejudice, and the lack of a migrant network—issues that we will also analyze in the following sections.

Moving along the U-curve

Every Zantoko family member in *The African Doctor* (2016) moves through different stages of intercultural adaptation in Marly-Gomont as cultural and racial outsiders. As Seyolo, Anne, Sivi, and Kamini journey through *anticipation*, *culture shock*, and *adjustment* in different ways and across disparate time frames, each of them stands as a cultural text for us to understand how the U-curve theory of acculturation works in the context of long-term migration. The first step in this U-shaped model of cultural adaptation is *anticipation*, or excitement that the migrant experiences coming into a new cultural space (Lysgaard, 1955; Sorrells, 2016). In Anne's case, she feels the excitement anticipating her future contact with a new culture and a cosmopolitan life in Paris.

In a somewhat comedic scene toward the beginning of *The African Doctor* (2016), Seyolo Zantoko calls home to Zaire from France hoping to inform his wife about his decision to move there on account of his new job. A shot of his kitchen fades in where the wall-hung dial telephone is ringing loudly. 'Kinshasa, Zaire (1975)' is scripted over the screen, as we see an older woman come into the kitchen and answer it. It is night time in France, and early morning in Kinshasa where Dr. Seyolo Zantoko's family live. The cultural and locational differences are visually set up for the audience right from the start. Anne comes to the phone and gets to know that Seyolo wants their family to live in France. Anne mistakenly thinks they're moving to Paris, and excitedly exclaims: "Paris? That changes everything. You should have said! Children! We're going to Paris with Dad!" Seyolo repeats that it's not Paris, but a village further north. However, his entire family, including his wife, children, in-laws, and other relatives are too excited to pay heed to him. The excitement of the anticipation phase that Anne experiences is seen when she passionately says, "I'll be the happiest woman in France, I'm going to Paris!," as her relations crowd around her, with their hands up in the air, clapping, cheering, and dancing. What sets the stage for the next phase in the U-curve process of intercultural adaptation is the scene ending with the phone hanging off the hook, and Seyolo repeating "Hello? Hello? Listen darling, it's not exactly Paris itself" [6:31–7:32].

The next phase in the U-curve model of cultural adaptation (Lysgaard, 1955) is *culture shock* (Oberg, 1954). Moving into a new culture with a different set of customs, traditions, behaviors, and value systems can be stressful and disorienting for an individual (Neuliep, 2015). Often, one also comes into conflict with their own native culture within an unfamiliar cultural space, finding it hard to balance the old and the new (Oberg, 1954; Winkelman, 1994). We see the first stage of culture shock at play in an early interaction that takes place between Seyolo and the mayor of Marly-Gomont. During the graduation celebration when the mayor comes to recruit a new doctor, Seyolo sees an ideal opportunity to escape Mubutu's dictatorial regime and secure coveted French nationality for himself and his family. The mayor's continued doubts about Dr. Zantoko's non-French lineage and his desire to settle for an insignificant job in a small French village that no doctor has accepted before make the mayor undermine Seyolo's French fluency and his assurance of how seriously he intends to permanently settle in Marly-Gomont. Seyolo reassures: "I would bring my family . . . I want to give my children the best future I can" [3:55].

Race also plays a big part in the mayor's hesitation to offer Seyolo the village doctor position. It seems not so much his own racial preference for a white French doctor, but his fear that in 1970s rural France a Black medical professional would be a cultural anomaly and a social outcast. Despite the mayor's forewarnings about potential racial othering, and a dismal picture of the village that he describes where "it rains, it's muddy and nothing happens," Seyolo's determination to move makes him exclaim, "So what? Now they will," to the mayor's continued disclaimer that "they've never seen a black person in Marly-Gomont" [4:30]. This incubation stage of culture shock starts with feelings of "optimism and even elation" (Neuliep, 2015, p. 448) similar to a honeymoon phase where the migrant is still in admiration of cultural differences in the host society (Winkelman, 1994). As the scene ends, Seyolo grins and tightens the knot of his tie as a comedic sign of him landing the job, proving that in the first *elation* stage of culture shock the "stresses associated with cultural differences are tolerated and may even seem fun and humorous" (Neuliep, 2015, p. 448), for both migrants and hosts.

The second stage of culture shock moves on to *crisis* (Oberg, 1954) that the individual faces in the new culture, also known as *hostility* (Smalley, 1963), *depression* (Richardson, 1974), and *frustration* (Kealey, 1978). In a scene that takes place shortly after the Zantoko family arrives in Marly-Gomont, Dr. Zantoko receives a phone call at his clinic summoning him to pay a visit to the Malaquin farm. Seyolo drives to the farm in his rickety old car, and starts walking across a large field toward a tractor that is apparently being driven by Mr. Malaquin, seeming happy that this could be his professional break in the French village. To our surprise, however, Mr. Malaquin pulls out his rifle and starts shooting at Seyolo, yelling, "Beat it! Get out of my field! . . . Dirtbag! Son of a Bitch!" as Seyolo frantically scampers across the field and to his car [17:30]. This episode is an example of a "failure event," marking Seyolo's entry into the second stage of culture shock where cross-cultural interactions that were once considered humorous or insignificant are "now perceived as stressful" (Neuliep, 2015, p. 449).

Another example of village locals rejecting the Zantoko family and creating cultural hostility can be found in a scene where they sit around the dinner table, eating soup. Following is the Zantokos' interaction [18:35]:

Sivi: At school they called me Black.
Seyolo: What's the problem? You are Black. Listen, it's normal. We just arrived,
    people don't know us. We have to make an effort if we want people to like us.
Sivi: They call me Darkie.

Kamini: And me Jungle Bunny or Jigaboo . . .
Anne: Unbelievable! Stick up for yourselves. Next person who does it, punch them.

What starts as a casual dinner table conversation, ends up making most of them feel "helpless, isolated and depressed" (Neuliep, 2015, p. 449). It is also true that different people experience culture shock in different ways and to different degrees. Seyolo tries to make sense of his own experience of getting shot at, and of his children's race-based isolation in school, as a form of "role shock" in that the "behaviors associated with their role in their [home] culture may be dramatically different from the behaviors of that same role in the new culture" (Neuliep, 2015, pp. 449–50; Winkelman, 1994). As a cultural outsider, Anne is more drastic (though typical) in her reaction to the crisis phase of culture shock and is "convinced that their troubles are deliberate attempts by the [locals] to disrupt their lives" (Neuliep, 2015, pp. 449–50).

The third stage of culture shock leads to cultural *recovery* (Oberg, 1954; Richardson, 1974), or *adjustment* (Smalley, 1963) or *coping* (Kealey, 1978) for the cultural outsider. The scene where the Zantoko family dines on soup on one of their first nights in Marly-Gomont marks a slight transition in their perception of being cultural outsiders in France. The family laughs imagining the sight of the prim and proper Seyolo hitting the ground to escape Mr. Malaquin's bullets [19:19]. Their laughter here is a combination of shock, exhaustion, and absurdity directed at the locals' prejudice, but it is a moment that relaxes the family, even if only briefly, during a tense transitional time.

Their use of humor is one way to cope with their culture shock and take a first step toward the *recovery* phase. Anne makes a weak attempt at the same, when she calls home (her mother, in Zaire) and pretends all is well, and that they are in Paris enjoying a cosmopolitan life surrounded by "The Eiffel Tower, the shops, the lovely outfits . . . And so many people," when in fact she's looking out of her old kitchen window onto a field of cows grazing, mooing, and urinating [16:30]. This *coping* stage of culture shock makes migrants slowly realize that the problems they are encountering in the new cultural location are not always created by locals, but because of "a real difference in values, beliefs and behaviors" (Neuliep, 2015, p. 451).

In the final stage of culture shock the migrant starts to move toward *full recovery* (Oberg, 1954) or *acculturation* (Richardson, 1974) in the new host culture. Taking advice from a friendly farmer he had met earlier, Seyolo visits a village pub to help himself fit in with local life, and hoping the upcoming mayoral election will help his cause. As he enters the pub and greets everyone, the men in the pub stare at him, laugh when he tries a local liquor, but eventually begin to bond over darts and drinking alcohol [24:15]. When Seyolo's first dart toss is wildly off target, the men laugh, but the friendly farmer emerges and says, "You gotta *saquer neddin*, kid!". This term isn't translated to English, but based on what the farmer says later, this French term seems to mean something along the lines of "go for broke" or "give it your all," in English. Seyolo is clearly trying to develop "a level of competency in communicating with the [locals]," which is an important part of the *acculturation* phase of culture shock (Neuliep, 2015, p. 451).

The third and last stage in the U-curve theory of cultural integration is *adjustment* where the migrant learns to first accept, and then appreciate the host culture. In the film, acceptance comes in layers, as the children gradually find friendships. We see this at play in consecutive scenes, including when Sivi and some children start to bond over soccer, a sport that Sivi used to play in Zaire and now desires to play in Marly-Gomont [41:03]. We also find Kamini making friends with a French girl called Sylvie who tells him that other kids call her "scabby," since she has a skin condition that causes scabs all over her body. Kamini warmly says, "I prefer Sylvie," and the two children smile and start developing a friendship, which is an indication that the children have started accepting the host culture. Later, in a comedic attempt to cure Sylvie's skin condition we see Sylvie standing in a bath as Seyolo and a woman, presumably Sylvie's mother, apply a black paste to her body as Kamini enters and jokes, "I didn't know I had another sister" [48:54]. In the adjustment phase, migrants or sojourners slowly become open to solving problems and resolving conflicts while living in a different cultural space (Neuliep, 2015). It may take time, and many slip into "mini-crisis stages," but cultural differences found in the host society start making sense to migrants (Neuliep, 2015, p. 451; Winkelman, 1994).

To make a migrant's adjustment to the new culture successful, appreciation, acceptance, and patience must also come from the host culture. In a scene where a local man tries to teach Anne how to drive a manual car, we see her struggling to get the car in gear and it glides backward, as smoke bellows from underneath [1:03:00]. As frustrated as the local French instructor is at Anne's poor driving skills, he patiently and sympathetically concludes, "Can I be honest with you? This will take a while." Sorrells (2016) ascribes a migrant's ability to adjust to a new culture to many factors including the cultural outsider's desire to acclimate and the "host culture's receptivity" (p. 135), such as we find in Anne's driving instructor in this scene.

**Migrant–Host Mobilities: Assimilation,
Separation, Marginalization, and Integration**

Seyolo and Anne have very different approaches to acculturation, and how well they fit into the cultural fabric of Marly-Gomont can be understood by interculturally reading the family's migrant–host relationships in France.

Migrant–host relations are determined by a person's "out-group contact and relations" or how much they communicate with others in the host culture, and also by their "in-group identity and maintenance," or to what degree they accept or reject their cultural heritage (Neuliep, 2015, p. 440). Each Zantoko family member has a different approach to adjusting to the village. Their approaches include *assimilation, integration, separation,* and *marginalization* (Berry, 1992), or the four strategies that determine migrant–host relations.

Seyolo is a firm believer in *assimilation*. During the Christmas mass in Marly-Gomont, Seyolo is embarrassed that his extended family, visiting from Brussels, broke out in their lively rendition of Silent Night. After the church service, a relative confronts Seyolo, asking: "What's your problem? We can't sing at Christmas?" [55:50]. Seyolo responds in anger, "For weeks I've done everything to get people to accept us. To see us as normal people." His relatives are shocked at the implication that Seyolo doesn't think his own family, and culture, are "normal." Anne chimes in from the group, "He's renouncing his origins!" Seyolo yells back, "Not at all! I just want them to see we're the same. So I'd rather my family didn't sing African gospel in front of the whole village on Christmas! . . . Now what do I do? I'll need a miracle to convince them!" In acculturation, a migrant, like Seyolo, makes continuous efforts to approximate dominant cultural norms, while distancing oneself from the "values, beliefs and behaviors" of one's cultural location (Neuliep, 2015, p. 440).

Seyolo's attempts at assimilation come with the villagers' attempts at acceptance. Following the birth of Felix, a local French woman's newborn Dr. Zantoko helped deliver on Christmas day, the villagers and Zantoko relatives gathered in the pub to celebrate with singing, dancing, and cheers for Seyolo [1:00:15]. As everyone leaves, people say goodbye and Kamini points out, "Dad, did you hear? They called you doctor!" Baby Felix, a metaphor for the birth of Jesus, has transformed the community. After the celebration, the villagers' perception of Seyolo changes. Suddenly, they trust him. In the scenes that follow, Seyolo's clinic is full of smiling and anxious patients, pushing and shoving each other to enter the clinic first, while Anne informs her relatives in Brussels how busy the clinic is and how Seyolo has regained his confidence. In assimilation, Coleman (1995) says, the migrant consciously seeks out communication with people from the host society to foster social ties with the end goal of fitting in. The Christmas miracle becomes that transitional moment for the characters in the story.

Yet, assimilation comes at a price, especially for a migrant like Seyolo who wants to get a new cultural identity in the host society at the cost of rejecting his home culture and earning early rejection from the hosts. This is a common fallout for those who seek assimilative migrant–host relations

(Coleman, 1995). In a series of events that lead up to the local elections in Marly-Gomont, Seyolo goes to a meeting with the village officials [36:33]. Lavigne, a mayoral candidate, expresses concern about "the medical situation," and says it's a problem that villagers are driving far away to another (French, white) doctor. Despite Seyolo's pleas for support, which the villagers can give him by visiting his clinic, Lavigne cuts back at him by using the very thing that Seyolo was doing to earn trust—spending time in the local pub. Lavigne continues, hatefully, "Here we're endangering people's health. It might be time to find a replacement, Mr. Mayor . . . Well, bring on the election." After the men depart, Seyolo begs the mayor for more time to make it work, but the mayor seems relentless giving Seyolo until Christmas to make progress.

Anne, unlike Seyolo, prefers the *separation* mode of acculturation. This is motivated in part by the villagers' perception that the Zantokos don't speak French or don't speak it well, and don't know the local French foods. We see this best in a scene when Anne goes to the produce market and a local vendor asks her, "Do you know cabbage? Very good." Before Anne can respond, he continues, "Or I have cucumbers," and he sounds out the word as if she doesn't understand French. He quickly moves on to leeks, ignoring Anne's shocked expression. Exasperated, Anne cuts in to tell him: "I'm not an idiot" [20:10]. Anne's pushback and separation from Marly-Gomont's locals is a deliberate effort to solely communicate with her own people, while consciously avoiding or feeling uncomfortable communicating with members of the host society (Coleman, 1995).

Anne's adoption of separation as the preferred mode of mitigating migrant–host tensions in Marly-Gomont is furthered by Lavigne's negative rumors about Seyolo, presumably to boost his support for the upcoming election [45:50]. Lavigne walks through the town square with a small group of locals spreading gossip that Seyolo performs abortions, which they find shocking and "against the word of God." A nervous woman in the group asks Lavigne, "What we gonna do if there's trouble. It's like we got no one." Meanwhile, Anne overhears their conversation and confronts them: "How do you know if he's a good doctor or bad? You'd have to try first! He has the same diploma as your French doctors. Have you seen yourselves with your holy-kamoleys and gosh-darns? You can't even speak French! My kids talk better than you! You don't even deserve a doctor. With your lousy Camembert breath . . . Bunch of ignoramuses!" Research suggests that migrants like Anne who adopt separation strategies often feel hostility toward the host society because of a history of social, cultural, and/or political discrimination (Coleman, 1995), which Anne clearly vocalizes in this moment.

Feeling like they'll never fit in is what led Seyolo to temporarily adopt acculturative *marginalization* from both his home and host cultures (Neuliep,

2015), despite his continued efforts to assimilate in Marly-Gomont. Early in the film, the Zantoko's relatives arrive from Brussels at an inconvenient time during a minute of silence in the village square, as locals were sharing a commemorative moment for the fallen during the First World War. Their arrival with a lot of car horn-honking and loud music shocks the locals who look on with disapproval, including one of them asking, "What is that racket?" [26:50]. Seyolo is embarrassed and tries to get them to turn down the music, while Anne cheerfully gives them all warm hugs. The family goes to the Zantoko house where a cousin explains who everyone is to Kamini, the women make food, and the family dines, sings, and dances throughout the day. While Anne and the children have a good time, Seyolo looks uncomfortable and disapproving of his relatives. This is a connection to home that Anne needs and embraces, and perhaps Seyolo also requires, but is unwilling to accept. Often, Neuleip (2015) argues, those who do choose to be marginalized from their original culture don't gain acceptance from the host culture that they want desperately to assimilate to.

Marginalization as a strategy to gain acceptance within the host society becomes more salient in situations where immigrants like the Zantokos don't have the support of a migrant network (Sorrells, 2016). This has been especially true for Seyolo, whose focus has been on fitting in rather than upholding his own cultural values. One way Seyolo wishes to push back against local prejudice is to insist that his children make more efforts to fit in by speaking only in French, and not Lingala, their local language [19:45]. In another scene following Seyolo's arrest that was orchestrated by mayoral candidate Lavigne, Seyolo is fired from his position. As he packs up his office, Mayor Ramollu brings in a white, French doctor to show around, while Seyolo and the mayor exchange disappointed glances, brokenhearted at the situation [1:11:58]. Soon after, the friendly farmer Jeannot finds Seyolo walking alone and drunk, in the dark. An inebriated Seyolo laments that the kids are on their own: "They're with themselves, they don't need me. No one does. Not even my wife needs me." Seyolo stumbles into a field as Jeannot chases after him, and says, "I did all I could to be accepted. And for what? It's true, I renounced my origins! Me, the orphan from Biongo." Marginalization, which Seyolo feels at this point, happens when migrants are neither a part of their own culture nor that of the host society (Neuleip, 2015), and thus feel lonely and go through acculturative stress.

Integration or the final phase of successful migrant–host relations comes from the villagers of Marly-Gomont who help the Zantoko family to fully integrate by learning the value of cultural acceptance. In a key scene, Seyolo takes the children to a soccer game [1:14:40], and as they walk into the field, Kamini's friend Sylvie and her family express their surprise that he is no longer allowed to work. Seyolo requests, "If you want a chance to get me back, vote Ramollu tomorrow." As Seyolo and Kamini watch the match, he asks for Sivi's whereabouts and is informed that she's with a friend. Seyolo is unaware that Sivi is pretending to be a boy and playing on the boys' soccer team. Meanwhile, the man next to Seyolo nudges him and referring to Sivi, knowingly says: "'He' really has a magnificent kick." Everyone on the Marly-Gomont stands, other than Seyolo, knows that Sivi is playing, including the school bully who is there cheering Sivi on, and some hold a banner that reads, "Sivi the Black Panther." Sivi is shown wearing an Afro (likely a wig) and ruling the game. Seyolo is in shock when he finds out, but also proud that his neighbors are cheering for her. Lavigne is also watching the match, but is uncomfortable and torn—he's not sure if he should force Seyolo out of the village and risk losing Sivi, and her soccer skills, that are bringing pride to Marly-Gomont, or if he should let him stay to keep Sivi on the soccer team and lose the election. As the team wins the match, a man hugs Seyolo and says through tears, "Thanks to her, we've made the minor league! It's beautiful!". At the same time, we see Lavigne trying to calm his son (the bully), who is excitedly chanting, "Sivi, Sivi, Sivi!". The soccer match serves as an example of cultural integration as we find both the villagers and the Zantokos to be a part of shared "activities that allow individuals from different groups to interact without the obstacle of social hierarchies" (Neuleip, 2015, p. 440).

For integration to work, hosts have to be respectful of migrants and their cultures, and also take steps to make them feel accepted (Sorrells, 2016). Shortly after the soccer match, Seyolo and the children go to the local bar while the polling place appears empty. It is election day in Marly-Gomont [1:19:30]. As the villagers at the bar congratulate Sivi on a great match and want to make sure their "champion" is in good health for the next one, they realize that Sivi won't be on their team once the Zantokos move and they are shocked. Seyolo complains, in feigned helplessness, "If only there hadn't been this election . . . Since the mayor managed to get a local doctor, Lavigne has tried to stop me working. There must be a solution, but." As they all stand there wondering what can be done, one of the villagers suggests: "We'll vote for Ramollu! If we keep the mayor, he'll support us." Seyolo, trying not to smirk, offers, "That could help." Integration is said to be related to reduced acculturative stress in migrants who do not necessarily have to abandon their indigenous cultural identities to be fully accepted into the host culture (Coleman, 1995; Neuleip, 2015). The soccer match and the gathering of locals in the pub following Sivi's win for Marly-Gomont show us that Seyolo and his family can now adopt a bicultural, Zairian-French identity that would ensure their integration into a society that is slowly appreciating cultural differences.

Racialization and Prejudice

Othering, especially in the form of racialization, is persistent among the villagers right from the beginning—from the mayor questioning Seyolo's medical credentials, to the pregnant woman bolting out of the clinic due to her fear of Seyolo. Although racialization may occur around attributes other than the color of one's skin, such as religion (Onasch, 2017), in this film it is largely centered around skin color. Some villagers are fearful of the Zantokos simply because they are Black and/or other villagers struggle to see Seyolo as the professional that he is.

Lavigne, the man running for mayor, preys on the villagers' fears in order to serve his own interest in attaining power as mayor. He is a central figure that reinforces and reproduces supposed differences between Seyolo and the villagers, while he also emphasizes villagers' shared commonality of Frenchness and, we can assume, white-ness. Lavigne does this by spreading negative lies about Seyolo that reinforce villagers' fears about him being different, by trying to influence the election, and searching for other ways to sabotage Seyolo's success at the expense of the villagers' health. Late in the film, after the Christmas miracle, as villagers are warming up to Seyolo despite Lavigne's best efforts to prevent such affection, an ally comments to Lavigne that his wife went to see Dr. Zantoko and "found him charming." The man then exclaims, "It's intolerable! We're talking about an African doctor here! It's a disgrace to French medicine" [1:04:30]. Not only is Seyolo's success a threat to Lavigne's political ambitions, but it is also a threat to this man's racist sense of social hierarchy where European (white) men should be the higher class professionals and Black men should be subservient. Seyolo's role as a trained medical professional challenges their racist ordering of the world and they respond by trying to *other* the Zantokos to either make them leave the village or force them into a lower class so that this supposed "order" can resume—after all, this social hierarchy serves the white villagers' interests, even at the expense of their health.

Aside from fear of the Zantokos, racialization is also part of why some people have difficulty seeing Dr. Zantoko as an expert medical professional. It seems children vocalize this doubt toward Sivi and Kamini because Kamini at one point asks Seyolo, "Are you a real doctor?" [39:30]. He explains to his father that "the kids at school think you're a witch doctor. They say there's no such thing as a Black doctor." Seyolo responds, "Soon they'll believe it, wait and see." But as he closes the door to the children's room, his face is sad, scared, and exhausted. In another scene where Seyolo's expertise is questioned, two men from the pub visit the clinic for treatment of various ailments. The men do not seem to be highly educated nor do they appear to be accustomed to regular personal hygiene, the latter of which is likely contributing to their physical ailments. When Dr. Zantoko gives them a bill for his medical services, they burst out in incredulous laughter, saying that if they knew they had to pay, they would have gone to see Dr. Vinquier—"He's a real doctor" [32:00]. There is a perception among the villagers, just as when the mayor questioned the authenticity of Seyolo's medical degree in the opening scenes, that a Black person couldn't possibly be a "real" doctor. Once again, racist perceptions of social hierarchy that place white Europeans at the top are challenged by Dr. Zantoko's presence and medical degree, and many of the villagers struggle to reshape their thinking. This is partly why the Christmas miracle birth of baby Felix was a key turning point, as Kamini pointed out—some of the villagers began calling Seyolo "Dr.," evidence that their perception of him as a true medical professional is finally becoming a reality.

Still, the price of this racialization is high and nearly leads the Zantokos to leave the village. Because the villagers are afraid of Dr. Zantoko, they initially refuse to go to his clinic, which means he isn't earning money. Meanwhile, Anne has been making regular phone calls to Kinshasa, not realizing how expensive long distance calls are, which makes their financial situation even more difficult. After a town meeting where the leaders refuse to support Dr. Zantoko and the mayor refuses to give him a loan, Seyolo turns to the friendly farmer (Jeannot) for work. Seyolo, however, is ashamed of their financial circumstances and the fact that he has become a farm apprentice to make ends meet, and doesn't tell Anne about this new job. Anne grows suspicious when she smells manure on Seyolo's clothes [41:32]. After a few mornings of Seyolo supposedly rushing off to the clinic, Anne follows Seyolo and makes her way to the farm, sees him undressing in a room, and presumably thinks he is having an affair. After weeping in a barn as Anne is about to leave, she stumbles upon Seyolo driving a tractor, and it all becomes clear.

In the next scene Jeannot enters the bar and looks agitated [44:54]. He gets a shot and turns to the men socializing to make the following declaration:

> Gentlemen. Tonight I raise my glass to my new employee, Seyolo, who had to accept a job on my farm due to lack of patients. A word of advice to those who'd like to cultivate something else next year [presumably referencing the election]. The soil around here is very fertile for stupidity. Idiots grow like weeds. Cheers.

Even as the villagers warm up to Dr. Zantoko, Lavigne and his cronies won't give up their efforts to push out Seyolo to serve their own self-interests and reinforce their racist perception of social order. Lavigne concocts some minor errors on Seyolo's paperwork from the Health Ministry [1:09:50], and uses it to suspend Seyolo's right to practice medicine and have him arrested, yet another tactic designed to feed racist suspicion around him and undermine his professionalism. Luckily, Sivi's soccer talents combined with some strategic politicking and voter mobilization by Seyolo and the children, villagers vote for the incumbent mayor so that the Zantokos can remain in Marly-Gomont. While it would be nice to think that people voted for the mayor purely because they wanted the Zantokos to remain, some people voted because they wanted their star soccer player, Sivi, to stay to help the local team win a championship. We find this detail in the storyline refreshing for its illustration of the varying ways that people may or may not overcome racism and prejudice—sometimes people change for virtuous reasons, and sometimes their changes are motivated by self-interest.

Lack of Migrant Network

Aside from the othering and racialization that the Zantokos experience in Marly-Gomont, another factor that makes their transition challenging is the lack of a migrant network in the village. The Zantoko family members are on their own, except for relatives that live in Brussels, about two hours away by car. Not only are they the only Black people in the village, but they also appear to be the only immigrants there at all. Migrant networks are key elements for newly arrived migrants to adjust to the new culture and build connections and community (Massey et. al., 1993; Sorrells, 2016). Without this social and cultural capital, migrants may feel isolated. Anne feels especially isolated during their first months in Marly-Gomont. As mentioned earlier, she regularly called Kinshasa while Seyolo was at the clinic and the children were at school. She yearned for social connections and the villagers were unwilling, at first, to build intercultural relationships with them. When they realize that the phone bill was over 3,500 francs, Anne and Seyolo argue. Anne explains, "I spend my life on the phone because no one here speaks to me! We should have stayed home. We were good there. We were at home. We were happy" [36:03]. But for Seyolo, remaining in Zaire is simply not an option. The next best thing is visiting with relatives from Brussels. Anne lights up when she is around their relatives, and seeks comfort in their support by discussing the challenges they face in Marly-Gomont during the Christmas celebrations. A family member insists that they come visit Brussels, but Anne reluctantly declines—"it's not in our budget" [49:09].

Despite benefits of having a migrant network visit, the film also depicts some of its challenges, in that tensions related to the home culture are bound to follow people and bubble up within the network of people living in a different culture. One of the party guests is visiting from Zaire and is intent on flashing his money and cosmopolitan airs, making smug jokes about the cold and the lack of luxury amenities in Marly-Gomont. The man even shows off photos of his mansion in Zaire, bragging about how expensive it is, to which

Seyolo critiques that it was "bought with people's blood, money and pain" [50:32]. The man reminds Seyolo that he too could have had such a life, and it comes out that he was offered a position as personal doctor to President Mobutu. Seyolo never told Anne about this prominent offer that he declined due to the political circumstances, and this new information leads them to argue in the next room while the guests sit awkwardly in the dining room. It is clear that a migrant network brings many benefits, which Anne especially aches for—connection to home culture, networks of support—and which she does not regularly experience in Marly-Gomont. However, the film also illustrates how such networks come with all the good, the bad, and the in-between of one's home culture that may ripple or even splash into the new context as migrants navigate old tensions alongside the new ones that emerge with settling in a new space.

CONCLUSION

Despite the challenges of adjusting to a new culture and the racism the Zantokos face, *The African Doctor* (2016) ultimately tells a touching story about a family and the trust, respect, affection, and even love that eventually grows among the Zantokos and the villagers of Marly-Gomont. This wry comedy was well received in the international film festival circuit, and selected in the feature film category at the Vienna Francophone Film Festival (2017), and the Tübingen-Stuttgart International French-language Film Festival (2016), where the Stuttgart Audience Prize was awarded to Julien Rambaldi, director of the *The African Doctor* (2016). The cross-cultural appeal of the film is evident in its international releases in Austria (2017), Belgium (2016), Germany (2017), Italy (2017), South Korea (2016), and Sweden (2016), following its parent release in France (2016) where the film was called *Bienvenue à Marly-Gomont* (i.e., "*Welcome to Marly-Gomont*").

In the film, the Zantokos indeed become Marlysians themselves, fully integrated as beloved members of the community. Villagers learn to accept Dr. Seyolo and his family, and the Zantokos learn to accept the villagers as they are. The children's play at the end of the film depicts this turning point. The children created a play that recounts the story of the Zantoko family moving to Marly-Gomont, and it is a plea for acceptance and forgiveness. As the film ends, the adult Kamini narrates: "I never knew if it was our play that did it. But if it was, I think it was a fitting turnaround when children can help their parents" [1:22:50]. Shortly after, the Zantokos obtained French citizenship and the adult Kamini recalls, "My parents remained loyal to Marly for the rest of their lives. And even if every night my mother barely slept, over time they became inseparable. Like my father and his patients, who he cared for until his dying day" [1:22:50].

Dr. Zantoko died in 2009 in a car accident and Kamini describes his funeral as one last appointment: "At his funeral, when I saw his patients arrive, it was like he'd given us all the same appointment. This last appointment was proof of what he always wanted . . . something that had transformed into love. A simple love that said here, we were at home" [1:22:50]. From the beginning Seyolo seeks assimilation, while Anne's approach is separation, and their different approaches to adjusting to their new home result in tensions—both with each other and with villagers.

Yet, Seyolo's approach to migrant–host relations is indicative of his yearning for acceptance and to "transform into love" the resistance that he and his family face when they first arrive. Although some drawbacks of this approach are depicted in that there are accusations of him giving up on his own culture, his persistence pays off and ultimately he, Anne, the children, and the villagers find a balance between their cultures that allows them to find acceptance, build rich intercultural relationships, and achieve the peace of knowing they are at home. This compelling story shows audiences that migration is difficult and often filled with conflict that causes people to change their thinking about themselves and how the world works. Yet, it ultimately illustrates that such transformation is worth it because, at least in this story, both migrants and hosts grew intellectually and emotionally, learned to love one another, and created a new sense of home.

Chapter 3

A Better Life

Immigration Industrial Complex, Conflict Styles, and Facework in a Mexican-American Family

A Better Life (2011) tells the story of one family's encounters with immigration systems in the United States as a father and son try to build a better life. Set in Los Angeles, Carlos Galindo (the father) is an unauthorized[1] immigrant working as a landscaper and tries to remain hidden as best he can given his status. Carlos works hard to support his teenage son, Luis, who is a U.S. citizen by birth. Luis is fully American from his citizenship, to his accent, to his ideas about handling conflict. In many ways, Luis sees his father as "a periodically embarrassing ambassador from a foreign land" (Dargis, 2011). After taking a risk with financial support from his sister, Carlos buys his boss' truck and tools, and he and Luis start to see new hope for building a more secure future. However, Santiago, an unauthorized immigrant that Carlos hired for a day, steals the truck and tools, leading Carlos and Luis on a journey to find their investment, their source of income, and along the way their different cultural approaches to handling conflict comes into view. While the father and son may differ in their individualistic–collectivist orientations, Santiago's actions reveal how situational factors (Sorrells, 2016), such as the desperation of poverty and unauthorized status, can push even a traditionally collectivist-oriented person to steal from one of his own.

In this film, migration-related conflict, stress, oppression, facework, and familial separation are also reflective of the current climate of legal uncertainty and anxiety that exists among unauthorized immigrants in the United States. Underlying this story about an intra/intercultural father–son relationship is an intercultural story about the impacts of the immigration industrial complex (Golash-Boza, 2009) as depicted in the fear Carlos and many of the characters face, the othering that white Americans thrust upon Carlos and others, and the systems of deportation and border crossings that become like additional characters in the film affecting everyone's relationships.

We continue this chapter by reviewing the impact of the immigration industrial complex on unauthorized immigrants like Carlos, and the severity and anxiety that deportation policies and unauthorized border crossings inflict on such migrants and their families. We then explore how different conflict styles, cultural values, and facework are adopted and adapted in familial communication, following which we analyze our case study of the film using these intercultural concepts in the mobile context of immigration and interpersonal relations.

IMMIGRATION INDUSTRIAL COMPLEX

As of 2017, the foreign-born population in the United States was 44.4 million, which is about 13.6 percent of the total population (Radford, 2019). Three-quarters of today's migrants are in the country legally and experts estimate that 23 percent are unauthorized. As of 2017, it was estimated that there were 10.5 million unauthorized migrants in the United States, or 3.2 percent of the total population, a number that has been on the decline since 2007 (Radford, 2019). The largest percentage of immigrants in the United States come from Mexico (25 percent), while the rest come from many different countries, including China, India, the Philippines, and El Salvador, which make up the remaining large percentages. Deportation of immigrants rose during the Obama administration, but declined in 2017 with that year being the lowest total of deportations on record since 2006 (Radford, 2019), a surprising fact given the Trump administration's rhetoric around immigration. With regard to crime, most of the immigrants (60 percent) deported between 2001 and 2017 were not actually convicted of a crime.

In terms of how people are getting into the United States, Warren (2019) reveals that visa overstays have "significantly exceeded illegal border crossings during each of the last seven years," with Mexico being the country with the most immigrants overstaying in 2017. In other words, the challenges with U.S. immigration policy are less about "illegal border crossing" and more about people entering legally and then staying after their visa expires. As Kamarck and Stenglein (2019) point out, approximately two-thirds of unauthorized immigrants have been in the country for ten or more years, according to 2017 data.

There are many industries in the United States that rely on immigrant labor, and some specifically rely on unauthorized immigrant labor. The kind of work that Carlos does in the film—landscaping—relies heavily on immigrant labor. Americans enjoy having well-manicured lawns, but finding people to do this difficult labor is hard for landscaping business owners (Campbell,

2016; D'Acosta, 2018). As a result, some business owners turn to unauthorized immigrant labor to meet demands. Unauthorized immigrant labor makes up approximately 22 percent of the employees in the "business and other services sector, which includes legal services, landscaping [and more]" (D'Acosta, 2018). The picture painted by these statistics comes to life in the cinematic story of Carlos Galindo and his family.

Now that we've established a statistical picture of immigration in the United States, and specifically unauthorized immigration, it is important to contextualize this in scholarly literature. A key concept framing our analysis of *A Better Life* (2011) is the notion of the immigration industrial complex. The *immigration industrial complex* is defined as "the public and private sector interests in the criminalization of undocumented migration, immigration law enforcement and the promotion of 'anti-illegal' rhetoric" (Golash-Boza, 2009, p. 296). Forming the basis of this concept is the notion that

> there exists a convergence of interests that drives the U.S. government to pass and then avidly enforce a set of immigration policies that have consistently failed to achieve their stated goals and have violated the human rights of migrants and their families in the process. (Golash-Boza, 2009, p. 296)

In 1961, President Eisenhower warned Americans about the growing influence of what he called the "military industrial complex" (MIC). He was referring to the close ties between corporations, politicians, and the military that combined to expand the military and enrich the arms industry in the midst of the Cold War, but which may detract from expanding other resources such as building schools and hospitals (NPR Staff, 2011). Eisenhower explained that due to these growing ties, "the potential for the disastrous rise of misplaced power exists, and will persist" (NPR Staff, 2011). Later, as the external threat of Communism waned, the perceived internal threat of crime emerged in political discourse, which became a justification for the growth of the prison industrial complex (PIC), referring to "vast network of prisons, jails, courts, police officers, and other elements that purport to reduce the amount of criminal activity in our society" (Golash-Boza, 2009, p. 301). Powerful stakeholders invested in the prison industrial complex include "media, private contractors, politicians, state bureaucracies, and private prisons," and those who suffer most are the poor and people of color (Golash-Boza, 2009, p. 302).

Like the MIC and the PIC, the immigration industrial complex is a joining of multiple powerful stakeholders, such as politicians, media, and private contractors, that perpetuate fearful rhetoric around some perceived threat (in this case, unauthorized immigrants). These stakeholders wind up enriching themselves by criminalizing certain people and creating a neverending cycle of apprehension, detention, deportation, and reentry. Indeed,

Golash-Boza (2009) points out that "many deportees, especially Mexicans, simply return to the United States . . . because of extensive family ties in the United States and because they know there are jobs available" (p. 304). In addition to the fearful rhetoric and the merging of powerful interests, shared features of these three complexes, othering is the third common feature (Golash-Boza, 2009). During the Cold War and the corresponding expansion of the MIC, the "others" were Communists. During the prison expansion and corresponding PIC, Black men were/are the "others" to be feared (Golash-Boza, 2009). With the immigration industrial complex, "the 'others' are 'illegals' (racialized as Mexicans)" that supposedly need to be controlled (Golash-Boza, 2009, p. 306). In creating an "other" to be feared, each type of complex has successfully generated support and obtained government funds to do their work of "safeguarding the nation" (Golash-Boza, 2009, p. 306).

How did immigration and criminalization become intertwined? It wasn't always so. While the United States has a long history of creating policies to keep certain people out (i.e., Chinese Exclusion Act, Johnson-Reed Act), with the passing of the Hart-Cellar Act in 1965, immigration policy shifted from a national origins quota system that was criticized for being racist, to a more open system that emphasized family reunification (Kammer, 2015). Ackerman (2014) argues that a more flexible immigration system, along with the Bracero program (a guest-worker program) and a growing intolerance for racism in the 1960s and 1970s, led a confluence of interested stakeholders to want to focus on illegality when it comes to immigration in the national and political discourse. The Immigration and Naturalization Service and Border Patrol officials saw these changes as a chance to increase their budgets, trade unions targeted unauthorized immigration "as a strategy to 'defend' their members," and "ethnicity-based organizations . . . sought to fight discrimination by emphasizing a differentiation between hyphenated Americans and immigrants" (Ackerman, 2014, p. 182). Over time, whether "the illegal aspect of unauthorized immigration was a problem in and of itself or not passed to the background as a generally accepted fact" (Ackerman, 2014, p. 196).

By the 1990s and 2000s, criminalization and immigration systems had increasingly blurred boundaries, but with incongruencies such that "immigrants are essentially tried twice for the same crime, once in a criminal court and again in an immigration court" (Martinez & Slack, 2013, p. 537). The confusion and inconsistency means that it is difficult for unauthorized immigrants to defend themselves and makes it more likely that their detention will ultimately lead to an adverse outcome—typically deportation or incarceration (Martinez & Slack, 2013). Indeed, this was Carlos' experience in the film—once apprehended and imprisoned, he was faced with a choice to either plead guilty and be deported or fight the charges and spend many months in prison before likely being deported anyway. The social consequences of this immigration system that criminalizes economic migrants such as Carlos include (1) reduced opportunities for legal and permanent status in the country and (2) "introducing migrants into illegitimate means structures" of drug smugglers, human traffickers, and other criminals that may draw in an otherwise law-abiding person who has become desperate to return to their family in the United States (Martinez & Slack, 2013, p. 539).

In fact, some scholars argue that the very fact of labeling certain forms of migration as 'illegal' creates the conditions to "employ *actual* forms of illegality" such as human trafficking and coyotes (Martin, 2012, p. 356, italics original). Migration and mobility are linked, but it is the nonsanctioned or "illegal" forms of corporeal movement that are the focus in this chapter—movement that is dangerous and requires constant circumventing of security networks (Martin, 2012). Movement and economic liberalization where ideas, goods, *certain* people move easily across borders may get a lot of attention, but these messages belie the reality that free movement for many people is "hampered at every turn, often by those most vocal about the importance of dismantling barriers to trade" (Bhattacharyya, 2005, p. 158). As a result, concealment is a key characteristic of "desperate mobilities," and reflects the ways that efforts to order human movement at borders is "continually undone at multiple sites" (Martin, 2012, p. 367). It is not possible to stop people from moving across borders, but borders "do ensure that they are disenfranchised when they arrive" (Bhattacharyya, 2005, p. 159). Given such movement, regardless of legality, it is inevitable that intercultural contact, and eventually intercultural conflict, are going to occur.

INTERCULTURAL CONFLICT, VALUE ORIENTATIONS, AND FACEWORK

Intercultural conflict is defined as "the real or perceived incompatibility of values, norms, expectations, goals, processes, or outcomes between two or more interdependent individuals or groups from different cultures" (Sorrells, 2016, p. 203). Globalization and the complex movement of people have "created unprecedented opportunities for and threats of intercultural conflict" (Sorrells, 2016, p. 203). Micro- or individual-based aspects such as interactants' cultural value orientations, specifically individualism versus collectivism, their communication styles and negotiations of face, as well as their situational factors determine how they deal with conflict. To make sense of the cultural and situational conflict styles, communication, and facework adopted by the father–son dyad in *A Better Life* (2011), we briefly explore relevant scholarship in this section.

To understand the nature of the relationship between communication and culture, anthropologists Kluckhohn and Strodtbeck (1961) proposed a value orientation model, which was an effort to investigate the innate system of values, beliefs, and/or worldviews that were collectively shared by most members of a specific culture. The most studied value orientation is relationships among humans, which can be individual (independence, individuality, self-motivation, higher degree for achievement, aspired equality), and/or hierarchical (unequal distribution of power and resources), and/or collective (prioritization of familial, group-based, communal and social relationships).

In the early 1980s, management researcher Geert Hofstede expanded Kluckhohn and Strodtbeck's (1961) research to propose a more complex value orientation model within organizational settings (Martin & Nakayama, 2013; Hofstede, 1980). Hofstede's findings led to the creation of the cultural value orientation model that had four dimensions, with others added later. This model was widely used in large organizational spaces and was particularly useful in the context of economic globalization (Martin & Nakayama, 2013). The individualism–collectivism dimension, which we address in the film, explains how people within a cultural group relate to each other—being somewhere along a scale of 'me-focused' or 'we-focused.' Hofstede's work highlights the ways these differences in values influence behavior and communication in the workplace, but it has also been used to explain other topics such as psychological and behavioral changes among individuals in different societies (Triandis, 1995) and the impact on familial communication, conflict, and facework across cultures and nations (Oetzel et al., 2003; Ting Toomey, 1994, 1999).

Individualist cultures focus on the needs and interests of the individual. People in individualist cultures like the United States and Western Europe are self-reliant and responsible for their choices and decisions. Family, friends, colleagues, and/or community are secondary. Collectivist or interdependent cultures, like many Asian, Central and South American, and African nations, focus on the needs and interests of the group (e.g., family, community, workplace). Individuals are relational to the collective, and in return, are protected by their group. These value orientations shape how individuals from different cultures communicate and manage conflict. In collectivist cultures, like Mexico, conflict is typically managed through indirect communication, and individuals are more focused on maintaining relational harmony with their group (Sorrells, 2016; Ting-Toomey & Oetzel, 2001).

In individualistic cultures, like the United States, individuals typically manage conflict using direct communication and are more focused on independence and meeting self-goals. However, increased human and technological mobility, and increased opportunities for intercultural interactions have blurred "national and ethnic cultural orientations to conflict" (Sorrells, 2016, p. 205). These culturally influenced communication patterns result in particular ways that communication is constructed—typically high or low context. High context is "where most of the information is already in the person, while very little is in the coded, explicit, transmitted part of the message" (Hall, 1976, p. 79). It is a communication style mostly seen in collectivistic cultures where communication between individuals and the group is part of previously held or shared knowledge. In low-context communication, the "information is vested in the explicit code" (Hall, 1976, p. 70) and is commonly found in individualistic cultures where the individual is more concerned with imparting new information in ways that are autonomous from the group.

In individualistic and collectivistic cultures, conflict is often predicated and managed based on an individual's level of uncertainty avoidance. Hofstede (1980, 2001) conceptualized uncertainty avoidance as the degree of uncertainty that individuals feel in an unfamiliar situation, and the steps they take to manage or avoid it. People in individualist cultures like the United States typically have low uncertainty avoidance and are comfortable confronting others and taking risks during conflicts. People from collectivistic cultures like Mexico typically lean toward high uncertainty avoidance, since "conflict is seen as a threat to both group harmony and effectiveness" (Sorrells, 2016, p. 109). To test Hofstede's (1980, 2001) conclusions about uncertainty avoidance and how different cultures negotiate face, Merkin (2006) analyzed survey data from six countries, including the United States, and found that "ritualistic, harmonious, and aggressive facework strategies" do impact an individual's avoidance of intercultural conflict and embarrassment (p. 213). The idea of *face* is key in the humanities and social sciences, and has been defined by Erving Goffman (1967) "as one's public self-image" (p. 7). Goffman's "face" is a nod to dramaturgy and Chinese anthropological studies (Hu, 1944), as well as a relational concept that refers to the "flow of events in the encounter" (Goffman, 1967, p. 7). We perform our ideal selves to/for others to seek approval or maintain and repair relations.

One can lose, save, or protect their face during conflicts, and when one's face is threatened they use facework "to restore one's desired identity" (Merkin, 2006, p. 69). Facework refers to the different communication strategies people adopt to negotiate face across different cultures, and "focuses on relational, identity, and substantive issues during conflict" (Oetzel et al., 2003, pp. 70–71; Goffman, 1967; Merkin, 2006). Many intercultural scholars have studied how people use facework in individualistic and collectivistic societies to manage situations like requests, apologies, conflicts, and embarrassment using theoretical frames such as politeness theory (Brown & Levinson, 1987) and face negotiation theory (Oetzel et al., 2003; Ting-Toomey, 2005). In a seminal study, Oetzel, Ting-Toomey, Chew-Sanchez, Harris, Wilcox, and Stumpf (2003) applied face-negotiation theory to conflict-managing communication between young adults and parents or siblings across four different cultures, including in families from Germany, Japan, Mexico, and the United States. Their findings revealed that families in individualistic cultures tended to value "self-face" (i.e., focus on self-image) and prefer dominant facework strategies in generic conflict situations, cooperating facework strategies to task-related conflicts, and self-honoring facework during aggressive conflicts. People in collectivistic families tended to value "other-face" (i.e., focus on other's image) and "mutual-face" (i.e., concern for both self and other face, or for 'image' of relationship) issues more, preferred avoiding facework strategies in general conflict situations, and liked cooperating facework during relational conflicts (Oetzel et al., 2003).

As we find in this film, and as far as national cultural orientations impact communication, Oetzel et al. (2003) suggest that Mexicans are seen to value collectivism and high-power distance to resolve family conflicts, whereas Americans prefer individualism and low-power distance. In conflict with siblings and parents, Americans (mostly of European descent) use direct forms of communication, but also prefer "mutually acceptable" strategies that help family members solve their problems in "calm and rational" ways (Oetzel et al., 2003, p. 73). However, when that doesn't happen they adopt aggressive self-defense strategies to resolve conflict (Oetzel et al., 2003). Mexican families like to "avoid conflict if possible, utilize indirect and avoiding strategies to resolve conflict, and have strong other- and mutual-face concerns" (Oetzel et al., 2003, p. 73; Cocroft & Ting-Toomey, 1994). In high-power distance cultures like Mexico, families typically function by children accepting parental authority, learning how decisional power and respect descend hierarchically from older to younger family members, resulting in greater "face concerns and face behaviors in conflicts with parents and siblings" (Oetzel et al., 2003, p. 76; Hofstede, 1991; Ting-Toomey, 1999). Research shows that in Mexican culture, since the family is the primary unit, individuals are expected to save face of/for their community during conflicts, and thus "they may not express their [own] feelings completely so as not to upset the harmony in the family" (Oetzel et al., 2003, p. 87). It's not surprising then that as children grow up in a Mexican household, they are first more at conflict with their parents or caregivers, but post-adolescence they learn to respectfully settle family or relational conflicts (Oetzel et al., 2003).

Brew and Cairns (2004) and Sorrells (2016) explain that situational factors also impact how individuals communicate or change their communication style when working through conflicts, based on their own and others' cultural values. In a study of interpersonal conflict resolution within five Western multicultural workspaces, Brew and Cairns (2004) found that situational factors such as time deadlines, work status, and cultural identity prompted traditionally collectivistic and high-context Thai and Singaporean employees to adopt direct communication strategies to meet the demands of globalization. The typically individualistic and low-context Australian employees, on the other hand, altered their communication style to a more indirect one in keeping with preferred cultural identities of their Southeast Asian colleagues. Increasing global migration is a situational factor that has led to heightened "cultural and ethnic diversification," meaning that people living and raising their families in other countries will experience and be affected by different cultural preferences (Judy & D'Amico, 1997; Oetzel et al., 2003, p. 68). Migrant families, particularly those whose children are born and raised in the host country, are more likely to encounter and manage family conflicts in the form of contradicting cultural value orientations, situationally brought on by immigration and its complexities, as we explore in the relationship between Carlos and Luis.

FILM ANALYSIS

To follow Carlos' and Luis' movements navigating complex systems of immigration, and the complexities of their interpersonal relationship, our film analysis is structured along the two major conceptual themes we have identified—*systems of immigration and deportations*, and *intercultural conflicts and facework*.

Systems of Immigration, Deportation, and Unauthorized Border Crossings

Although the film's protagonists are Carlos and Luis, "La Migra" or immigration authorities act as a third central character that structures and haunts the lives, interactions, and communication between not only the father and son at the center of the film, but all of the characters. From subtle, indirect references to directly stating it, the La Migra follows these characters and influences many of the large and small decisions they make in their lives.

Concerns about legal status and immigration authorities surface in the first full conversation we see between Carlos and his boss, Blasco. Blasco is trying to persuade Carlos to buy his truck and tools, saying it's not just about buying the truck, "What you're buying is the American Dream" [7:11]. It seems like a conversation they've had before and Carlos remains unconvinced. Blasco warns Carlos that someone else will buy the truck, and then Carlos will be out of a job, "back on that corner where I found you six years ago. Begging for work with all the other desperate wetbacks.[2] Ducking La Migra. Not knowing where your next dollar's coming from." But if Carlos buys the truck and the tools, he can keep all the same customers and be his own boss. "Look at me," Blasco says with pride, "I came here with nothing, but I'm going home to my very own farm."

In a later scene, Blasco continues the pressure campaign while he brags about the booming business he has set up in Mexico, including sending packages. Carlos jokingly asks, who is he sending packages to, since "we're all here [in the U.S.]" [11:42]. From Carlos' perspective, there is nothing and no one for him in Mexico—his home is in the United States. He can't afford the truck, he explains, "Remember the lawyer who took all my money? He said he'd get me my papers. No papers, no driver's license. What if the cops stop me for a broken tail light? You know what'll happen. They'll send me back. And then what will happen to Luis?" Blasco is relentless and turns the questions around, saying, "Think about what happens if you *don't* buy the truck. What happens if La Migra gets you and you're not making money? They don't care about separating parents from their kids. Since 9/11 things aren't the same. It's not a little drive through Juarez anymore. It's three days in the desert . . . You want to get your papers? You want to be legal? Buy the truck, brother, in a few months you'll have enough money to hire a real killer lawyer" [12:48]. However, Carlos decides to "stay invisible" rather than take the risk. What Carlos describes is the kind of living in the shadows that so many unauthorized migrants do. Concealment is a central feature of unauthorized immigration (Martin, 2012), and Carlos has structured his life to live in this way, understanding that his ability to earn money is limited due to his unauthorized status and he has to seek employment through hidden means.

In these early scenes, Carlos' backstory reflects what the research shows about immigration in the United States, and specifically migration from Mexico. His joke that there is no one to send packages to in Mexico, because everyone is in the United States, reinforces the statistics showing that most immigrants in the United States are from Mexico (Radford, 2019). Moreover, Blasco's comment that he hired Carlos six years ago suggests that Carlos has been in the country for a long time, and research shows that two-thirds of unauthorized immigrants have been in the country for ten or more years (Kamarck & Stenglein, 2019).

The pressure that La Migra puts on everyone and the widespread efforts at concealment start to become more clear in the scene when Luis has been arrested for fighting at school [13:42]. The officer prepares to release Luis to a parent, but Luis explains that he doesn't have a mother and quickly asserts that his father is unreachable because he's working. He is quick to protect his father from any contact with the police, knowing that it could put his father at risk of deportation if they know who he is. Luis, too, wants his father to remain invisible. In a later scene, Carlos wakes Luis up for school only to learn that he has been suspended. They argue and then Luis rolls over in bed saying, "Go mow some lawns" [19:27]. On the one hand, Luis' response to his father is rude, dismissive, and insulting with the way he brushes off his father's hard work. On the other hand, we know that Luis wants to protect his father from encounters with authorities like the police or the school, so his dismissive approach may also be shaped by his desire to protect his father from getting involved in the institutions that structure Luis' daily life. Luis was born in the United States and as a citizen he does not need to worry about immigration authorities for himself, but it is a central feature of his relationship with his father, and he communicates with others in ways that attempt to shield his father from being discovered.

Unauthorized immigrants' need to hide influences their job options once in the United States. Low-wage work is readily available, but from Luis and his friend Facundo's perspectives, it is a sore spot used to insult people, as Luis did to his father. Mowing lawns as an insult appears again later when Luis and Facundo discuss the fight that got them suspended from school. Facundo tells Luis that he's not a "gangster" and all he's going to do is "mow lawns like your pops" [22:12]. Facundo's insults about types of work communicate his and Luis' perceptions of the honorable, but low-wage work that Carlos and many other unauthorized migrants do. The boys see this kind of work as demeaning, disgraceful, and below them. Instead, they seem to value the lives lived by the gang members around them—the boys perceive them as tough and self-respecting. After all, gang members, from their perspective, are rich, and being rich seems to be the ultimate goal. In these interactions about types of work, the immigration industrial complex is not directly brought up; however, it looms in the background knowing that a central reason Carlos and other unauthorized migrants work in these jobs is to hide from La Migra while still earning money. Gang members, on the other hand, intentionally stand out in their demeanor and their visible tattoos, and stand up to the authorities from the boys' perspectives.

For Carlos, the path to success and becoming an authorized immigrant lies in buying Blasco's truck. Anita, Carlos' sister, offers a generous monetary gift allowing Carlos to make the investment. She and Carlos both see the truck as Blasco described—a way to earn enough money to get papers, to live as an authorized migrant, and to have a better life. But the threats of the immigration industrial complex come into clearer focus when Santiago steals Carlos' truck and tools, and Carlos has to find alternate means to reclaim them since he cannot go to the police.

Once Carlos owns the truck and tools, it is his turn to hire workers for the day. He drives to the same corner where he has waited to be hired. As he approaches, men anxiously gather around the truck hoping to be selected.

Santiago, the elderly man who had kindly shared food with him the day before, waves from the back of the crowd and Carlos chooses him. Carlos and Santiago work side by side throughout the day, and when Carlos climbs a tree, he leaves the car keys on the ground. Step by step, Carlos slowly makes his way up the tree as Santiago watches nervously from the ground. He calls down to Santiago to send up a saw, but when he looks down he sees that Santiago is not there, nor are the truck keys. Panic sets in as Carlos looks around to see Santiago running toward the truck. Carlos climbs back down and tries to catch him, but is unsuccessful. He runs into town hoping to find the truck or some kind of help. He sees police officers, but because of his unauthorized status, Carlos is unwilling and unable to ask them for help. Santiago stole the truck knowing that Carlos wouldn't be able to go to the police. Although Santiago also suffers at the hands of the immigration industrial complex, he uses that vulnerability to steal from another unauthorized migrant who appears to be a little better off.

Carlos and Luis find a man who takes them to where Santiago lives. At the apartment, Carlos politely begins asking about Santiago, but Luis pushes through the door and yells for Santiago. Luis snatches down a curtain from a window and sees that the bedroom is full of people sleeping in bunk beds and crowded on the floors, not to mention the many people sleeping on beds and floors throughout other rooms. Luis is shocked but he remains angry and demands that his father, "Tell these fools if they don't 'fess up, we're calling La Migra" [48:10]. Luis is using fear of La Migra to threaten people that he associates with the man who stole from them. He knows that, as a citizen, he cannot be deported, but he can threaten vulnerable others as a means to gain cooperation.

Upon finding the restaurant where Santiago works, Carlos enters to confront him. Santiago looks startled and ashamed at seeing Carlos, but then runs outside. Luis easily catches up with the elderly Santiago and tackles him to the ground, beating him until Carlos drags him away. They find a receipt for a wire transfer; Santiago sold the truck and sent $2,800 to someone in El Salvador. Luis kicks Santiago again and Carlos once again pulls him away. Luis yells at Carlos, "You want to be nice to this bitch? Huh? What about all that shit you said about moving to a better neighborhood? To a better house? To a better school? How the hell are we going to do it now?". The truck as a symbol of their escape, their chance to improve their circumstances and to have Carlos stop hiding, reemerges in their conflict.

Direct interaction with the immigration industrial complex comes after Carlos and Luis have taken back their truck. The father and son go to Patriot Auto Mart where Santiago sold it—a place that looks like a chop shop where they disassemble stolen vehicles. The father and son sneak in and take the truck, and back on the street as the excitement wears off, Carlos drives slowly noticing a police car. Tensions rise as Carlos' unauthorized status once again rears its head. "Drive, apa, drive," Luis says nervously and Carlos replies, "Yeah, yeah, tranquilo, tranquilo [calm, calm down, or chill]" [1:12:33]. As they drive past the police car, Luis looks back and we see the car pull out and order them to pull over, lights and siren blaring. As the officer approaches Carlos and Luis look at each other in desperation, knowing they are about to be separated, possibly forever. Here the story changes. Carlos is no longer hiding. He has been discovered and is apprehended, and the first link in a chain of systems is set into motion.

We next see Carlos entering a prison where an officer explains that each of them will be processed "into the Department of Homeland Security's immigrant database" [1:15:43] and that their information will be shared with federal and international law enforcement agencies. Whereas Carlos was able to live under the radar before, now he is known to immigration authorities. The first images we see of Carlos entering this immigration industrial complex are stark, intimidating, and reflect the way that immigration and criminalization have become intertwined (Martinez & Slack, 2013). Carlos is not a gang member and he is not committing crimes—just working unauthorized—yet he is treated as a criminal, shackled, and thrust into prison with people who appear to be gang members (based on their display of tattoos). The social consequences of blurring the boundaries between immigration and criminalization include reduced chances of getting legal status once entered into this system and introducing migrants to criminal elements (Martinez & Slack, 2013), and we can see both of these consequences playing out for Carlos in the prison.

The confusion of this system that tends to result in either incarceration or deportation (Martinez & Slack, 2013) is also depicted in Carlos' story when he meets with a lawyer. The lawyer is provided by an NGO that represents "illegal aliens" because the government won't offer any representation for them. It is disconcerting to hear Carlos being labeled an "alien"—after getting to know him and feel affection for him throughout the film, the term sounds sinister (Hiltner, 2017) and inapplicable to the loving father that Carlos is. The lawyer says that Carlos has a choice to either contest his "removal" (deportation) or not. If Carlos chooses not to contest removal, then Carlos will be deported immediately. If Carlos wants to fight deportation, he'll be detained at this cold, gray, intimidating facility for at least three months but probably six months, until the removal hearing after which he'll likely be deported anyway. Carlos asks the lawyer for his honest opinion about the chances of winning the case and being permitted to stay in the United States. The lawyer says, his chances are "zero. Not exactly zero, but only 3% of all removal hearings result in the alien being granted asylum. Thousands of people are deported each year with children younger than yours. Even aliens who pay taxes with clean records" [1:19:25].

The lawyer goes on to explain that Carlos has to make a decision soon, and then warns that, "even though it would be quicker and cheaper to have a coyote bring you back here, there would be legal consequences" [1:19:53]. The lawyer seems to be giving Carlos a message. The words are that of a warning, but the tone and the look on his face suggest that this was his way of legally telling Carlos what he ought to do—let himself get deported and then hire someone to bring him back home by crossing the border illegally. The lawyer follows his warning message with, "Do you understand me? I want you to understand me" [1:20:03], as Carlos looks at him picking up on the real message. The cinematic story here reflects what research tells us about the realities of unauthorized immigration—that oftentimes people who have been deported, especially Mexican nationals who have been deported, simply return to the United States because of their far-reaching family connections and the regular availability of jobs (Golash-Boza, 2009). Regardless of how well the border is patrolled, people continue to find more and more remote areas to cross. As Golash-Boza (2009) argues, the immigration industrial complex is one that feeds on itself, enriches powerful stakeholders at the expense of migrants, and ultimately is unsuccessful in managing unauthorized immigration, and Carlos' story illustrates that from one migrant's perspective.

The effects of Carlos' direct contact with the immigration industrial complex on the whole Galindo family can be seen when Luis listens to a voicemail from his father and when they say farewell at the prison. Luis returns to their home and listens to an answering machine message from his father. On the recording Carlos says, "Listen, mijo [my son]. I'm going away. I can't help it. I don't know when they're sending me away, but you have to come soon. It might be the last . . . It might be . . . Puede ser la última vez que te vea, mijo [It might be the last time I see you, my son]. They say I can have one bag with me. Mijo, come soon, please" [1:23:15]. Carlos switching to Spanish here is significant—when the words are too difficult to say, he changes to the language that is not so familiar for him and Luis to speak to each other. The idea of them being separated is more than either of them can bear and the language used to talk about it is the one that they tend not to use as much with each other.

While sitting together in the prison, Carlos reminds Luis of earlier in the film when he asked why he and Luis' mother had him. Carlos explains:

> You know, back in the village [in Mexico], you just did what any man would do. You found a novia [girlfriend], got married, and then you headed north. That's what I did 'cause I didn't know any different. So we came here. And then, we had you . . . You are the most important thing in this world to me, mijo. I . . . I wanted you to be able to be anything you wanted to be. That would make me

feel worthy. If you became somebody. That's why I had you. For me. For me. For a reason to live. [1:28:05]

Carlos' perspective that "going north" was the typical thing people did at a certain age in his village reinforces the way movement across the U.S.–Mexico border is so fluid and indicative of the deep links that migration and mobility have, regardless of border militarization efforts. During this painful farewell the officers waiting in the background, who occasionally bark about needing to hurry up, stand in stark contrast as embodiments of the callous systems that make up the immigration industrial complex. As the officers take Carlos away, Luis weeps and begs for his father to promise that he'll return "home."

The United States as Carlos' home appears one final time in the last scene when he and a group of people gather in a desert landscape. A man that appears to be a coyote leading the group says to them, "Listos? [Ready] Al otro lado. [To the other side]." Carlos responds in English, "Let's go home" [1:32:22]. For Carlos, home is no longer Mexico, even if the U.S. government sees it that way. For Carlos, Luis, and their family, home is in the United States. And like many others, Carlos returns to the United States after deportation. Borders won't stop people from moving, but they can ensure that certain people are marginalized when they cross that border (Bhattacharyya, 2005). Ultimately, trying to control people's movement at borders is fruitless because people find other ways, sometimes illegal, to cross a border if the need is high enough (Martin, 2012), such as it is for Carlos to reunite with his son.

Moving in between Conflicts, Face, and Cultural Values

Carlos and Luis Galindo are father and son who are in constant conflict. Recall that intercultural conflict is the learned and/or innate disagreement between individuals' cultural beliefs, needs, behaviors, and/or goals that affects their relationship or communication (Ting-Toomey, 1994). Carlos and Luis represent contradictory orientations of cultural values that influence how they perceive and handle conflict, as well as negotiate face in difficult situations.

We see this conflict at play early in the film, in a long interaction that Carlos and Luis have while Carlos is in the kitchen, getting ready for the day [3:36–7:00]. Luis asks Carlos for money, saying he needs it to buy things for school. Carlos retorts, "Since when do you go to school?". Luis seems annoyed and says "Everyday." Carlos asks how many days of school he's missed so far this year, and Luis reluctantly says, "I don't know, 18, 19?". Carlos pushes back saying, "School's important. It's everything." Luis retorts in Spanish, "Si, professor?"—irreverently suggesting that Carlos doesn't have a right to lecture him about the importance of education. Carlos continues, "You wanna end up like me?" Luis turns the conversation back to the money he wants, and Carlos says that if Luis wants money, he needs to work. He explains, "If you need money in this world, Luis, necesitas trabajar. You need to work. Get yourself an education." Luis jokes that he can always "jack an old lady in the street." Carlos, a bit exhausted from the conversation by now, chides Luis saying that it's not funny to joke like that.

Their interaction indicates two culturally conflicting communication styles, with Carlos wanting to be more involved in his son's life and decisions, while Luis desires to be left alone to make his own way. Carlos displays a high-power distance parenting style common in collectivist Mexican families, using heightened "emotional expressions during interactions . . . [since typically] Mexicans value passion and spontaneity" (Condon, 1985; Oetzel et al., 2003, p. 73). Luis, on the other hand, presents as a second-generation migrant youth who is influenced more by mainstream American individualism and prefers his 'self-face' and direct style of communication when involved in family conflicts (Ting-Toomey & Kurogi, 1998). Carlos' way of telling Luis that he needs to work to earn money reflects the high-power distance, while Luis' quick retort questioning his father's authority and focus on getting the conversation back to money reflect a low-power distance and direct communication style.

In the film, intercultural conflict is used as an oppositional metaphor that introduces nuanced binaries of relational complexities within families, but can also expose cultural differences or perpetuate stereotypes. Oppositional metaphors are "rigid and polarized dichotomies" that are typically used as media artifacts that perpetuate interethnic and international divisions among cultural groups (Sorrells, 2016, p. 213). In *A Better Life* (2011) socioeconomic differences are depicted as an important aspect of intercultural conflict by contrasting scenes of the characters' constant movements between low- and high-income neighborhoods of Los Angeles. In the first minutes of the film, we see Carlos get into a truck, presumably to go work for the day, with the sun still rising [0:00–2:24]. On the truck's radio, we hear a DJ speaking in Spanish, and as Carlos and the driver make their way to work the camera shows the view from Carlos' window. The neighborhoods gradually change from lower income to higher income as they drive from Carlos' home to the localities where they work. To reinforce this socioeconomic dialectic, a later scene starts with aerial shots of Los Angeles mansions surrounded by tall green trees [3:36–7:00]. As the camera pans out, it becomes clear that the image is from a TV show that Luis is watching at home. The TV show is about the "dopest cribs in the world" and the imagery on the TV is a stark contrast to the dark living room where Luis sits. Visual juxtapositions of rich and poor neighborhoods function as markers of vastly different social and economic realities that unauthorized migrants like Carlos have to live in and are constant reminders that he works in places where he can never get real access.

These juxtapositions of social and economic realities also appear in character interactions and some conflicts. Carlos is at a landscaping job with Blasco and climbs up a tall tree using a strap and rope system [8:04–8:51]. Meanwhile, on the ground, their client, Mrs. Donnelly, asks Blasco to tell Carlos to be careful. Blasco assures her that it's safe and after some back and forth, Blasco claims that he is fully insured and bonded, even adding, "This is the way we do it in Mexico. It's safe. Believe me." Blasco's lies, or at least stretching of the truth, become clear when Carlos says to him in Spanish from up in the tree, "If it's so safe, why don't you climb up here, fatty?" Blasco smiles and Mrs. Donnelly takes a deep breath as if reassured. Blasco plays on Mrs. Donnelly's stereotypes of Mexicans when he says that this way of climbing trees is how it's done in Mexico and what he probably knows is her assumption that Mexico is an underdeveloped place lacking access to basic machinery.

Intercultural conflict styles can also be seen within the confines of Luis' school, which resembles a prison. We see a building from the outside and the sound in the background is reminiscent of prison doors opening and closing [8:52–11:14]. On this school's campus, Luis and Facundo are angry with another boy, Ramon, because he accepted Facundo's payment for "yesca" (marijuana), but then didn't give him the product. Ruthie, Luis' girlfriend, marches over to Ramon and says, "Yo, my man, you know who I am?" Ruthie is part of a well-known gang family, and she threatens him saying, "I'm gonna have you killed." Ramon pushes back at first, but then quickly relents, and then hits on Ruthie after returning the money. Luis, by now seething, loses patience and punches Ramon in the face multiple times. A school police officer breaks up the fight but apprehends Luis in the process. Luis' violent actions and Ruthie's hostile communication are evidence of an aggressive conflict style (Merkin, 2006). Posthuma et al. (2006) rationalize that "Mexicans' higher level of collectivism and close interpersonal space would actually foster less trust due to the increased social comparisons" (Gomez & Taylor, 2018, p. 37), as we find in the violent interaction among Luis and his school mates, and the prison-like mise-en-scène (guards, gates, police etc.) that their Latinx-predominant school depicts.

Oppositional metaphors of the urban and familial sociocultural divide are recurrent visual motifs in the film and return in a scene where Carlos and Blasco are ending their long day of work [14:54–19:41]. As they drive home, Carlos looks out the window at the white-presenting men gathering to surf in the setting sun, a white-presenting woman on an evening jog with her dog along sidewalks next to perfectly manicured lawns, a group of friends meeting in front of a restaurant, and a family out for an evening stroll. The montage then changes to a less residential and more low-income neighborhood where an Asian-presenting group engages in a fistfight, people waiting at a bus stop in front of a run-down church, and a group of Latino-presenting men gathered on a street corner in front of a dilapidated building. This montage moves in reverse order from the beginning of the film when Carlos is going to work. Here he is returning home, leaving the wealthy white neighborhoods where he works, back to the low-income area where he lives.

After Carlos learns that Blasco is planning to sell his truck to the buyer with the best price, Carlos reluctantly calls his sister Anita to ask for money. The scene cuts to Anita who says, "12 thousand. That's a lot of money. I can barely afford to put gas in the car" [17:38]. As she walks from her car to the house, it is clear that her home is in a middle-class neighborhood and seems larger than Carlos' one-bedroom apartment. Anita is unsure and needs to discuss with her husband. She warns Carlos, "But don't get your hopes up. You know what he's like. He's the cheapest man on the face of this earth" [18:02]. Carlos is disappointed but insists that he'll figure out another solution. Carlos' facework here indicates the avoidance strategy of communication suggesting that it's more important to maintain relational priorities than approaching a conflict directly (Oetzel et al., 2003).

Carlos returns to day labor and takes the bus to the corner where men gather in hopes of getting hired for the day [19:55–21:31]. Later the only two men left on the street are Carlos and Santiago. They were not selected for work that day. Santiago breaks open his lunch and offers to share with Carlos, who does not have lunch with him. Carlos initially refuses, but upon Santiago's insistence, he accepts the food. Here, Santiago's behavior leans collectivist. In this situation of labor uncertainty, Santiago prioritizes the group over his own goals (Oetzel et al., 2003). Santiago knows they both will not earn money on this day, but seeing that Carlos does not have food, shares the little piece of bread he has.

Carlos arrives home after dark to find his sister Anita waiting at his doorstep [24:01–27:09]. Anita nervously hands Carlos an envelope filled with money so he can buy Blasco's truck. Carlos is shocked and worried about her husband's reaction. She tells Carlos that the money comes from a savings account they started a long time ago in case of emergencies, and that Humberto doesn't have to be made aware of it. Carlos is moved but refuses to take the money. Anita insists, saying that she completely understands the risks. Anita's generosity reflects an other-face, collectivist mindset (Merkin, 2006). Giving this money may be putting her family and herself in financial trouble if she or Humberto loses a job or gets sick, but the risk is worth taking if she can help lift Carlos out of the cycle of poverty and the shadows of unauthorized status that he currently lives in. Anita is thinking about the whole family, not just her own needs. Both Carlos' refusal to accept Anita's future savings and Anita's insistence on helping her brother's survival reveal "high mutual-face concerns that lead to cooperating conflict strategies during relational interactions" (Oetzel et al., 2003, p. 72).

After buying the truck, Carlos drives to meet Luis at school to share the good news. Carlos is beaming with pride sitting in the driver's seat, but Luis still thinks it's Blasco's truck. Carlos explains, "it's ours now." Carlos' words here are important—the truck is theirs—his and Luis'. For Carlos, purchasing this truck is an investment for both of them, for the entire family. Luis, unimpressed, says, "Good for you" and Carlos redirects him—"No, mijo [my son], good for us" [30:00]. For Carlos, it is something he did for the whole family, to be able to help improve their circumstances—it is not something he did solely for himself. Luis reluctantly agrees, "Sure, good for us." Luis' reluctance here is more typical of individualism, yet his condescension that the truck is not Carlos' alone supports previous research about there being different levels within collectivistic thinking among Mexicans, who often use more competing face negotiation to communicate that "while they were concerned for others, this may not translate to them being willing to concede to others" (Gomez & Taylor, 2018, pp. 47–8; Posthuma et al., 2006).

Soon after, we do find Luis' competing facework turn to 'compromising' and 'considering the other' (Oetzel et al., 2000), when Carlos comes home drunk after having his investment (the truck) stolen out from underneath him by Santiago [40:50–43:30]. As Carlos passes out, Luis asks "Are you going to be ok?" For one of the first times in the film, we see the affection that Luis has for his father. In the morning while Carlos showers, Luis makes him breakfast, but Carlos thanks him explaining he can't stay. He says, "This is my problem," but Luis counters: "No, this is our problem." Here the tables have turned. Earlier Carlos saw the truck as theirs, but now that it's stolen, he takes the blame and doesn't want to burden his son with this trouble. For Carlos, the stolen truck is his problem. But, Luis has changed his outlook—now the truck is theirs and from that perspective, Santiago stole from all of them. Luis too feels robbed.

Cultural identities are fluid, however, and move between values as situations demand. This is seen in the different conflict styles presented by Luis and Carlos when they first go to look for their stolen truck [43:32–45:02]. As they get off the bus and arrive at the corner where men anxiously gather trying to get day labor, Luis scoffs at them, "Look at these pendejos [idiots, morons] out here ho-ing themselves." Carlos retaliates, "You think they want to do this? That was me out there. That's going to be me out there." Carlos is redirecting his son to show respect for these men and their efforts to earn an honest living, even if it's not the kind of work they want to be doing.

Carlos' reaction suggests that when it comes to issues of respect and integrity, Mexicans have a "strong independent self," despite having an interdependent mindset (Oetzel et al., 2003, p. 73). Luis retorts, "Yeah, well it's also the bitch that stole your truck." For Luis, Santiago has stolen from him and does not deserve his respect, nor do the other men at the corner who are now inadvertently associated with Santiago in Luis' mind. Luis' reaction suggests that his individualistic "self-face concern" is predominant in this situation and is prompting him to use dominating conflict strategies (Oetzel et al., 2003, p. 72). Carlos, on the other hand, has a more nuanced perspective having been one of the men there asking for work and having firsthand knowledge of the anxiety the men are experiencing.

Carlos' and Luis' culturally divergent conflict styles come to a climax, soon, after they leave Santiago's crowded apartment and Carlos wants to pay Jesus, the man who led them to the building where Santiago lived. Luis resists and reaches for Carlos' hand with the cash before he gives it to Jesus, trying to convince him to give Jesus only half the promised payment. Carlos says, "Stop talking like an ass!". Here, Carlos is showing Luis what being a man means to him. It's not about being angry at everyone and getting payback for every wrong. For Carlos, being a man means taking care of his family, as we already know, but it's also about keeping his word and respecting the people around him. Having the truck stolen is certainly a significant loss of face for Carlos, but he also knows that it is not right to take that out on people who were not involved in Santiago's betrayal. For Luis, this significant loss of face is something he wants to take out on anyone he associates with Santiago. Luis' perspective of face is rooted in his experiences of being American and being loosely associated with a gang via Ruthie. From that perspective, a wrong toward their group requires an aggressive response to rectify the situation and regain face. But Carlos' perspective is different. In this situation Carlos leans toward a compromising conflict resolution strategy, common to the collectivistic mindset of high uncertainty avoidance, while Luis displays competitive facework, common among individualists who prefer low uncertainty avoidance (Oetzel et al., 2003; Hofstede, 1980, 2001).

Carlos' 'other-honoring' and Luis' 'self-honoring' facework (Oetzel et al., 2003) comes out more in the scene where father and son walk into a charreada [Mexican rodeo], while they wait for the restaurant where Santiago works to open. Inside the charreada, people are dressed in traditional clothing and ride horses. Luis jokes that they look like they're going to a Halloween party. Carlos explains, "This is where I'm coming from. This is your people. Charros [horsemen]. They're you" [53:18]. Luis snubs Carlos, insisting this type of culture isn't him. He identifies more as American than Mexican. As they watch the horse performances and competitions, traditional music plays in the background. Luis says, "I hate this kind of music," and then goes on to complain about not understanding what the announcer is saying. Carlos is startled and realizes that Luis doesn't understand as much Spanish as he'd thought. Luis' difficulty understanding Spanish, combined with his reluctance to embrace his Mexican heritage, is quite a shock for Carlos and he encourages Luis to try harder to listen to the announcer and understand the words. Luis focuses and can understand most of what the announcer says.

Later, while still at the rodeo, a song is heard in the background and Carlos asks if Luis remembers it. The song is called Zapatero [shoemaker]—a traditional Mexican folk song. Luis doesn't remember the song, but Carlos explains that his mother used to sing it to him when he was a baby. Luis shuts down because he doesn't want to discuss his mother, and though Carlos finds it hard to accept his son's response, he yields because of his high-context sensibility. What Carlos symbolizes here is Mexico's 'normative' orientation in long-term cultural values (Hofstede Insights, 2019). The long-term cultural value explains the degree to which societies consider their past in connection with their present and future, ranging between normative (low) or pragmatic (high) orientations (Hofstede Insights, 2019). Among other beliefs, Mexicans like Carlos show a lot of respect for their ethnic heritage and cultural traditions, as we see in this context with Carlos' nostalgia about the charreada, the Zapatero folk song, and his efforts to make Luis understand Spanish and appreciate the important aspects of their cultural identity. That said, we also see Luis slowly beginning to appreciate this aspect of Mexican culture and this part of his heritage, the more he gets into the charreada performances.

The gradual cultural transition in Luis also changes his conflict style and preferred facework. In a scene later in the film, Luis goes back home and he hears a voice message from Carlos, who by then is in prison [1:20:44–1:24:15]. While listening to the message, Luis stands weeping over the answering machine. Suddenly, Facundo appears at the door asking for Luis while Ruthie and some young men wait in the distance. Luis hides out of sight and as they leave, we can see that Facundo has a new neck tattoo and injuries on his face. It seems he has now joined the gang, having experienced an initiation beating. When faced with the choice, Luis chooses his father instead of the gang. Luis' change of heart and his decision to stand by family—as we see more of in the following scenes when he meets Carlos in prison, expresses regret for past behavior, sings Carlos the Zapatero song from his childhood, and pleads him to return—indicates Luis' movement to collectivistic conflict-resolution strategies like apologizing, compromising, considering the other, having private discussions, and talking about the problem (Oetzel, 2003).

Luis has now reached the phase of his cultural identity that he manages through integrating facework, which "emphasizes both the resolution of the conflict and the preservation of the relationship" (Oetzel et al., 2003, p. 71). In a scene that, in cinematic time, opens four months after Carlos' deportation, we see Luis playing soccer on a lush, green field and wearing the jersey his father had bought him earlier [1:31:37]. As Luis' movement from an individualistic to collectivistic orientation seems complete, it becomes apparent that Luis is now living with his aunt and fulfilling his father's dream of being part of a good school in a good neighborhood with their family.

CONCLUSION

For Carlos and other unauthorized migrants, the fear of being caught weighs heavily on them, and it also weighs heavily on their citizen children who fear that their families will be broken up because of deportation. The threat of the immigration industrial complex looms large and haunts all of the characters. Almost a decade later, these themes continue to resonate in the American political climate. *A Better Life* (2011) earned many accolades for its depiction of these themes, including an Oscar nomination and a Screen Actors Guild Awards nomination for Best Actor in a Leading Role. The film was also the winner of the American Latino Media Arts award for Favorite Movie, and earned eighth place with the African-American Film Critics Association's list of Top 10 films in 2011.

The theft of Carlos' truck is the turning point in the film, and in Carlos' life, shifting his low-key existence into one filled with the fear that so many unauthorized migrants feel living on the margins. It is also the juncture that changes how Carlos, like Luis, settles, heightens, withdraws, intimidates, or confronts other individuals, and defends self- or others' face during conflicts, moving in between cultural values (Merkin, 2006; Oetzel et al., 2003). We see movement in both father and son's cultural orientations, and associated conflict styles, as the film progresses, inferring that Mexicans and Mexican Americans can also use more competing conflict resolution in specific situations while aiming for an integrative resolution (Posthuma et al., 2006; Gomez & Taylor, 2018).

In the film, Carlos' truck, Los Angeles' complex urbanscapes, gang life, and the prison function as cinematic symbols of Carlos and Luis' precarious survival, and their movements, along borders of mobility and immobility. The recurrent visual comparisons of starkly different urbanscapes, moving from Carlos' low-income community, his run-down home, Luis' prison-like school, and Santiago's overcrowded apartment where unauthorized immigrants live, to the expensive Los Angeles mansions where Carlos works, function as oppositional metaphors of *what* his labor is, and the spaces *where* his labor actually takes place—a jarring reality that many unauthorized migrant laborers like Carlos experience.

The dream of social mobility toward a better life turns into the dread of legal immobility when La Migra takes on a life of its own, affecting the

Galindos' movements and interpersonal relationships. A comment from 'Celo, a high-level gang member, encapsulates this dread: "That's all they know how to do. Lock us out, or lock us up" [23:01]. 'Celo is referencing various kinds of authority that want to keep Latinx individuals like them out of institutions that could be used for advancement (i.e., schools), or deny their entry into the country in the first place (border wall), or imprison or deport them (DHS/ICE). From the xenophobic rhetoric about Latinx individuals as 'other,' to the cruel separation and imprisonment of migrant families and children, to the ending of temporary protected status for refugees of natural disaster and war, and more, the message of the current U.S. administration is that Latinx individuals are unwelcome (Varela, 2018), but it is also a message that has been brewing for a long time.

What personifies the immigration industrial complex in the film, and provides a lens into the demonization of unauthorized immigration that Trump's administration is currently legitimizing through its "'anti-illegal' rhetoric" and material border wall (Golash-Boza, 2009, p. 296), is the incarceration and eventual deportation of Carlos to Mexico. As we see playing out for Carlos in prison, the real outcome of disappearing boundaries between immigration and criminalization minimizes the odds for many to gain legal status in the United States, or pairs them with criminal others (Martinez & Slack, 2013), and/or leaves little recourse than to resort to unlawful means of reentry to the United States (Bhattacharyya, 2005). Like many deported immigrants, Carlos makes the return journey to the Mexico–U.S. border, on foot, with the help of a coyote, and through treacherous desert terrain. Carlos' movement, at the end of the film, may not be free and unencumbered, but it is a movement toward "home." Even if Carlos is disenfranchised at every turn, it is movement in pursuit of his family's (re)unification and survival.

NOTES

1. We use the term "unauthorized" throughout this chapter (except in direct quotes), as opposed to illegal or undocumented, based on terminology used in the literature reviewed. Additionally, per *The New York Times*, "illegal" has a "sinister" tone, and "undocumented" is acceptable but may be interpreted as a euphemism for 'illegal' (Hiltner, 2017). Even "unauthorized" sounds a bit "bureaucratic" (Hiltner, 2017). To remain consistent with the literature informing our analysis as well as the norms of immigration journalism, we use the term unauthorized.

2. The Amazon Prime Video translation of this conversation uses the term "wetback." The character says, in Spanish, "mojados" which is slang for unauthorized migration. The word mojado also literally means wet. It seems that when a Latinx person uses the term "mojados," it is generally acceptable, but when a non-Latinx person says "wetback" it is an offensive and derogatory use of the term (Gerber, 2013).

Part II

MOVEMENTS

COLONIALISM, POSTCOLONIALISM, AND CONFLICT

Chapter 4

Rabbit Proof Fence

Kidnapping, Colonization, and Segregation of Australian Aboriginals

"No! This my kids! Mine!" screams Maude as a white Australian police officer takes her daughters and niece, and claims that "it's the law." In this painful scene, in the opening minutes of *Rabbit Proof Fence* (2002), audiences see the trauma of Aboriginal mothers and their children being forcibly separated, but this separation is legal. What follows is the story of three half-caste Aboriginal girls: Molly (fourteen), her sister Daisy (eight), and their cousin Gracie (ten), as they are abducted from their families and taken to a colonial Christian school that will teach them to assimilate into "civilized" society as domestic workers. Grief stricken at the loss of their home, heartbroken to be separated from their mothers, and repulsed at the colonial whitewashing that was determined to beat the indigenous out of their bodies, minds, and souls, the three girls escape and chart a 1,500-mile northward journey across the West Australian desert.

How could such abduction be legal? This dramatic scene is rooted in the true history of Australia's treatment of Aboriginal people—treatment rooted in cultural othering and its history of colonization. In this chapter we pay homage to the Australian drama *Rabbit Proof Fence* (2002), directed by Phillip Noyce and set in 1930s British Commonwealth of Australia. We explore the film's conceptual interplay of racial othering, white savior narratives, assimilationist policies, and the movement of contested identities and spaces, in the context of "conquest, colonization, and the rise of capitalism . . . [as] the terrain on which race, racial identities and racial hierarchies were forged . . . that justified and promoted domination and exploitation" (Sorrells, 2016, pp. 60–61).

The film is based on the true story inspired book *Follow the Rabbit-Proof Fence* (1996) by Doris Pilkington (Aboriginal name: Nugi Garimara). After being abducted, the girls strategize an escape from the missionary settlement,

Moore River. Guided by Molly's sharp tracking skills along with help from sympathetic strangers, they largely evade the colonists and their Aboriginal tracker, Moodoo. The girls follow a rabbit proof fence north to Jigalong in the hopes of reuniting with their mothers. While Molly and Daisy manage to hide from the removalists, Gracie is mercilessly reabducted and sent back to Moore River. Molly and Daisy battle the remaining journey and are reunited with their mother and grandmother in Jigalong.

We explore how the film's symbolic use of the fence and the freedom movement of half-caste Aboriginal children belonging to the Stolen Generation marked a cultural breach and mobility against the colonial discourses of assimilation and segregation (Parry, 1995; Sorrells, 2016). The movements shown in *Rabbit Proof Fence* are multilayered and cut across geophysical planes, generational spaces, racial labels, and colonial realities, as three half-caste Aboriginal girls travel in search of their lost cultural identities despite oppression and familial separation.

In this chapter, we start with a brief review of the history of colonization and racial othering in early twentieth-century Australia, its role in separating indigenous families, how power impacts physical and spatial mobilities, and finally move to exploring our case study of the film using these conceptual frames.

COLONIZATION AND RACIAL OTHERING

"Are we to allow the creation of an unwanted third race? . . . Will our children be black?" (Noyce, 2002) asks A. O. Neville, the chief protector and legal guardian of "every aboriginal and half-caste child" (Aborigines Act 1905, 2016). In *Rabbit Proof Fence* (2002) Neville addresses a room full of white Australian settlers, in post-independent 1930s Australia, to convince them that the "continuous infiltration of white blood stamps out the black color." Australia gained independence in 1901, yet remained a part of the British Commonwealth for years after. Colonial masters were replaced by white missionaries who took a moral resolution to remove, institutionalize, and "civilize" indigenous Aborigines, believing that "white 'blood' fitted them for a better life" (Parry, 1995, p. 141). Racial othering of Western Australia's Aborigines by white settlers, in particular the kidnapping and forced assimilation of half-caste children (of mixed Aboriginal and white parentage) largely informed their removalist policies from the late nineteenth century until the 1970s.

Discourses on race and racial hierarchy as markers of biological difference have been debunked for some time, yet the exclusionary impact of their social construction is rather grim. Intercultural communication scholar

Kathryn Sorrells (2016) explains how European capitalist conquests of other nations for over 500 years, up until the nineteenth century, created opportunities for close cultural interactions between settlers and indigenous people. Differences in physical appearance (skin color, facial features) were leveraged by colonizers as divine justifications for creating a racial hierarchy with whites on the zenith and nonwhite racial others way beneath. History bears witness to how European colonizers have authored dominant discourses about "racial purity" of white blood, and obscured histories of "non-Christian, 'uncivilized,' and soon enough non-white 'others'" (Winant, 2001, p. 22), dominating, exploiting, and oppressing the latter on claims that were economic, political, religious, cultural, and moralistic (Said, 1978).

In *Orientalism* (1978), Edward Said traces the *othering* of the *Orient* (non-European, nonwhite cultures) to the *Occidental* (Western/European) imagination. The Western construction of the Orient was not as much a true account of its cultures, people, and society, as it was a representation of what the colonizers wanted it to be. Ideologies of power, hegemony, and oppression, whether grounded in capitalism, religion, and/or Darwinism, were leveraged by European colonizers to position their cultural, moral, racial, and social superiority against that of the colonized (Said, 1978). The rationale of their "colonial project" was to "'civilize' and 'save'" the supposedly uncivilized indigenous people (Sorrells, 2016, p. 63). To this end, coerced or consensual assimilation of indigenous groups in European colonies became a common political tool used by colonizers to validate dominance and perpetuate a hierarchy of difference.

The *hierarchy of difference*, or German anthropologist Blumenbach's eighteenth-century social construct that grouped people along a superior to inferior racial continuum (Sorrells, 2016), from light to progressively darker skin tones in descending order, informed the white supremacist ideals of European colonizers (Winant, 2001). White supremacy points to the historical and systemic persecution and othering of countries, continents, and communities of nonwhite people, independent or colonized, by white Europeans whose intercultural contact with the former was for acquiring capital, labor, power, and authority (Martinez, 1998; Sorrells, 2016). Often dressed up to look like benevolence or philanthropy, especially for Christian missionaries in non-European colonies, the white man in particular took it upon himself to salvage nonwhite, indigenous people who were apparently in dire need of being *saved* from themselves. Thus emerges the trope of the *white savior*, in reality an empire-driven, self-serving colonial strategy that finds its early allusions in Rudyard Kipling's poem, *The White Man's Burden* (1929). Originally detailing America's role as a white savior in the Philippine–American War (1899–1902), Kipling's plea to white colonizers: "Take up the White Man's burden, Send forth the best ye breed . . . To serve your captives' need . . . Your new-caught, sullen peoples, Half devil and half child" (1929), explains the white savior narrative we find in *Rabbit Proof Fence*, particularly in Neville's proselytizing to half-caste children: "We're here to help and encourage you in this new world. Duty, service, responsibility. Those are our watchwords" [23:20]. Masking disenfranchisement as progress, the Eurocentric claim that "non-whites are childlike innocents in need of white men's protection" (Rieder, 2008, p. 30) served as Neville's and the Australian assimilationists' justification for continued dispossession of indigenous Australian people from their land, cultures, and traditions.

SEPARATING FAMILIES

In the Australian context, race and racial hierarchy placed whites at the top and Aboriginals at the bottom. The question then became—how to categorize those with mixed Aboriginal and white heritage, or the *half-castes*? The answer was to abduct these children from their families and train them for domestic service. Beginning in 1869, during British colonial rule and with the passage of the Aboriginal Protection Act, the government took control of Aboriginals' lives. Subsequent acts, even after Australia's independence in 1901, clarified and extended that control ("Bringing them home," 2007).

The argument for kidnapping half-caste children was that their supposed 'white' blood made them superior to their Aboriginal families. As Parry (1995) describes, the thinking among whites was that half-castes were "salvageable because a white heritage gave them a limited, diluted as it was, intellectual heritage which could be cultivated" (p. 145). Typical of these racist systems of oppression, whites obscured their deep-seated racism, even from themselves. They did this by convincing themselves it was their *duty* to maintain racial separation and to protect mixed-race offspring from their Aboriginal heritage and family. The result was that children born to Aboriginal mothers were routinely taken from their families and placed in missions where they were brainwashed to believe in this system of racial hierarchy, and to train for work as domestic labor for white households. According to white Australian law, Aboriginals and their children were considered wards of the state, meaning it was legal for state officials to take Aboriginal and mixed children from their homes and place them in state care.

Assimilationist policies outlined in the Aborigines Act of 1905 were "designed initially to protect " Aboriginal people, but in reality "separated them from the group which accepted them and offered them love" (Tilbrook, 2007, p. 55). In addition to having a white colonial protector who would control the indigenous Aborigines, the Commonwealth Constitution also guaranteed that "Aboriginal natives shall not be counted . . . [and] the Commonwealth would legislate for any race except Aboriginal people"

("Indigenous Australia Timeline," 2018). In fact, the Act of 1905 granted government delegates, like A. O. Neville, the authority to abduct Aboriginal and Torres Strait Islander children from their families and take them to settlements. As seen in the film, Moore River, where Molly, Daisy, and Gracie were taken to be indoctrinated into Eurocentric-Christian ways of life, was in reality founded by the Government of Western Australia in 1918. Such missionary settlements had a number of problems, including health and sanitation issues, with more than 200 children between the ages of 1–5 years dying in the Moore River settlement. It has also been recorded through oral histories and survivor testimonies that indigenous children frequently tried to escape the Moore River Native Settlement to return to their families ("Map," 2018).

In 1997, the Australian government released a nearly 600-page report about the history of the tragic separation of Aboriginal and Torres Strait Islander children from their families, which was updated in 2007. Some findings from the report were that: (1) families and their children were discouraged from communicating, (2) officials falsely told children that their families did not want them or that their parents were deceased, (3) children were taught to repudiate Aboriginal culture and heritage, (4) living conditions at missions and placement homes were extremely poor, (5) many never received wages promised to them, and (6) many children were subjected to physical and/or sexual abuse. Ultimately, the report argues that the state failed the Aboriginal community, and these children in particular, and that there are numerous legal grounds for reparations ("Bringing them home," 2007). The generations of children who were forcibly separated from their families are known as the *Stolen Generation* because they were stolen from their families, and their culture was stolen from them. By 1931, when the backstory of *Rabbit Proof Fence* (2002) takes place, these racist systems were well underway.

SPACE AND POWER

Power, from the perspective of Foucault, is understood in terms of knowledge and discourse rather than physical force. In fact, power and knowledge are deeply intertwined for Foucault and they function together to produce certain kinds of discourse (1980, 2012). One tool of power used to control and regulate people's thoughts and actions is discipline. Restrictions on movement within spaces, forcing people to live in specific areas, and surveilling their actions are tools used to discipline people into behavior, actions, and even thinking that suits the powerful group's interest. Foucault famously made these arguments by analyzing institutions such as prisons and medicine, but his ideas can be used to see how knowledge and power dynamics operate within physical spaces. This thinking opens up ways of seeing the "disciplinary components" of state uses of power, and of recognizing how certain practices are "part of a shifting field of power and knowledge in which we can see the gradual self-formation of a class, a nation or a civilization" (Rabinow, 2003, p. 355). Colonization and the racist systems therein are archetypal examples of discipline and power implemented on a population—by physical force as history has shown, of course, but also through knowledge, ideological systems, and discourse as well. The formation of the Australian nation is rooted in its original sin of forcibly taking the land from indigenous inhabitants and then using power and discipline to control their movements and every aspect of their lives.

Colonial and postcolonial spaces are deeply imbued with social, cultural, and political tensions and discourses. But, one of the challenges of postcolonial theory is that it does not always adequately address the impacts of colonization on indigenous populations, bodies, and subjects (Moreton-Robinson, 2003). It is valuable for analyzing the power dynamics of "the dispersed, or diasporic, subject" (Moreton-Robinson, 2003, p. 28)—locations where colonial settlers left after colonial rule ended, and that may be experiencing postcolonial migration where citizens from former colonies migrate to colonizing countries (Sorrells, 2016). But in cases where settlers established colonial rule and then remained after it ended—such as Australia and the United States—the notion of *postcolonizing* may be more suitable because it captures the fact that the dispossession of land continues (Moreton-Robinson, 2003).

Space, in terms of land and land rights, is at the center of *Rabbit Proof Fence* (2002), and land dispossession is an original sin at the heart of Aboriginal suffering. The land that we call Australia can be considered a contested space, or a location where "conflicts in the form of opposition, confrontation, subversion, and/or resistance engage actors whose social positions are defined by differential control of resources and access to power" (Low & Lawrence-Zuniga, 2003, p. 18). Beginning in 1788 when white, European migrants first arrived in Australia, they claimed that the land belonged to no one (*Terra Nullius*, in legal terms). This formed a legal basis (from their perspective) for white possession of the lands, and so began the oppression, domination, and control of Aboriginals' lives (Moreton-Robinson, 2003). The lands are contested because conflict and resistance exist between whites and Aboriginals, and whites largely retain power. Aboriginals have little power and they remain the most impoverished group in the country (Moreton-Robinson, 2003).

Even the question of who can claim Australian national identity is tied to racialized social hierarchy. It is rooted in the capitalist accumulation of wealth, which subsequently afforded the accumulation of "social worth, authority, and ownership," and Aboriginals were excluded from these systems (Moreton-Robinson, 2003, p. 25). White Australians developed a sense of a right to, and ownership of, the land, through their perception of their own hard work and their contributions to building the nation (and the false presumption of taking unpopulated land). That is, the formation of this nation is bound up with power, discourse, and disciplinary tactics designed to marginalize the indigenous population. Aboriginals are not afforded this same right of national identity. Indeed "who calls Australia home is inextricably connected to who has possession, and possession is jealously guarded by white Australians" (Moreton-Robinson, 2003, p. 27).

When it comes to the social relations in this land, this national space, power, and possession is spatially illustrated by policies such as those that forced Aboriginal groups to live in specific areas and restricting movement across spaces. Scholars can think about space and social relations in at least a couple of ways—social production and social construction. *Social production* of space refers to the political and economic formation of space, while *social construction* refers to the "transformation of space—through people's exchanges, memories, images, and daily use of the material setting" (Low, 1996, p. 862).

Another way to think about space is to differentiate between strategic and tactical uses of space, as argued by de Certeau (1984). Strategic space refers to spatial practices associated with power, while tactical space refers to practices associated with individuals lacking power, but generating their own meaning within spaces that are strategically beyond their control. Those in power implement strategic uses of space by creating systems of classification and division, declaring and forming territories and boundaries (Cresswell, 1997). Simply put, powerful subjects "depend on the certainty of mapping" (Cresswell, 1997, p. 362). By contrast, tactical uses of space by weak subjects involve "furtive movement, short cuts and routes ... [that] contest this spatial domination" (Low & Lawrence-Zuniga, 2003, p. 32; Cresswell, 1997). Such tactics "refuse the neat divisions and classification of the powerful and, in doing so, critique the spatialization of domination" (Cresswell, 1997, p. 363). The spatial tactics of weak subjects include "mobility and detachment from the rationalized spaces of power" (Low & Lawrence-Zuniga, 2003, p. 32). By so doing, disempowered subjects enact tactical uses of space by challenging dominant and strategic systems of categorization, and forming fluid territories and mobile borders.

FILM ANALYSIS

In this chapter, we frame our analysis of the film along two intercultural themes, following its characters' movements across geographical and ideological spaces—*whiteness and half-castes*, and *borders and fences*. These themes depict the oppressive, colonial contexts that frame the journey of three Aboriginal sisters who share, suffer, lose, and grow a great deal as they make their way home to reclaim their families and cultural identities.

Whiteness and Half-Castes

A low-key, high-angle shot of A. O. Neville is interestingly placed toward the end of the film. Molly and Daisy have finally reached home. Neville's department has no more funds to continue looking for the girls, so he orders the search to end. Resignedly, Neville dictates a letter to his secretary: "We face an uphill battle with these people, especially the bush natives who have to be protected against themselves. If they would only understand what we are trying to do for them" [1:23:49]. As Neville sits alone in his ominously furnished office, clutching the arms of his chair, the audience is primed to look down on him, and on all that he represents—a bitter colonial legacy of ethnic oppression, racial othering, and white supremacy.

Constant visual references to othering and captivity are found in *Rabbit Proof Fence*, starting with the scene when the girls, Molly, Gracie, and Daisy, are on a truck going to the Moore River Native Settlement, after being abducted from Jigalong [9:29–11:55]. The dark, menacing soundtrack accompanying their truck ride through barren lands is followed by a long shot juxtaposing the church in the background and the truck in the foreground, as it pulls into the settlement. The camera moves to an almost tilted, medium shot of the girls all huddled up in the truck's hutched trunk. The condescending tone of the nun, as she says "poor dears, such a long way, you must be exhausted" [15:46], and leads them to the dormitory with her lantern, is reminiscent of a warden leading prisoners to jail. Related imagery of large iron locks on dormitory doors meant to prevent escape, and the consistent insistence of hall monitors and nuns that indigenous children speak only in English at Moore River, function to remind audiences that "the Aboriginal has simply been bred out . . . to be given the benefit of everything our [colonial] culture has to offer" [13:12–13:44].

Lies, separations, abuse, and whitewashing are key to understanding the tremendous grief, trauma, and loss of identity felt by Australia's Stolen Generations. Whether by compulsion, duress, or undue influence, half-caste children were taken from their families by government-delegated protectors and police officers upon legislative orders. We find this happening in the film when unsuspecting Molly and her sisters are mercilessly abducted by a white officer working on Neville's removalist orders, while their mother and grandmother are collecting rations from a supplier in Jigalong [9:29–11:55].

The forced movements from home and family to oppressive spaces controlled by white colonists had debilitating effects on indigenous populations. It resulted in a deep sense of loss, depression, anxiety, mental illnesses, and health problems, not only for those removed but also for Aboriginal mothers and families who were forced, tricked, and/or guilted into giving up their children (Human Rights and Equal Opportunity Commission, 1997). According to Sir Ronald Wilson, president of the Human Rights Commission, this act of nonconsensual familial separation was nothing short of genocide. Wilson quotes the fifth clause in the description of the Genocide Convention, defining it as the "removing of children from their communities with a view to extinguishing their culture" (Australian Human Rights Commission, 2014). It was not only their families and cultures the children were separated from, but they were dislocated from their connections with indigenous spaces and ethnic languages that were closely tied to their spiritual identity (Australian Human Rights Commission, 2014).

"There are Westerners, and there are Orientals. The former dominate; the latter must be dominated, which usually means having their land occupied, their internal affairs rigidly controlled, their blood and treasure put at the disposal of one or another Western power" (Said, 1978, p. 44). We see this unapologetic conviction in racial superiority in the film, when A. O. Neville addresses a room full of white Australian female settlers, convincing them that, "in spite of himself, the native must be helped" [13:45]. Neville's moralistic stance as a white savior is reminiscent of Edward Said's critique of twentieth-century British imperialist Balfour, who describes colonized Egyptians as, a "subject race, dominated by a race that knows them and what is good for them better than what they could possibly know for themselves" (1978, p. 42).

The labels *white savior*, *white savior complex*, and more recently *white savior industrial complex* also finds place in popular culture in its association with nonwhite races. It shows up in critiques of films, news, shows, and social media that feature Caucasian characters as saviors, both of white racial purities and as benevolent messiahs for people of color (Keesey, 1998; Cole, 2012). In the Australian bush melodrama film genre of the 1920s, white male heroes were heralded as saviors who would "ensure cultural continuity" (Keesey, 1998, p. 333) to safeguard their patriarchal rights, and the heroine's purity, via "rescue of the young [white] woman taken by the aborigines" (Tulloch, 1982, pp. 177–78). It is only in Australian new wave films like *Picnic at Hanging Rock* (1975), and later in twenty-first-century postcolonial cinema like *Rabbit Proof Fence* that white, colonial protagonists are progressively presented as the ambivalent *Other*, oppressor, and as a patriarchal dual embodiment of the "white savior and primitive rapist" tropes (Keesey, 1998, p. 334).

In the early twentieth century, Eurocentric racist mindsets undergirded assimilationist Aboriginal policies (Parry, 1995, p. 145), along with a premonitive system of colorism that preferred light-skinned half-castes over dark ones. A specific scene from the film, when A. O. Neville is at the Moore River settlement checking "for the fair ones," resonates this colonial mindset. The sisters, and the rest of the half-caste children, wait in an assembly-like formation for Neville and the nuns to decide their future, based on the color of their skin. Nina, another inmate of the colonial settlement, explains to Molly how the fair-skinned ones are "more clever than us . . . they can go to a proper school" [21:49]. Lighter-skinned indigenous children were often adopted by white, European families, and a large number of them were taken as wards, overseas (Australian Human Rights Commission, 2014). Since the "white body was the norm and measure for identifying who could belong" (Moreton-Robinson, 2003, p. 25), dark-skinned half-castes were sent to missionaries, and mostly went on to become domestic servants and farm laborers. They were institutionalized, often being mistreated, flogged, raped, sexually abused, chained, locked up, and kept in solitary confinement (Australian Human Rights Commission, 2014).

"Patriarchy was the basis of state power, economic rationalization and family structures" (Parry, 1995, p. 143). It was no different for the Northern Territory, than it was for other states in the Australian Commonwealth, that growing concerns about its sparse white population were made stronger by a colonial abhorrence that "children of white fathers were growing up amongst Aboriginal people in the poorest of circumstances" (Parry, 1995, p. 144). The inimitable strength, endurance, and independence of Aboriginal mothers was presented as antithetical to Western, patriarchal ideals of "loving, self-sacrificing and virtuous" motherhood. Aboriginal motherhood became *othered*, for white settlers, and sadly for many institutionalized children of the Stolen Generation. Nina, the older girl at the settlement, has internalized the colonial erasure of indigenous motherhood when she claims to Molly and her sisters, "nobody here got any mothers" [26:37].

The film also presents a social commentary on the role of patriarchy in Eurocentric and Aboriginal worldviews, where "Aboriginal women threatened the power base of Australian society by making the men redundant" (Parry, 1995, p. 144). Toward the end of the film, Neville is upset at losing the girls again, and angry that they're "making fools" of the government. His reputation is at stake, and he is indignant that they are unable to understand his benevolent efforts at helping society by kidnapping, converting, and training half-caste children for domestic labor, for "civilized" white households [1:01:00]. The fundamental threat is that Neville and his patriarchal policies are being outsmarted by girls—indigenous women of color—turning the white savior myth on its head. Aboriginal women were a direct threat to white men and their dreams of nation-building in colonial Australia. Even those Aboriginal mothers who bore mixed-race children, as a result of rape, prostitution, and/or consensual coupling, "survived and continued to produce and raise children independent of a white male" (Parry, 1995, pp. 143–44).

Borders and Fences

From the opening scenes when the camera pans over the remote lands of Australia it is clear that this land, and the women and girls the audience first meets, are "geographical selves" tied closely to the land that they inhabit (Casey, 2001). And yet this is land that is controlled, and inhabitants' movements are governed and restrained. White colonists use strategic space to implement their power to discipline Aboriginals into submission and marginalization. The so-called rabbit proof fence at the center of this film serves as a physical barrier that restricts movement of wildlife according to white society's interests and agricultural needs. However, from a tactical perspective, it also serves as a guide that brings the girls back to their home. The very thing meant to restrict and control movement becomes a navigational tool leading Molly and Daisy back home.

The fence functions at a literal level, but it is also a metaphorical tool—a comment about colonial and postcolonizing efforts at controlling and dominating the indigenous population. As the opening text of the film explains, after years of resistance, white settlers eventually invaded Aboriginal land and by 1931, when the film takes place, white settlers had created laws to "control [Aboriginals'] lives in every detail." While place and space are regulated and monitored throughout the film, the girls use space in tactical ways to elude forces of power and oppression and find their way home. Such different uses of space can be seen in the contrast between Neville's methods of searching for the girls and the girls' movements. Neville is depicted, several times, frantically referring to his large paper maps of the region, trying to determine where the girls are. His position of power makes him comfortable with "classification, delineation, division," and the resulting mapping that complements it (Cresswell, 1997, p. 363). In fact, the entire system of classifying Aboriginals and half-castes is founded on such thinking, and on classifying people by color (lightness) of their skin. The darker someone is the more their life is controlled and restricted, notably in terms of the spaces they are allowed to inhabit.

By contrast, the girls interact with space in tactical ways. They quickly escape the camp where they've been placed and where their lives are controlled. The girls do "not obey the laws of the place, for they are not defined or identified by it" (de Certeau, 1984, p. 29). That is, the girls and their mothers reject the colonial and postcolonizing laws of Australia—physical capture and placement in Moore River cannot beat the indigenous out of them. As Moreton-Robinson (2003) would argue, their connection to this space, to this land, ultimately transcends white colonizers' attempts at controlling it. The girls escape by taking advantage of an impending rainstorm, which Molly knows will cover their tracks and provide them a good start to escape the tracker, Moodoo. By relying on her knowledge of the land, the environment, and tracking skills, Molly leads the girls to escape.

There are repeated visual uses of "furtive movement" (Cresswell, 1997, p. 362) throughout the film as the girls stealthily evade Neville's goons and Moodoo. They are depicted as endlessly walking, running, crawling, and climbing with aching, scraped, and dusty legs toward home, toward safety, and away from oppression.

Shortly after their escape, the girls learn where the rabbit proof fence is and they realize that they can use that to guide them home. A fence that powerful subjects designed to divide becomes reimagined by weak subjects as a tactic to unite. In one particularly poignant scene about halfway through the film, the girls finally locate the fence and they run to grab hold of it. Meanwhile, back in Jigalong, Maude (Molly and Daisy's mother) grabs hold of the fence there, and it is as if they can feel each other's presence along the fence so many kilometers apart. The fence changes from a physical barrier to become a physical line that connects the girls and their home. In subsequent scenes, Maude and her mother are seen praying and chanting beside the fence, willing the girls to return home.

Later in the film, Molly and Daisy practically crawl through the desert, exhausted, dehydrated, and famished [1:12:40]. The fence suddenly ends and they stand staring and astonished. Daisy says, "I want mother." Here, it becomes even clearer that not only is the fence reimagined into a tool to lead the girls home; it is more specifically reimagined from being a strategy for (white) men to divide, and into a tactic for (Aboriginal) women to unify. There is a gender dynamic, and particularly a mother–daughter dynamic, that challenges whites' conceptions of space and the social and cultural relations therein. Much like Moreton-Robinson (2003) would argue that Aboriginal connection to land and space transcends whatever boundaries migrant colonizers put in place, so does the fence remind us that the connection between a mother and her child knows no boundaries and no matter the barriers of separation people might implement, these strategies can always be subverted and used against them to draw us home. Molly's response to Daisy is to insist that the fence "will come back." Her faith in the power of their connection to Maude and with their land is depicted as they push on, collapse, pass out, then reawaken to find that the fence did indeed resume just outside their home.

The film comes to a close as the now-elderly Molly recounts what happened after she and Daisy made it home: the girls, their mother, and grandmother left to hide in the desert. Molly eventually married and had two daughters. She and the girls were captured and sent to Moore River, following which she escaped with her youngest daughter. Neville captured the daughter again when she was three years old, and Molly never saw her daughter again. The film ends with footage of Molly and Daisy as elderly women living in and walking through their country, Jigalong, and Molly declares that they're "never going back to that place" [1:25:44]. White colonizers forced separation of these families, implementing spatial strategies to discipline Aboriginals into submission. Yet, the film tells the story of how weakened subjects can fight back, challenge such systems of domination, and use space in tactical ways to reject certain forms of oppression.

CONCLUSION

> The histories we trace are complex and pervasive. Most significantly the actions of the past resonate in the present and will continue to do so in the future. The laws, policies and practices which separated Indigenous children from their families have contributed directly to the alienation of Indigenous societies today. (Human Rights and Equal Opportunity Commission, 1997, p. 4)

A key lesson to learn from the study of intercultural communication is how history has shaped our social and political realities. It is only by questioning dominant histories written by those in power that we can arrive at a fuller and more nuanced understanding of silent and/or absent histories (Sorrells, 2016). This award-winning film has earned many accolades, including Audience Favorite at the 2002 Aspen Film Fest; Best Film, Best Original Score, and Best Sound in 2002 from the Australian Film Institute; a 2002 Golden Globe nomination; and Audience Award at both the 2002 Edinburgh International Film Festival and the 2002 Durban International Film Festival, among other honors. These awards reflect the recognition of the power of film to question dominant histories and tell a more complete story of our past. We find in *Rabbit Proof Fence* (2002), a cross-cultural microcosm of silenced history—a glimpse into stories of struggles, constant movements, and subjugations of Australia's indigenous Aborigines by white colonists.

More than a century passed before the government of Australia, in particular the Human Rights and Equal Opportunity Commission, conducted a *National Inquiry into the Separation of Aboriginal and Torres Strait Islander Children from Their Families* in 1997, to implement support and reconciliation services for children of the Stolen Generation (Human Rights and Equal Opportunity Commission, 1997). Their aim was to bring to light oral histories of half-caste children who were forcibly separated from their families, and who have returned home decades later, or even learned the truth about their identity and origin, as ways for us to witness the debilitating impact of forced assimilation and the colonial erasure of indigenous cultures. A year after the *Bringing Them Home* report (1997) was published, the Australian government announced the observance of *National Sorry Day* on May 26, and created *Sorry Books* with personal apologies from the Australian public to indigenous communities, for their historical mistreatment (Passi, 2013). Other social justice measures were taken to further cultural reconciliation, including the founding of *The Aboriginal and Torres Strait Islander Healing Foundation* in 2009 to help and heal affected people from the Stolen Generations ("Our History," 2018). A revised, national *Australian Curriculum* that would teach all students about the histories, cultures, colonization, and impact of forced assimilation policies on Aboriginal and Torres Strait Islander communities was also approved and implemented (Rogers, 2014).

Yet, as we find in the report and the supporting documentary, reconciliation of cultural differences is not an easy task, especially when the site of racial oppression are the bodies of children, many of whom were not old enough to remember their mothers when they were taken away (Australian Human Rights Commission, 2014). To attempt partial reconciliation many Aboriginal Australians from the Stolen Generation shared stories of being forcibly assimilated, separated from parents and siblings, and being relocated multiple times to different missionary settlements or foster homes, often with little to no knowledge about who they were, where they were from, or where they were going next (Australian Human Rights Commission, 2014).

Stories of the Stolen Generation as told in the report, and in films like *Rabbit Proof Fence* (2002) and other texts, are important for people to consume for recognizing the tragic, heartbreaking, and long-lasting impact that oppressing a group of people and separating their families can have. In fact, the highly publicized detention of nearly 70,000 migrant children in 2018 and 2019 in the United States (Chalabi, 2018; Kopan, 2018; Sherman, Mendoza & Burke, 2019), up from just 2,400 in 2017 (Dickerson, 2018), is reminiscent of the story of the Stolen Generation. Certainly, there are contextual differences. The migrants being oppressed in the former case went to the United States to seek asylum and some of the detained children traveled alone versus being indigenous populations already living in Australia when European migrants arrived to dispossess them. But the rhetoric surrounding the U.S. controversy, with claims of enforcing the law and invoking biblical justification for such inhumane treatment, wreak of colonialism, and othering (Zauzmer & McMillan, 2018), only this time from the perspective of keeping 'others' out, rather than going to communities to impose supposed 'civilization' upon them.

Movements in the story of *Rabbit Proof Fence* (2002), the Stolen Generation, and the resulting intercultural communication are important to recognize for the ways that one group can oppress and violate the human rights of another group under the guise of doing good, even doing "God's work." Citizens living in former colonies like the United States and Australia need to recognize how their sense of national identity may be tied to racialized social hierarchy and capitalism, rooted in accumulation of wealth. Such systems subsequently afforded the accumulation of "social worth, authority, and ownership," while indigenous populations were excluded from these systems (Moreton-Robinson, 2003, p. 25). In the case of Australia, white Australians developed a sense of a right to the land and ownership of it through their perception of their own hard work, and their contributions to building the nation. Ironically, their false presumption of taking unpopulated land ignored the fact that *they* are the migrants on this land. There is a sense of having a right to this land that is not afforded to Aboriginals, and the entire existence of the nation is based on this stripping of place from original inhabitants by migrants (Moreton-Robinson, 2003).

Migration and movement can have many positive outcomes, including rewarding intercultural interactions and relationships. But the story of the cross-cultural film *Rabbit Proof Fence* (2002) and the Stolen Generation reminds viewers of the tragic dangers that migration and mobilities have had in some cases. What we should learn from bearing witness to these stories is that we need to recognize the humanity of those we encounter who are different, and if we are in a position of power, it is our responsibility to avoid or mitigate behavior, communication, and policies that create injustice. When we fail to recognize the humanity of others, when we fail to care about how our actions impact others, and when we set up zero-sum migration policies, we fail ourselves and our neighbors. Such myopic thinking sets the framework for national tragedies like the story told in *Rabbit Proof Fence* (2002), and like the United States faced in 2018 and 2019, where the federal government detained tens of thousands of migrant children, many of whom were forcibly separated from their families.

Chapter 5

A Borrowed Identity

Religious and Ethnic Relationships in an Israeli High School

> Identity is our legacy and not our inheritance, our invention and not our memory
>
> —Darwish, *A Borrowed Identity* (2014)

This prophetic quote from Palestinian poet Mahmoud Darwish appears in the opening credits of Eran Riklis' Israeli drama *A Borrowed Identity* (2014). The film centers on a bright, Palestinian-Muslim boy, Eyad, who is raised in the Israeli town of Tira in the 1980s. Eyad is the brilliant son of a university-educated Israeli Arab fruit picker. Later, during the early 1990s, while attending a reputable high school in Jerusalem, Eyad becomes romantically involved with a Jewish classmate, Naomi. He also forms a lasting friendship with Yonatan, who is suffering from muscular dystrophy, and develops a close bond with Yonatan's mother Edna, who later in the film *lends* Eyad her deceased son's Jewish name and identity.

Riklis' film, also known as *Dancing Arabs*, is adapted from Sayed Kashua's (2002) novel of the same name. It is worth mentioning that the actors in the movie speak in Arabic and Hebrew. Direct quotes and dialogues from the movie that we furnish in this chapter are drawn from its English subtitles. The key role of ethnoreligious identity for Eyad is portrayed from the opening scenes of the film with the image of a pensive Eyad smoking on an empty terrace with a mosque in the background and the sound of an *azaan* (Islamic call to prayer) reverberating in the night skyline. The reel time of *A Borrowed Identity* (2014) is the early 1980s and follows the progression of Eyad's life and conflicted identity up to the mid-1990s. Politically, this period in Israel coincides with the first Palestinian *Intifada* (insurrection against Israeli occupation) leading up to the Gulf War.

Palestine has long been the subject of geopolitical and religious conflict, and its mobile identity as a nation within Arab states has been historically questioned. However, "many of those that do not recognize the State of Palestine do recognize the Palestine Liberation Organization as 'representative of the Palestinian people'" (Jandt, 2016, p. 222). As Sorrells (2016) points out, ethnoreligious fundamentalism has an effect on "political, legal, social, and intercultural relations in many areas of the world" (p. 210). Placed in the context of globalization, political mobility, and the "disaffection and isolation" it can produce, a sense of identity via ethnic kinship and religious fundamentalism is understandable (Sorrells, 2016, p. 210).

Conflict, compromise, and constant movements of cultural identities along interethnic and interreligious lines abound in *A Borrowed Identity* (2014). Such movements are particularly evident in Eyad's interpersonal relationships with his patriotic Arab-Muslim family in a Judaism-predominant Israel, in his father's political protests to secure an independent identity for Palestine, in the minoritization of Eyad's religious identity, in Yonatan's terminal disability and his invisibility fueled by ableism, in Naomi and Eyad's clandestine romance that meets with parental and interreligious disapproval, and most poignantly in Edna's sacrifice of a Jewish burial to her deceased son so Eyad could 'borrow' Yonatan's identity to move into a life of religious and socioethnic acceptance. The narrative of the film surfaces as a site of contention, familial and social separations, and religious anxiety for Eyad, whose minority identity is continuously developing, moving, changing, rejecting, and adapting to intercultural challenges.

In this chapter, we first survey the history of ethnonationalism and ethnic democracy in the Israel–Palestine conflict, its social and political implications on spatial- and state-based identification, and how it shapes the identity of minority groups and individuals, following which we analyze our case study of the film using these intercultural communication concepts.

ISRAEL–PALESTINE CONFLICT: ETHNONATIONALISM AND ETHNIC DEMOCRACY

Ethnicity alludes to people who have descended from the same tribes or regional groups, sharing common cultural traits and social habits across generations (Jandt, 2016). They usually show "such distinguishing features as language or accent, physical features, family names, customs and religion" (Jandt, 2016, p. 13). Grounded in ethnicity is the construct of ethnic identity, which "refers to identification with and perceived acceptance into a group with shared heritage and culture" (Jandt, 2016, p. 13; Collier & Thomas, 1988). In the case of Israel, the two main ethnic groups are Jewish, the ethnic majority (Judaism is also a religion, of course), and Arab, the ethnic minority.

The historical ethnic tensions between Israelis and Palestinians are established within the first few scenes of the film. "The Jews are coming to visit us next week, so tell your parents to get ready. We don't want to be embarrassed. You hear me, morons?," chides the principal of Eyad's school in Tira, mistranslating the American guest's spiel to students about promoting peace between Israel and Palestine [5:30]. The American representative from *Children for Peace*, talks about the youth building cultural bridges, in particular encouraging Muslim (Palestinian Arab) children living in Israel to be that bridge. The principal reluctantly translates, and chastises his students for speaking out of turn, telling them they'll "never be anything but street cleaners and fruit pickers" as the American smiles in ignorance [5:30].

Rouhana and Bal-Tar (1998) have termed the long-standing political and ethnoreligious dispute between Israel and Palestine as an *intractable ethnonational conflict*—intractable because a mutually beneficial compromise between them has been almost impossible to achieve. An ethnonational conflict is marked by recurrent national, religious, linguistic, and ethnic strife taking place within a state or a nation (Connor, 1994; Rouhana & Bar-Tal, 1998). Other examples of ethnonational conflicts can be seen in Northern Ireland, between Protestants and Catholics; in Sri Lanka, between Tamils and Hindus; and in Northern India (Kashmir), between Hindus and Muslims. The actors of an intractable ethnonational conflict fundamentally disagree on what caused the conflict and/or who was responsible for it (Rouhana & Bar-Tal, 1998). While there may be agreement on many historical facts and a shared understanding that Jewish people went to Palestine to recreate and preserve their Jewish homeland, the two sides' perspectives and narratives diverge from there (Rouhana & Bar-Tal, 1998).

The UN declaration of 1947 to split Palestine into two states, one Jewish and the other Arab, resulted in their erstwhile regional conflict to morph into a full-scale Israel–Palestine war. While Palestinian leaders opposed the UN verdict, the Jewish state accepted it, resulting in the formation of the State of Israel in 1948 (Rouhana & Bar-Tal, 1998). In 1967, the war between Israel and the Arab states of Egypt, Jordan, and Syria brought the remaining Palestinian territory including the West Bank and Gaza Strip under Israeli control. The appropriation of the West Bank and the Gaza Strip brought with it opportunities for reuniting Palestinians living on either side of the Green Line.[1] However, it was also concerning that "nineteen years of living under Israeli rule had produced a variant of Palestinian identity that was different from that developing in the West Bank and the Gaza Strip" (Pappé, 2011, pp. 111–12).

After the six-day war of 1967 Israel annexed East Jerusalem, then claiming Jerusalem as its capital, in its entirety. Interestingly, despite being one of the oldest cities in the world and a site of global reverence for three religions—Judaism, Christianity, and Islam—Jerusalem still holds a disputed location as the proclaimed state capital for both Israel and Palestine. Palestine's resistance to Israeli occupation of Palestinian territories in 1967, their continued efforts to reclaim the West Bank and Gaza Strip with claims on East Jerusalem as their capital, and their goal to form an independent State of Palestine reached its climax in the 1987 Intifada (shaking off), resulting in a six-year-long insurrection against Israel (Rouhana & Bar-Tal, 1998). It was only with the signing of the Oslo Agreements in 1993, a "secret channel of negotiation in Norway between Israel's Labor government and the Palestine Liberation Organization" (Rouhana & Bar-Tal, 1998, p. 763) that Israel and Palestine agreed on a truce.

Following the 1967 war, the State of Israel's Arab population was granted the status of residents, but not citizens (Rouhana & Bar-Tal, 1998). From the 1980s and into the twenty-first century, ethnic discrimination against Arab employees at workplaces forced many Palestinians to do jobs they were overqualified for, despite many being college or university educated, a dilemma characterized in the film by Eyad's father, Salah (Pappé, 2011). Palestinians in particular "developed a flawed national identity," one that was equally shaped by the segregated realities in Israel and by their allegiance to Palestinian nationalism (Rouhana, 1997).

It is the 1987 Intifada for an independent Palestinian state, and its aftermath in Israel during the early 1990s, that forms the backdrop of *A Borrowed Identity* (2014)—a political reality personified in this visual text through conflicted identities, personal struggles, and spatio-cultural movements of its characters, who are in different ways tied to the complex Israeli–Palestinian dispute. In his review of the film, Turan (2015) compares complexities in both the protagonist, Eyad, and his father, Salah, whose involvement in Palestinian liberation politics compels him to become a low-income fruit picker, despite being university educated. Eyad, on the other hand "lives in a world of mixed messages" (Turan, 2015). He lives with his Palestinian family in Israel, learns about their Islamic heritage from his beloved grandmother, brings home a Jewish friend as part of his school's peacekeeping initiative, gets upset on finding an old Hebrew news-cutting that labels his father an Arab terrorist, yet still receives "clandestine messages about Palestinian nationalism and he and his family root for the Arab side during the region's frequent armed clashes" (Turan, 2015).

SPATIAL AND IDENTITY MOVEMENTS

When Eyad attends this new school, his spatial surroundings change as he adjusts to life in Jerusalem. The ethnic tensions are even more pronounced in Jerusalem than we had seen him experiencing in Tira. In this chapter we draw on Lefebvre's work on the power and social dynamics of space, as well as identity development models to frame our analysis of the film.

"Space *is* Political"

For Lefebvre, space is not an empty vessel that we fill as needed; rather space is an active agent in shaping and in being shaped by social relations and the power dynamics therein. As he writes, "Space is permeated with social relations; it is not only supported by social relations, but it also is producing and produced by social relations" (Lefebvre, 2009b, p. 186). Embedded within those social and power dynamics are political processes, which brings up an often quoted point of Lefebvre's "space *is* political" (2009a, pp. 170–71). Many times space is thought of as a neutral and empty container, but this association with impartiality is mistaken, likely because it has been planned that way based on ideologies, systems, and strategies that are no longer detectable. As he explains, "Space has been fashioned and molded from historical and natural elements, but in a political way" (Lefebvre, 2009a, p. 171).

The state is a critical player in the making, shaping, and maintaining of spaces, in terms of the physical built environment, the social relations therein, and the privileges or disadvantages that people have for moving among those spaces (Brenner & Eldin, 2009). Certain regions, cities, neighborhoods, or even buildings may become sites of racial, ethnic, or religious conflict with different groups and stakeholders claiming rights to it, asserting control over it, and/or understanding the space's position/history/value in different ways. When tensions rise, the state steps in to discipline those acting out of turn (Foucault, 1980; Rabinow, 2003) and the state may reassert control over how individuals can behave, communicate, move through, or access specific spaces. In the film, Jerusalem is portrayed as a space in conflict, at least from the perspective of the protagonist, Eyad.

In the context of Israel as depicted in the film, Arabs are a minority group and they are marginalized within social spaces, relegated to low-wage jobs out of sight—fruit pickers, dishwashers, and so on. In the film, Arabs occupy what Yiftachel (2009) calls gray spaces. Gray space refers to physical spaces and the people therein that fall "between the 'lightness' of legality/approval/safety and the 'darkness' of eviction/destruction/death . . . pseudo-permanent margins of today's urban regions, which exist partially outside the gaze of state authorities and city plans" (p. 243). They are areas that are somewhere between the secure, privileged dominant position in a society and the dangerous, underworld, criminal parts of society—areas that are overlooked because the people in those locations are not valued by the state. But then comes the paradox of such spaces—this oppression and/or abandonment can breed radicalism among those who occupy gray spaces that may result in disruption and destabilization stemming from the very policies designed to control and oppress the space (Yiftachel, 2009). Marginalized people in gray spaces are not necessarily powerless, though power is largely "skewed in favor of the state" and middle classes. People occupying gray spaces use them "as bases for self-organization, negotiation and empowerment" and they have some hand in "shaping cities and regions" (Yiftachel, 2009, p. 243).

What these conceptions of space reveal is that space is fundamentally social and political, and it plays a role in shaping one's identity and vice versa. A person's identity (or identities) may influence which spaces are open to them and which are closed off based on social hierarchies and political structures. Likewise, the spaces a person occupies shape their identity, say as a member of a dominant social group versus as a member of a marginalized group. Many models attempt to explain and predict a person's identity development based on their status within a social space—whether a member of a majority or minority group.

Minority Identity Development (MID)

Identity development among minority groups has drawn attention from numerous scholars. For example, there is Helms' (1995) people of color racial identity model, Phinney's (1989) ethnic identity development model, and Atkinson's (2004) minority identity development (MID) model. For our purposes, because the film addresses minority status in terms of both ethnicity and religion, we apply Atkinson's more general five-stage model of minority identity to unpack Eyad's developing sense of identity during his adolescence. Atkinson (2004) points out that although the model marks five distinct stages, in practice the stages blend and a person's experience is likely more of a flow from one stage to another with fluid boundaries between them. Nevertheless, for the purposes of analysis, we review the five stages of the model, which we use to follow Eyad's identity development as depicted in the film.

Stage one from Atkinson's model, called conformity, is characterized by a minority individual conforming to the dominant group. There is a preference for the dominant culture, to the detriment of their own cultural group. An individual in this stage may belittle or diminish their own cultural group in favor of the dominant group. As Atkinson (2004) explains, in this stage the person's attitude toward the self is "self-deprecating" and their attitude toward the dominant group is appreciative (p. 40).

Stage two, dissonance, emerges when an individual encounters a situation or a person expressing pride in the minority identity, which creates dissonance between the individual's previously held negative attitudes from the conformity stage. Movement to this stage may be triggered by a significant world event, by the individual experiencing discrimination firsthand, or by meeting someone who challenges their previously held assumptions. In this stage, a person's attitude toward the self is "conflict between self-deprecating and self-appreciating" while their attitude toward the dominant group is "conflict between group-deprecating and group-appreciating" (Atkinson, 2004, p. 42).

Stage three, resistance and immersion, is characterized by an individual fully embracing their minority culture and rejecting the dominant culture. There may also be an interest in "eliminat[ing] oppression of the minority group" (Atkinson, 2004, p. 42). A person reaches this stage once they have resolved the dissonance from the earlier stage and may experience guilt, shame, or even anger at their adoption of dominant group culture and values from stage one. In stage three, a person's attitude toward the self and group has reversed from stage one—here, there is a strong sense of self-appreciation combined with group depreciation (Atkinson, 2004).

Stage four, introspection, is when an individual has developed a greater sense of security within their own sense of minority identity and they begin to challenge the sweeping beliefs about the dominant group (e.g., "All [x-group] are bad"), and come to see that the dominant group contains both positive and negative components (Atkinson, 2004). Like with stage two, stage four is characterized by some conflict—there is a sense of conflict between group loyalty and personal autonomy. In this stage, a person's attitude toward the self is "concern with basis for self-appreciating attitude" (Atkinson, 2004, p. 43), which reflects the individual's work toward balancing pride in their own cultural group with a sense of autonomy that allows them to move beyond a blanket endorsement of their own cultural group. A person's attitude toward the group is "concern with the basis of group depreciation," reflecting the movement from total distrust of the dominant group toward "selective trust and distrust" based on a dominant group member's behavior (Atkinson, 2004, p. 44).

The final stage five, synergetic articulation and awareness, is when an individual has achieved a sense of self-fulfillment and the conflict and discomfort from earlier stages is largely resolved. An individual in this stage is both comfortable with themselves and others. Attitudes toward self are self-appreciating and attitudes toward the dominant group are selectively appreciating. Individuals in this stage use experiences from earlier stages to gauge acceptance or rejection of minority or dominant group cultural values on a case-by-case basis. Finally, in this stage, an individual has a drive to "eliminate *all* forms of oppression," rather than only oppression toward their own cultural group (Atkinson, 2004, p. 45).

We conceptualize movement in this film largely in terms of identity. More specifically, we analyze movement and identity in two contexts: (1) Eyad's evolution along the MID model as a type of movement, and (2) a person's opportunities for, or exclusion from, movement within social spaces based on their identity within their ethnocultural location. The prejudice and power dynamics that exist around marginalized identities in specific cultural, religious, and social contexts often prevent people with those identities from freely moving within society. Such exclusion is evident in Eyad's experiences throughout the film, as we explore further in our analysis.

FILM ANALYSIS

In this chapter, we organize our analysis of the film along two intercultural themes, following the protagonist's complex and recurrent geopolitical and relational mobilities—*spatial shifts and identity movements*, and *ethnic and interpersonal conflicts*.

Spatial Shifts and Identity Movements

Spatial shifts and movements across minority and majority identities predominantly frame the narrative of *A Borrowed Identity* (2014). It isn't until Eyad moves to Jerusalem that he begins to move through the stages of identity development. Between his time as a teenager experiencing adolescent identity development, and the move from Tira, a largely Arab town in Israel, to a Jewish-dominated Jerusalem, this is a stage in life when Eyad begins to feel his marginal status more prominently. This also kick-starts his identity evolution, which we track along Atkinson's MID model. However, his friendship with Yonatan and romance with Naomi ease the challenges of Eyad's identity evolution, for example, in the lighthearted ethnic teasing that Yonatan and Eyad engage in, and in Naomi's willingness to teach Eyad correct Hebrew pronunciation.

The scenes depicting Eyad's early days at the high school with teachers and classmates mispronouncing his name, his culture shock with food customs, and ethnic taunting by Jewish boys from another school illustrate his marginal status in Jerusalem. Moreover, the appearance of military personnel and military checkpoints where identification is required are the film's attempt to illustrate the power of the state to create and maintain the built environment and the social dynamics therein. In Jewish-dominated Jerusalem, Eyad does not have the freedom of movement that he enjoyed in Arab-dominated Tira. Under these conditions, Eyad's MID commences.

The stage one of MID, conformity, is prominently visible in a scene two years into Eyad's time at the high school in Jerusalem. It is 1990 and he is in class learning about the formation of Israel. The teacher asks him (as he turns his head to admire Naomi), "What led to the war that then broke out?". Eyad replies, "The war? Oh, the Arabs. Of course," as his classmates laugh. Eyad continues on with further details about the war:

> The Arabs rejected the Partition Plan and tried to prevent the establishment of the Jewish state. When the Plan was accepted, in 1947, the Arabs launched a series of hostilities against the Jewish community, starting the War of Independence. [34:35]

Eyad's communication here reflects his position in the conformity stage of MID. He talks about Arabs as if they are the "other," a distant group of troublemakers who changed their minds about a global agreement and started a war. His joke at the beginning, "the Arabs, of course," reflects a willingness to conform to the notion that Arabs are the source of problems in the region, in order to be accepted by the majority group. Eyad is seeking to fit in, not yet ready to challenge the status quo.

Later in the film, two scenes reflect Eyad's movement to somewhere between stages two (dissonance) and three (resistance and immersion) of the MID model. The dissonance stage is when someone starts to move away from the negative attitudes toward their own minority group and desire to fit in with the majority, exhibited during the conformity stage. The resistance and immersion stage is when someone embraces their minority identity and rejects the majority culture. As noted by Atkinson (2004), movement between stages is often rather fluid in practice instead of being a clear-cut jump from one stage to the next. This fluid movement is illustrated in two scenes when Eyad and Yonatan explore an Arab neighborhood of Jerusalem [35:20] and when Eyad and his school friends are seen running a bustling small business selling hummus and pita/bagels to their fellow students [37:55].

During their time in the Arab neighborhood, Eyad assists Yonatan, who is using a wheelchair, as they look at street vendors' goods and stop at a cafe for hummus and pita. Yonatan teases Eyad about being an Arab tracker, seemingly referencing Bedouins who protect Israel's northern border ("Muslim Arab Bedouins," 2013). Meanwhile, Eyad retorts with a jab at Yonatan's Jewish identity, using a long-standing negative stereotype about Jewish people being cheap—a stereotype that dates back to at least the Middle Ages when Jewish people were forced to be money lenders based on rules set by the Catholic Church (Balser et al., 2006). Eyad is comfortable in this part of town and seems happy to share his culture with Yonatan. Yonatan enjoys the outing, but it is clear that he has never been there before—it is another world for him even though he lives in Jerusalem. The neighborhood appears more crowded and run down than other parts of Jerusalem that have appeared in the film thus far. As depicted in the film, this neighborhood may be something like a gray space (Yiftachel, 2009) that is overlooked by the dominant culture, but the occasional appearance of military personnel in the background reminds the inhabitants (and viewers) of the ever-present power of the state to control spaces throughout the city, especially neighborhoods where minority groups gather.

The boys get hummus and pita, which they then enjoy eating in the car with Edna. In the Israeli cultural context, hummus is often thought to be made best by Arabs, although Arabs and Jewish individuals both enjoy eating it (Moser, 2010). The boys' mutual teasing and the common ground established by eating hummus illustrate both Eyad's distancing from Jewish culture by teasing Yonatan (stage two), and an embrace of his own Arab culture while rejecting the majority culture (stage three), at least to some extent.

Hummus resurfaces as an intercultural leveler a few scenes later when Eyad sells hummus and pita along with Jerusalem bagels[2] to his classmates. By *intercultural leveler*, we mean an artifact or person that works toward resolving cultural, ethnic, and/or religious differences by addressing the causes, symptoms, or products of such conflicts. In these scenes, hummus serves as an artifact that establishes common ground and tastes. In selling hummus with bagels, possibly purchased from the Arab neighborhood of Jerusalem portrayed earlier, Eyad is embracing a part of his own Arab culture. In doing so, he begins to create an understanding with the majority culture in Jerusalem by selling the food to Jewish students. Again, Eyad appears to be somewhere between stages two and three in that he is no longer fully conforming to the majority culture, he is open to critiquing and questioning the dominant culture, and he embraces parts of his minority identity, at least in terms of food heritage.

The classroom is another space where Eyad's identity development is illustrated. As a young boy in Tira, the classroom is a gray space where his teacher surreptitiously teaches the children about Palestinian history. In one scene [5:14] the teacher shows a map of Palestine and asserts that Palestine is the real name of the country, not Israel. He then hears someone coming down the hall, stops and pulls down an Israeli map, and starts speaking of Israel. The classroom in this Arab town is an overlooked, undervalued space where inhabitants push back and attempt to destabilize the system—in this case by teaching children a different version of history. But, as Yiftachel (2009) argues, power in gray spaces is ultimately in the hands of the state, reflected here in the way the teacher quickly reverts to teaching a state-approved version of history as soon as a supervisor is within earshot. This reluctant deference to the state is reinforced in the previous scene when Eyad's grandmother tells him that despite his father being a gifted student, he is relegated to being a fruit picker "because of the State . . . because [he] got involved in politics" [4:50]. The grandmother's message seems to be that only so much disruption is permitted; when someone goes too far, the state will step in to discipline and punish.

Perhaps this awareness of the consequences of pushing too far explains why through most of the film, Eyad rarely disrupts or makes trouble. As Eyad's identity development evolves, he is seen to gradually move into a space between stage three (resistance and immersion) and stage four (introspection). Recall that stage three is when an individual embraces their minority identity and rejects the dominant culture. Stage four is when an individual has a more secure sense of themselves and their minority identity, and they come to see that there are both good and bad aspects to the dominant culture. But in this stage the individual is still working to balance their personal autonomy and desire to make judgments about their group and other groups independently, with an allegiance toward their own minority group and a desire to protect it.

In a classroom scene [53:41], the teacher is leading a discussion about a literary work by an Israeli author Amos Oz, featuring Arab twins in a character's vision (Weissberg, 2014). The teacher asks about the meaning of the twins in the character's (Hannah) false vision, suggesting they are perhaps Hannah's fantasy or childhood friends. She calls on Eyad to respond and he asks if he can opt to not answer. The teacher refuses and accuses him of having not read the book. At this point, Eyad's transformation becomes clear. He politely offers the response that he knows is expected and that is the typical and accepted majority group interpretation, but then goes on to eloquently challenge that interpretation. He chooses to defend the twins' identity and marginalization in the narrative, and he does so, consciously, in a room full of Jewish students who listen intently to his thoughtful critique. Eyad explains:

> Because when I read it, I think of the Arab twins and not of Hannah. When I read it, I see two poor, violent, ugly Arabs who've become the sexual fantasy of a woman who's losing her mind. I think about how they never did anything wrong, apart from being Arabs. I think about what they represent to the author, to the reader and to the Israelis. I think about the primitive Arab who's only interested in sex. That image of the wild, animalistic, primitive Arab, who's only motivated by his phallus. [54:30]

The teacher attempts to interject, but then Eyad continues with his critique. Referencing the book's author, Eyad asserts, "To him, Arabs just destroy everything. It's easier for the authors and their readers when an Arab makes a move on a Jewish girl. After all, we all know how Arabs stink." The teacher, quite awkward by now, tries to change the subject, but Eyad says: "I really would have preferred to keep silent. We're more polite that way." The scene ends in a rather surprising way as Naomi gets up from her seat and kisses Eyad on the lips, in a genuine show of affection, and we hear an excited round of applause from the rest of the students in class.

Here, stage three is illustrated in the way that Eyad rejects the dominant culture's interpretation of the narrative as yet another stereotype and form of discrimination toward the minority group. He does not necessarily offer a blanket endorsement of his own culture, but he defends it by calling attention to offensive stereotypes and patterns of discrimination, which suggests an interest in "eliminat[ing] oppression of the minority group," that is characteristic of stage three (Atkinson 2004, p. 42). Remarkably, though, this classroom scene is one of the only moments where Eyad openly "question[s] Israeli hegemony" (Feinstein, 2015). It is a moment when the audience can see Eyad's "transition from awkward outsider to metaphorical shape-shifter," who is now adept at being polite when unprovoked, and political when pushed (Weissberg, 2014). The classroom serves as a space throughout the film where, either in the scenes with Eyad or memories of Salah's experiences, protest and disruption of the state must be navigated carefully.

At the same time, the way that Eyad attempts to opt out of this conversation to seemingly be "more polite," and his passionate kiss with Naomi, both suggest that he does have respect for the dominant group, which is indicative of stage four. Clearly, given his relationships with Naomi, Yonatan, and Edna, he knows that there are many beautiful aspects of Israeli Jewish culture and people. Stage four is characterized by a "selective trust and distrust" for the dominant group (Atkinson 2004, p. 44) and that is seen in the way that Eyad trusts Naomi in this scene, perhaps even trusts some of his other classmates, but does not seem to trust the teacher. He tries to avoid the conflict because he believes the teacher will not want to hear his critique and/or it will make her uncomfortable.

Eventually, after leaving school, Eyad lives on his own in East Jerusalem and his identity development remains at stage four until he realizes that his best chance for success is to adopt Yonatan's identity. It is this decision that leads him into stage five, or synergetic articulation and awareness. During Eyad's time working in a restaurant as a dishwasher, some of the cooks and dishwashers (who are all Arab as well) assert that the waitstaff make more money than them, and they are relegated to the back of the restaurant where customers do not see them because they are Arab. When one kitchen worker asks, "You know how to become a waiter?" another man responds, "Die a martyr and then ask Allah to send you back as a Jew" [1:11:20]. This interaction and Eyad's work in the restaurant show him that his employment options as an Arab in the Israeli cultural context are limited.

This interaction taking place in the back of a restaurant, in the kitchen where Arab cooks and dishwashers remain unseen, reveals another kind of gray space in the film—the kitchen. The film has already established that

Arabs in Israel often do low-wage jobs like becoming fruit pickers and street cleaners, and here the audience sees another kind of low-wage job reserved for the minority group. In this conversation, Eyad realizes that he will never get a higher paying server job as an Arab. But when, in the next scene, he sees the opportunity to adopt Yonatan's identity in order to get that higher paying job, he takes it. After all, by now his understanding of the culture and his pronunciation of Hebrew makes him well equipped to blend in.

In a key scene Eyad visits Yonatan, whose health has deteriorated and he lies in bed immobile and unable to speak. Yonatan's identity card lies on the desk and as Eyad looks at the picture, he smiles and remarks, "We really look alike, right?" [1:12:55]. The audience learns what Eyad was thinking in the next shot when he is seen working as a server, wearing a name card that reads "Yonatan." He has adopted his friend's identity. Suddenly, Jerusalem is open to him—he now has social and physical freedom of movement in the city and beyond. It is in borrowing Yonatan's identity that Eyad has progressed to stage five of synergetic articulation and awareness. In this stage the individual is comfortable both with themselves and in their relationship with the dominant culture. Here, minority identity is fully realized. Eyad is comfortable with who he is, but he also needs to survive and has come to realize that being Arab limits his options in Israel. His entry into stage five is complete when Edna, who initially felt betrayed by her son's identity theft, comes to support Eyad and encourages him to sit for both his own school exams as well as Yonatan's. She tells Eyad, "It's alright. No one needs to know. No one" [1:20:30]. Her nod of approval and weighted silence signifies that she has forgiven him. Eyad's minority identity movement is now almost complete, but it is also a barrier in the social spaces of Jerusalem and Israel more generally, something that Edna too understands.

Eyad cements his minority identity when he registers Yonatan's death as his own with the Islamic Religious Council in Jerusalem. As the clerk stamps Eyad's (in reality, Yonatan's) death certificate, Eyad asks: "Can you please wrap him in these shrouds from Mecca?" [1:32:24]. The shrouds are those that Eyad's late grandmother had left for him (the same ones that she had desired to be buried in). The clerk says: "Don't forget to return the ID to the Ministry of the Interior." Eyad registers his own death in order to fully take on Yonatan's identity. However, in doing so, he is not conforming to the dominant culture nor is he walking away from his Arab identity. He is making a deliberate and informed choice in order to improve his chances at success in life, the very thing that his father wanted for him at the beginning of the film. And, he is making this choice with the support of his beloved Jewish friends. Moreover, in burying Yonatan in his grandmother's sacred shrouds, he shows respect for his friend and Edna, and the sacrifice they make in giving up a Jewish burial for Yonatan.

Such fluid movement between Muslim Arab and Jewish Israeli cultures that occurs in Yonatan's funeral and Edna's support of Eyad's identity adoption reflects their deep respect and love for each other, and Eyad's fully realized minority identity. That is, he can both deceive Israeli hegemony, institutions, and laws by taking on Yonatan's identity and by doing so critique and call attention to injustices. But, at the same time, he's done so because of his fully realized minority identity and through the support of the positive, enriching, and loving relationships he has formed with two Jewish individuals. In other words, Eyad is both comfortable with his own identity and is able to selectively accept or reject aspects of the dominant culture and the individuals therein.

In adopting Yonatan's identity, Eyad himself becomes a kind of metaphor for gray spaces. As Yiftachel (2009) argues, an irony of these types of spaces is that the oppression and marginalization that creates gray spaces often results in a kind of radicalization of the individuals that occupy them, resulting in efforts to protest and disrupt the state. Eyad takes advantage of how the gray spaces in his life are overlooked to improve his circumstances by deceiving the state in order to make himself more socioculturally mobile within their society. Borrowing Yonatan's identity is a radical form of protest, but Eyad does so in a quiet way, with the support of his ally in Edna.

Ethnic Conflicts and Interpersonal Relationships

A Borrowed Identity (2014) pays homage to opportunities presented for and against social and relational mobilities that an individual receives based on their ethnic identity, and the interpersonal connections they form in the process. Early in the film, Eyad and a Jewish boy are partnered as part of a cross-cultural peace initiative at his school in Tira. The boy visits Eyad's home, and as they head to the terrace asks Eyad if he wants to play "Sharon and Arafat". This points to the normalization of the Israel–Palestine conflict and the impact it has had on impressionable youth, symbolized here by these boys wanting to role-play Ariel Sharon, then prime minister of Israel, and Yasser Arafat, ex-leader of the Palestinian Liberation Organization. Soon after his young Jewish friend gets scared thinking Eyad's father is a terrorist, after reading about it in an old Yiddish news cutup that Eyad shows him [10:37–11:00]. This scene presents an interesting dilemma that conflates religious and ethnic identity and the power of linguistic labels. Despite having shared historical claims on the same territories, both religious and geographical, the intractable ethnonational conflict "encompasses the meaning and implications of these facts and extends [it] to names, language, main actors, causes, and responsibilities" (Rouhana & Bar-Tal, 1998, p. 763).

On the surface of the film, we have these "frustrating, seemingly irresolvable conflicts facing Israeli Arabs trying to reconcile Arab ethnicity with Israeli nationality" (Feinstein, 2015). The backstory of Eyad's father, Salah, presents some of this identity conflict. Salah is driving Eyad to begin school in Jerusalem. Eyad asks his father why he was in Jerusalem in 1969, and Salah explains that he, along with other students, was arrested after a bomb had exploded in the city. He wasn't charged or brought to court, but was detained for more than two years and spent a year in house arrest. Sadly, he wasn't allowed to go back to Jerusalem, or even attend university there. "It wasn't easy. In fact it was very hard. We thought we could liberate Palestine from the Jews," laments Salah, when disclosing to Eyad that he didn't have any regrets about his past life [22:31]. Salah's experiences of religious othering, his political activism for Palestinian liberation, and the educational and economic opportunities he missed are evident in his reply to Eyad, "Now we just want them to let us live with dignity." He convinces Eyad that attending the Jerusalem Arts and Science Academy is a rare, if privileged, opportunity for an Arab boy like him, and because, as Salah exclaims, "I want you to be better than them. In every way. Understand?" [21:00].

Eyad and Naomi's relationship seems to resemble the impasse between Jewish people and Arabs in the conflicted state of Israel. Ironically, their alliance starts on a positive note with a distinct possibility of moving toward a happy ending. She makes the first move to befriend "Ayid," as he's known in his Jewish-dominant school, and later corrects his pronunciation of 'P' (Arabs tend to pronounce *P* as *B*) with a useful trick [29:50–31:20]. They begin a secret romance, often meeting in their school's theater. Even as a group of rowdy Jewish teenagers bully Eyad, singing a discriminatory song: "Muhammad's dead, yo, ya; He had several daughters, yo ya; His daughters are ugly, yo ya; Just like monkeys, yo ya," we find Naomi standing by Eyad in silent support, though both are disapprovingly awkward in that situation [31:50].

Eyad, Yonatan, and Naomi attend a musical performance that is politically radical. Naomi gets upset, not only with the offensive lyrics but also with an inebriated Yonatan, who gives her a hard time for dating an Arab [34:45]. Later that night Eyad tries to pacify Naomi, blaming her discomfort on Yonatan's dark, but harmless humor. Naomi is calm, but laments at the truth in Yonatan's teasing. She convinces Eyad of her love for him, but also feels frustrated that she can't disclose their romance. She recalls an earlier conversation with her mother, about what their reaction would be if they found out she was dating an Arab. Her mother's reaction to this hypothetical question was "Naomi, darling, tell me you're a lesbian, tell me you're a drug addict, or that you have cancer, but don't ever tell me you have an Arab boyfriend" [43:55]. This conversation marks the start of a growing divide between Eyad and Naomi.

Naomi and Eyad's relationship ultimately ends. A close shot of her in a military uniform suggests she has joined the Israeli army. Not able to keep up with their lies anymore, Naomi asks him to let her go [1:27:40]. Interestingly, the camera's close up of Naomi ending their romance, in her Israeli military *artifact*, proposes a nonnegotiable solution to the conflict that their ethnonational differences present. Given Naomi's new role and responsibilities, there can be no compromising movement, personally or politically, within their interpersonal dyad.

Eyad's first meeting with Yonatan and Edna becomes a turning point in his ethnoreligious identity movement. Eyad is given a service learning assignment from school. He is to help a Jewish student with special needs, Yonatan Avrahami, with his school assignments. Yonatan seems skeptical to meet Eyad, perhaps because he is wary of strangers, or tired of the condescension he has received from able-bodied people, or even circumspect of young Arabs as can be surmised from the TV news coverage of Palestinian terror attacks playing in the background. Whatever the reasons for his skepticism, Yonatan is goaded into meeting Eyad by his mother, Edna. As an icebreaker, Yonatan tests Eyad's knowledge of music and introduces him to a new band. Alluding to his muscular dystrophy Eyad asks Yonatan, "Were you born that way?". As he moves away from Eyad, Yonatan's wryly retorts: "Were you born that way? . . . Arab . . . Is it contagious?". They both laugh, Yonatan lends a music CD to Eyad, and the scene ends with the possibility of a cross-cultural friendship between the two [27:00–29:40].

Yonatan and Eyad are awkward at first, but soon find common ground in alternative music, dark ethnocentric humor, and in their *otherness*, the former from his degenerative disability, and the latter from being an ethnoreligious minority in Israel. Eyad's friendship with Yonatan moves beyond the mundane as he eventually "serves as nurse, nurse's aide, and pipeline to the outside world" (Feinstein, 2015). Is their relationship symbolic of the peaceful cohabitation and identity mobilization that Israelis and Palestinians secretly desire in the future? Perhaps such is the director's intention, though presently distant it may seem.

Could Eyad's relationship with Edna be seen as a model for how best to resolve ethnoreligious conflict? There are two scenes in the film that can help answer this. In the first scene, Edna functions as a cultural broker, or mediator in the face of complex, intercultural interactions or conflicts (Sorrells, 2016). Edna is seated next to Eyad in the car that he is driving at night, in Jerusalem. An Israeli guard at a security check post stops the car and asks for their identity cards, and they comply. As the guard studies the first ID card, calling out "Yonatan Avrahami," both look at him, and Eyad gently nods. Next, the guard presumptively enquires: "Edna, you're his mother?". She nods her head, as Eyad turns to look at her. All seems well, and the security officer lets them go. The rest of the scene, which is also devoid of interpersonal dialogue, shows Edna smile in approval as Eyad quietly drives on [1:26:19].

In a key moment, Edna becomes what we have earlier referred to as an intercultural leveler. Although a secondary character, she plays a crucial role in the film's outcome and Eyad's life (Feinstein, 2015). This penultimate scene starts with a long shot of an Islamic burial ground and a small procession of people carrying a body wrapped in a *kafan* (burial shroud) and chanting Islamic prayers, accompanied by Eyad and Edna. As Yonatan's shrouded body is placed next to an empty grave, the Imam recites the funeral prayer: "Eyad, son of Fahima. When the angels of death ask: What is your religion and who is your God? Say: '"Allah is my God, Islam is my religion and Muhammad is my prophet"'" [1:33:24]. As Jewish Yonatan's body is placed in a Muslim grave, an aggrieved Edna rests her head on Eyad's shoulder and looks away, as the last piece of this complex identity puzzle gets sorted for Eyad (who is now Yonatan, in public eye). In a final act of sacrifice, Edna has helped Eyad move toward social acceptance. As an intercultural leveler, she has allowed Eyad to borrow her deceased son's complete identity.

CONCLUSION

The five intercultural stages of minority identity movement in Eyad are closely tied to his mobility across the social spaces he inhabits at different times. Space is always social and political (Lefebvre, 2009a; Lefebvre, 2009b), and the space one occupies invariably impacts one's sense of identity. The film depicts the restrictions on movement that Arabs experienced in 1990's Israel—the economic immobility incurred by only being able to get low-wage jobs; the social immobility of being teased, taunted, and discriminated against; and the physical immobility of being stopped and detained by military personnel. The kinds of immobility in this cultural context are inextricably linked to ethnic and/or religious identity. As such, these restrictions on mobility invariably shape one's minority identity and its development.

Indeed, *A Borrowed Identity* (2014) is not only about the characters' movements across tangible spaces. The movement illustrated largely concerns an individual's identity and ability to move within a space or a culture based on that. It also has to do with the prejudice and power dynamics that exist in relation to those identities. Adopting Yonatan's identity gives Eyad freedom of movement, such as easy movement through security checkpoints. He also gets better access to systems in Israel—a higher paying job as a server, increased economic opportunities, and perhaps the ease of getting into and attending college in Berlin, which we later find out he has achieved.

The borrowing of cultural, ethnic, and religious identities across social spaces aren't the only conflicts informing the film. The original title of the movie, *Dancing Arabs*, was also a subject of conflict. With the exception of Canada, where it was released under the original name, the film released worldwide using different titles including *My Son*, *My Sons*, and *My Heart Dances* (Feinstein, 2015). It received critical acclaim globally, being featured in many countries and film festivals including Israel's Jerusalem Film Festival (2014), Brazil's São Paulo International Film Festival (2014), Norway's Arabian Film Days (2015), and secured festival entries (2014–2017) in the UK, France, Switzerland, Belgium, Spain, Poland, Netherlands, Germany, Czech Republic, Slovakia, Argentina, Canada, and also the United States, where it was released as *A Borrowed Identity* (Feinstein, 2015). Telling a tale of conflict and borrowed compromise, its U.S. title "assesses the process of labeling, the possibility of unloading associated baggage, and the consequences of taking action, what is lost and what is gained" (Feinstein, 2015).

Ironically, what is lost is also what is gained, which in this case is the protagonist's sense of identity. Eyad's interpersonal relationships with Salah, his grandmother, Naomi, Yonatan, and Edna, are at the same time personal and political. His hot–cold relationship with his father is grounded in Salah's hankering for an independent Palestine. His closeness to his grandmother indicates a yearning for the past and for a revival of their religious heritage. His tumultuous romance with Naomi is indicative of the intractable ethnic conflict that Israel and Palestine grapple with. Eyad's ties with Yonatan and Edna are both symbolic of what the future can hold for Israel–Palestine, a relationship that could be built on trust, codependence, interethnic respect, and interreligious understanding.

Intercultural communication teaches us that religion is one of the strongest, and oldest, forces shaping identities, yet also causing conflicts globally (Cannadine, 2013; Jandt, 2016). As in real life, the mobility of spaces and connections that we find in this cross-cultural film are full of complexities and relational compromises. Here, too, we see how religion and ethnicity can function as a regulator of people's lives and create a sense of clarity in terms of identity (Jandt, 2016). The possibility of peaceful coexistence between Israel's Jewish and Arab communities is cinematized by Eran Riklis in Eyad and Edna's mobile relationship. It moves from friendship to a simulated and complicated mother–son bond, but with the final ethnoreligious swapping of identities, "substitution replaces coexistence as a cure for the Israeli-Palestinian impasse" (Feinstein, 2015).

NOTES

1. The *Green Line*, also known as the 1949 Armistice border, was a result of the 1949 Armistice Agreements between Israel and the Arab states of Egypt, Lebanon, Jordan, and Syria following the 1948 Arab–Israeli War, which separated the State of Israel's political boundary between the years 1949 and 1967.

2. The bagels depicted in the film appear to be specifically Jerusalem bagels, which are larger, thinner, and oblong as opposed to American style bagels (Kaufman, 2014).

Part III

SOJOURNING

NON/VERBAL COMMUNICATION, CULTURAL DIMENSIONS, AND INTERCULTURAL BARRIERS

Chapter 6

Outsourced

Holi, Kali, and Capitalism in an Indian American Call Center

A suggestion, Mr. Todd. You need to learn about India.

—Asha, *Outsourced*, 2006

This practical advice, between an employee and her manager in a fictitious Indian call center, lies at the heart of John Jeffcoat's romantic-comedy film *Outsourced* (2006). It is in the context of economic globalization, business sojourning, and the U-curve model of adaptation that this chapter turns its focus on this Indo-American film. *Outsourced* (2006) is a story of an American man, Todd Anderson's movements across professional and personal spaces, and of his struggles and experiences as he navigates culture shock, regional and organizational cultural symbols, and tries to adjust to India—a culture that is very different from his own. Yet, he grows acclimated to the Indians he befriends and starts appreciating their lived insights on India.

In the film, Todd is an employee of a Seattle-based novelty products company whose job is outsourced to their Indian call center where he is sent to train his local replacement in ways commensurate with U.S. corporate culture. Todd lives and works in India as an interim supervisor and a culture/accent-coach in the fictional town of Gharapuri, to train the low-wage employees of his order fulfillment division, including their future manager, Puro. During his professional sojourn, Todd falls in love with coworker Asha, which becomes the turning point in the film. Puro's and Asha's influence on Todd, and their suggestions that he learn about India, makes Todd more accepting of India's cultural uniqueness, as he gradually begins to understand and appreciate the value of his intercultural experiences. Ultimately Todd's sojourn in India does end as the call center shifts to yet another low-wage service location in China, but this time he journeys back to America changed and grown for all his experiences in India and the relationships he built there.

Sorrells (2016) emphasizes "how economic globalization has magnified the need for intercultural awareness, understanding and training at all levels of business" (p. 36). Globalization has made it possible for multinational corporations to outsource their support services to developing nations where labor is substantially less expensive, but also where there is an increased possibility of intercultural differences creating "difficulties of 'translating' business practices, products and markets across cultures" (Sorrells, 2016, p. 36). Todd's sojourn in India as he navigates the ups and downs of culture shock, and tries to connect his experiences of Hindu cultural symbols like Goddess Kali and Holi with American pop-culture symbols like cheesehead hats and McDonalds, makes it imperative for audiences "to critique media representations of non-Western cultures not merely because they may be false or stereotyped, but because 'representation as ideology' constitutes and defines the creation and production of knowledge about these cultures" (Parameswaran, 1996, p. 71). In *Outsourced* (2006), we see familiar South Asian and American stereotypes being touted, including visual markers of an impoverished and uber-traditional India versus a capitalist and ultra-individualistic American work–family ethic. But, we also find a challenging and changing of intercultural assumptions, and positive identity movements for most characters and their relationships, within a diverse workplace and beyond.

We begin this chapter by outlining an overview of economic globalization in the twenty-first century and the opportunities for outsourcing that it has created in the Global South. The implications of such labor and capital movements on sojourners and stages of the U-curve model of migrant adaptation that they navigate are also explored, after which we move onto our case study of the film, connecting and analyzing these intercultural communication concepts.

ECONOMIC GLOBALIZATION AND OUTSOURCING

Globalization creates "a world market in goods, services, labor, capital, and technology," equally impacting the home and host cultures that are party to the movements of its people, principle, and local practices (Martin & Nakayama, 2010, p. 17; Lipsey, 2004). Economic globalization tightens networks of capitalistic interdependence among global economic structures and across geopolitical, informational, marketized, scientific, and technological borders. In the 1990s, economic globalization also ushered in outsourcing and offshoring practices. *Outsourcing* refers to businesses contracting jobs to international locations, for reasons spanning lack of adequate in-house resources, to cheap foreign labor and/or other cost-cutting factors. *Offshoring* usually accompanies outsourcing, and prompts companies to move some departments or business processes to a foreign location, for the same reasons as outsourcing.

The 1990s also brought in a significant change in the global landscape of commerce, particularly with trade liberalization, large-scale privatization of industry, ICT expansion, political visibility, and economic capitalism taking strongholds in developing nations like India and China (Liu & Trefler, 2008; Gandhi, 2002). These changes compelled employees of developed economies, like the United States and United Kingdom, to professionally compete with "educated but low-paid foreign workers," many of whom were entrepreneurial enough to provide the same services from an offshore, outsourced facility, but at a substantially lower cost incurred by the parent company (Liu & Trefler, 2008, p. 1; Antraás & Helpman, 2004). Countries like India and China also created the capacity to strategically impact where service work could be located.

As a result of liberal capitalism, India's increased international trade with the United States, and a series of economic reforms, India became an obvious choice for outsourcing and offshoring (Gandhi, 2002). Transnational companies like GE, HSBC, Motorola, and American Express, among others, started offshoring business services to India in the early 1990s and later many U.S. technology startups also sought out the low-cost labor available in developing countries (Dossani & Kenney, 2006). Yet, in practice, setting up successful offshore businesses is not as simple as it may seem (Taylor & Bain, 2005). The service industry and MNCs in the United States were no exception to the cross-cultural fallout of economic globalization.

As with any market trend, which by definition is economically mobile and contingent on current business needs, shifts in industries and occupation change the nature and movement of human labor across physical and technological borders (Liu & Trefler, 2008; Neal, 1995). The limitations of offshoring can be categorized as a dialectical tension between movement and stasis. In moving jobs to another country, human capital in the company's original nation is destroyed (Liu & Trefler, 2008), while some jobs require in-person service and so cannot be offshored (Reich, 1990).

This "contradiction between mobility and fixity" underlying networks of outsourcing in the global marketplace is also found in call center offshoring (Taylor, 2012, p. 8). A *call center* functions as a stand-alone company, or the client-serving site (internal help lines) of a large organization or MNC, "in which the main business is conducted via a telephone whilst simultaneously using display screen equipment (DSE)" (Sprigg, Smith & Jackson, 2003, p. 1). Calls are taken by trained call handlers who "spend a significant proportion of their working time responding to calls" (Sprigg et al., 2003, p. 1).

Media coverage and early research on call centers described them as *electronic sweatshops* producing "'low-quality' and heavily routinised forms of work," while call handlers were termed *battery hens*, to expose the "intensive and stressful nature" of their jobs (Garson, 1988; Fernie & Metcalf, 1998; Sprigg et al., 2003, p. 1). Other research traced the progression of call centers from 'production line' processes that have now "moved away from this 'mass production model' (maximise volume and minimise costs) and adopted more high involvement work practices" (Sprigg et al., 2003, p. 1). Yet they remain a far cry from the bespoke knowledge workers that are needed to meet the demands of an evolved twenty-first-century marketplace (Huselid, 1995; Batt & Moynihan, 2002).

Notions of 'spatial elasticity' (Ritzer & Lair, 2008, p. 40) that have explained the geographical fluidity of call center operations are often a result of "mistaken versions of globalization" (Taylor, 2012, p. 8), which essentially feed its propensity for cultural essentialism and support the conjecture of a "genuinely borderless" world where, "the 'death of distance' (Cairncross, 1997) means that finance, capital and technology can flow uninhibited across a 'weightless world'" (Taylor, 2012, p. 8). And technology, though indispensable in our current market of information networks, is not enough to explain contradictory movements of capital and labor across "geographical mobility" and "relative fixity" (Taylor, 2012; Harvey, 1989, p. 294, 338). Instead, place becomes prime in a postglobalized map of the world and not as a point fixed within temporal and spatial borders.

India, with its "supplies of university-educated and, indispensably, English-speaking labour," at first proved to be a viable relocation option for global companies looking to invest 'mobile capital' in a material place where, "migratory flows follow the contours of linguistic and cultural compatibility" (Taylor, 2012, p. 9; Rainnie et al., 2008). Yet this was not always the case, whether in Indian call centers or other locations that were selected for their labors' cumulative skills in language and education. This is because MNCs did not always take into account social, cultural, political, and accent-dialect differences, which much like call center services "do not 'slice through' national borders equally" (Taylor, 2012, p. 9).

MIGRATION, SOJOURNING, AND U-CURVE

With so much investment in outsourcing and offshoring, it is inevitable that employees will be traveling among locations. Often this type of migration is specifically sojourning, meaning someone who travels to another place for a designated period of time, usually for a specific purpose, like a business person or an international student. A sojourner is different from a tourist, who spends only a brief period of time abroad, and a sojourner is also different from immigrants or refugees who (voluntarily or involuntarily, respectively) live in another country for long periods of time (Lynch, 2013). For the purposes of this chapter, we focus on sojourning as a specific type of migration that informs and shapes cultural adaption.

International migration is on the rise. There are 272 million international migrants around the world, most of whom are labor migrants (World Migration Report, 2019). Migrants tend to move from developing countries to developed ones, including the United States, France, Russia, Saudi Arabia, and United Arab Emirates, but more than half of the world's international migrants reside in North America and Europe (World Migration Report, 2019). Interestingly, in 2019, of all the countries that migrants originated from, India was the largest with 17.5 million migrants living outside of the country (World Migration Report, 2019). *Outsourced* (2006), however, tells a story of an American man sent to India by his employer for a specific professional purpose. This plot trends with the realities of business travel. Travel, specifically business travel, is a trillion dollar industry and it is only expected to increase over the years with the United States being one of the top spenders on this type of travel (Lock, 2018). But what happens when people arrive in a new culture and have to figure out how to do their jobs?

In this chapter, we revisit a popular model—the U-curve model of intercultural adaptation (Lysgaard, 1955), for how sojourners adjust to a new culture. Lysgaard (1955) identified three stages that comprise the migrant adaptation process, including (i) anticipation, (ii) culture shock, and (iii) adjustment. Recall from chapter 2 that the first stage, *anticipation*, is marked by the initial enthusiasm that a migrant or sojourner feels coming into a new cultural space, and the second stage, *culture shock*, is an uneasy feeling of unfamiliarity, anxiety, and stress one can feel in a new environment or culture. *Adjustment* is the final stage when the individual "learns to negotiate the verbal and nonverbal codes, values, norms, behaviors, and assumptions of the new culture" (Sorrells, 2016, p. 253).

As discussed in chapter 2, the term "culture shock" was coined by Oberg (1960) who describes it as being like a disease that has symptoms and can be cured. Although Berry (1997) proposes and prefers the term "acculturative stress" over culture shock because it links the term more closely with psychological models of stress and eliminates the negative implication embedded in the older term, we use culture shock because it is more widely known and understood. Oberg (1960) explains that culture shock is "the anxiety that results from losing all our familiar signs and symbols of social intercourse," and explains how the hundreds of small and large social interactions that we have each day become more challenging in a new cultural environment because we don't fully understand all of the verbal and nonverbal cues that are happening (p. 77). From greetings to communicating with housekeeping staff at a hotel, to whether or not to tip a server, these small and large interactions can feel like puzzles. The symptoms of culture shock that Oberg (1960) identifies include a sense of helplessness; excessive anger at small annoyances; excessive fear of the people, food, and so on of the new culture; and a yearning to return home. Culture shock can be "cured" by getting to know the people in the new culture—learn the language, understand why they do things certain ways, learn about their interests, and try to get involved as a sort of participant observer (Oberg, 1960). Moving past culture shock in this way is what can lead a migrant to the last phase of the U-curve—adjustment to the new culture.

It must be noted that the U-curve model and Oberg's research on culture shock have come under criticism. Specifically, Oberg (1960) argued that there is an exhilarating "honeymoon" stage at the beginning of the U-curve as a migrant is preparing for and first arriving in the new culture. This is what Lysgaard termed as the anticipation stage. However, research has shown that this is not necessarily the case, with some studies showing that participants experienced distress as quickly as 24 hours after arrival to a new culture (Ward, Okura, Kennedy & Kojima, 1998). Longitudinal studies have shown that "sojourners commence their overseas stay in a state of at least moderate psychological distress" (Ward et al., 1998, p. 287). These findings are important for the purpose of our analysis because Todd, the protagonist of the film, does not begin his business trip in a happy state of anticipation. Rather, his trip begins with distressing anticipation, in line with recent research on the U-curve.

For the business sojourner, the experiences of being in a new culture are framed by specific sets of expectations related to one's organization and the tasks assigned for the time spent abroad. An international business traveler, such as Todd, is someone who is abroad to accomplish a certain task and is sent by an employer for a designated period of time (Ward, Bochner & Furnham, 2001). While in the foreign location, business sojourners need to interact with local stakeholders that may positively or negatively influence their careers (Ward et al., 2001). Yet, business practices are culturally inhibited just like any other human activity (Hofstede, 1998), and so business practices that are common in the United States may not transfer well to other cultural contexts. These cultural differences in business behaviors mean that international business travelers need to adapt to local practices. But this adaptation raises a dilemma for the organization—do they force "uniform corporate-wide policies and practices whose functional benefits may be lost" in a different cultural context, or do they adjust their business practices at the risk of diluting the corporate culture that "drive their particular multinational organization" (Ward et al., 2001, p. 171)? The business sojourner must weigh these risks and benefits, and his or her career may well depend on the outcomes. For Todd Anderson, such dilemmas are some of the key plotlines that drive the film.

FILM ANALYSIS

To trace Todd's cultural, professional, and interpersonal movements between America and India, we organized our analysis of *Outsourced* (2006) following the two key conceptual themes we have explored in this film—*outsourcing labor and cultures*, and *U-curve movements of cultural adaptation*.

Outsourcing and Capitalism: Moving between Work and Cultural Spaces

Outsourced (2006) sets the stage for intercultural connection right with its opening scene when we hear the music of a sitar, a sound that stereotypically signals 'India' to Western ears, then quickly changes to Western guitar music that sounds like the uplifting Indie music of Seattle's music scene. We then see iconic images of Seattle—the Space Needle, Public Market, and the city's streets. The audio in the background is of a salesman on the phone with a customer negotiating shipping charges for something s/he has bought. The man, named Todd Anderson, is at a fictional company, Western Novelty, which sells kitschy products, like the hotdog clock on his desk. These novelties stand as symbols of American consumerism that fill employees' cubicles and the larger workspace, indicating America's impersonal and material corporate culture [1:16].

Todd's boss, Dave, summons him into his office and the interaction between them is indicative of American low-power distance, where communication between people at different levels in a hierarchy can be more casual. For example, Todd openly plays solitaire on his computer between calls and tells Dave that this meeting needs to be short. Dave explains, "Todd, we've decided to restructure order fulfillment . . . Offshore the whole department." Dave excitedly explains the expansive cost savings their company can make by outsourcing the order fulfillment jobs, while Todd remains incredulous and in disbelief. He says, "You can't outsource order fulfillment, half our catalog is patriotic knick-knacks. If a factory worker from Wisconsin calls the 800-number to buy this [Todd holds up a plastic bald eagle with an American flag painted on it] and gets a person in another country, he's gonna flip out." Dave counters flippantly, "That's where the accent training comes in" [2:15].

Todd is not needed in Seattle and he is needed in India to train his own replacement. Recall that outsourcing is a process of economic globalization, aided by technology and capitalism, where companies in developed countries like the United States set up branches in developing countries like India to manufacture, manage, or provide cost-effective labor and services to customers in the parent country (Taylor, 2012). In this context, if Todd chooses not to go, he'll have to quit. Todd asks what the new manager gets paid, and it's only a small fraction of Todd's salary, which Dave announces with glee and laughter. Dave's demands are typical of North American managerial methods that among other practices promote "emphasis on task achievement" and "negotiation based on rational, factual grounds" (Ward et al., 2001, p. 170). In these scenes, the aggressiveness and coldness of capitalism are personified in Dave—he has his vulnerable employee in a difficult spot that he manipulates to get Todd to sojourn in India.

Todd arrives in India and meets the man he is to train, Purohit N. Virajnarianan—Puro, for short. Puro arranged for Todd to stay at Auntie Ji's charming guesthouse instead of the "lonely" hotel. After Todd settles in at Auntie Ji's, Puro drives him to the Gharapuri office, explaining that they work from 6:00 p.m. until 6:00 a.m. local time, which is daytime in the United States. When asked if that disrupts their sleep, Puro explains that they are "accustomed to the problems by now" [18:12–20:38]. Puro's testimony is indicative of the differences between real working conditions and professional aspirations that outsourced call center employees like him face, including "a work intensity consisting of relentless, routinised and pressurised work, exacerbated by nocturnal working patterns" (Taylor, 2012, p. 15).

As they arrive at the office, Todd is shocked to realize that the office is still under construction. Puro explains that, "There is no office to rent in Gharapuri, so we had to build one. Because of outsourcing, all the real estate in Bombay [Puro says Bombay, not Mumbai], Madras, Bangalore, even Gharapuri is taken" [19:18]. Gharapuri is a fictional town, yet it may have been visually modeled after more recently developed IT sectors like Navi Mumbai, a newer suburb of Mumbai, or Rajarhat, a large-scale IT hub on the outskirts of Kolkata, or even Gurgaon, a suburb of Delhi that was developed in the 1980s (Marantz, 2011). What is common to these spaces is that they all were former rural areas, or on the margins of cities and suburbs.

Inside the office, about 15–20 people donning headsets work at small cubicles fulfilling orders. Todd walks around, sees the supervisor station that lacks a glass window, then glances into another room still under construction to see a cow wandering around. Todd looks at Puro in shock, and Puro eventually realizes that Todd is referring to the cow [20:27]. At first glance, a situation like a 'cow in the office' is comical, even stereotypical of a foreigner's perception of India as a place where elephants, cows, and snake charmers supposedly still roam the streets. On a closer look, however, it becomes obvious that this bovine situation is suggestive of the organic, material, high contact, and inadequate living conditions of India's larger population that live and work in rural, liminal, and suburban areas, of which Gharapuri is a microcosm.

Later, Todd returns to the office and introduces himself to the staff. He says:

> I'm Todd Anderson, from Western Novelty, and I'm here to help integrate you into our business. Now I gotta tell you, this center's numbers are nowhere near what they should be, and based on the customer complaints we've been having, it's a culture thing. Basically, you people need to learn about America. Now it's all about bringing down the MPI [minutes per incident]. Things go faster if the customer feels they're talking to a native English speaker. [22:43]

Research suggests that early decisions of multinational companies to outsource client-side services were based not only on lower labor costs (where countries like China could easily trump India and Philippines), but also on employees' linguistic competence (English-speaking ability) that was a major "criterion driving overseas location," and why India was a popular go-to for call centers (Taylor, 2012, p. 9). Here, Todd's spiel to Indian employees about their culture being a deterrent to mastering American English is typical of the multinational work ethic and of factors such as skills, language, and cost savings that go into outsourcing decisions.

A young woman in the group speaks up to challenge Todd on his ignorant and ethnocentric comment. She says, "But we are native English speakers. English is the official language of our government. You got it from the British and so did we, we just speak it differently" [22:41]. Todd points out that he wants them to be able to speak like an American in terms of pronunciation, as well as familiarity with slang and the general culture—"Learn about America." Here Todd relies on direct performance feedback, characteristic of North American management practices (Ward et al., 2001). Todd's cultural bias illustrates the bias held by many Western multinationals that English language competency is one thing, but employees also need cultural empathy to connect with customers in the way MNCs prefer (Taylor, 2012). Part of Todd's job is also to teach them enough about American culture to successfully manage customer calls, but Todd is ill-equipped at this stage to be a cultural broker, as is illustrated by his vague, imprecise, and confusing definition of small talk.

As the film progresses, Todd is starting to find a rhythm in India. But a call from Dave pressuring him to get the MPI down faster and explaining that he is expected to get the MPI to 6:00 exactly rather than "in the sixes," as Todd had understood his assignment, sets Todd off course from the rhythm he was starting to build in his new life. Todd snaps at Dave, calling him a "corporate slimeball" [32:27], to which Dave responds by again threatening lost stock options and unemployment. Dave's threats represent one extreme of North American corporate practices in that it assumes those practices are universal. When such rigid work practices like "reliance on written and unwritten rules," and "treatment and reward of employees based on individual achievement," are applied to other cultural contexts, as Dave pushes Todd to follow in India, it may not translate well—culturally or organizationally (Ward et al., 2001, p. 170).

Later in the film, Todd experiences a transformation as he is pulled into the public revelry of Holi, the Hindu springtime festival of colors, on the streets of Gharapuri. Todd expresses his change to the staff that evening when he says, "I want to apologize to all of you, and especially Asha. She was right. I need to learn about India . . . Now our first mistake has been trying to run this like an American office. So, I want to ask you, how can we do things differently? What would make your work day a more positive experience?" [45:11]. Sanji asks to bring family photos, Krishna asks to bring *murtis* (statues of gods and goddesses), Madhuri asks if they can wear Indian clothes instead of Western clothes, and Rani asks if they can get a discount on the products they're selling. Todd agrees to everything, realizes that they're actually interested in Western Novelty's products, and sets up an incentive program wherein whoever improves their MPI the most each day gets to choose any product they want.

Todd's apology, the steps he takes to change the office culture, and his regard for his employees' unique needs and identities, all confirm that "Global personnel management implies understanding local constraints" (Hofstede, 1998, p. 7). However, as Todd leaves, he nervously eyes a cow in one of the rooms under construction—a brief reminder to the viewer that he's still American and still finds some things about Indian culture to be unusual. This persistent theme with the cows comes off at times like pandering to American viewers, and a perpetuation of their stereotypes about India.

In a later scene, Todd approaches Asha asking why she hasn't signed up for the incentive program even though everyone else has [51:56–55:18]. She points out that she does not need products like the hotdog cooker since she is a vegetarian. Asha says to him, "You Americans have more choices than anyone in the world. Why would you choose this?" [52:55]. Todd has found a like-minded person in Asha in that they both think the products they're selling are tacky. She doesn't neatly fit into her company's ideal 'global' (universal, indistinguishable) call center employee model. Her character emphasizes the impact of unique cultural values within contemporary organizations where "Nobody can [truly] think globally," and when, if applied without considering the culturally diverse makeup of local workforces, both "national and organizational cultures [can] constrain personnel management" (Hofstede, 1998, p. 7). Todd's incentive program mostly pays off as he realizes and accepts the global–local value differences across American and Indian work contexts, suggesting that he has adopted a more mobile approach to managing the cultural complexities of outsourcing (Hofstede, 1998).

The organizational reality that "Management in general, and personnel management in particular, are culturally constrained" (Hofstede, 1998, p. 7) is apparent toward the end of the film. It is apparent in the different managerial styles and value orientations of Dave, who has newly arrived from Seattle with his corporate American work ethic, and Todd, who by now has adopted a culturally sensitive work ideology in the Indian call center. In this scene, Todd is awoken by his cell phone ringing [1:19:00–1:23:42]. It is Dave and he is waiting at the Gharapuri train station, much to Todd's surprise. He demands that Todd pick him up immediately. At the train station, Todd (who is now wearing a blue *kurta*) gets out of the taxi and smiles knowingly as he watches Dave eat the same *gola* that Todd mistakenly ate when he first arrived, and which took a toll on his digestive tract.

They take a taxi to the call center and Dave critiques, "It looks like a storage center" [1:20:18], and Todd quips back, "You get what you pay for" in a jab at the way that Dave (and by extension Western Novelty and corporate America, more broadly) treats people and takes advantage of them. Dave is there in part because he doesn't trust that Todd has successfully led the team to a six MPI and that he's somehow "rigging the system" [1:20:38]. The scene cuts to them walking in the office, which is flooded and the MPI is up to 12:17. The irrigation from the farm next door caused the flood in the call center. The computer stations are going down and as Puro frantically tries to get the water out, another station sparks, lights flicker, and two more stations go out of commission. Dave says to Todd, "I'm going to shred your passport," meaning Todd is never going to leave India because he'll never get this office running properly.

Todd thinks quickly and says they can transition all the stations up to the roof. Dave says it's impossible and Todd fires back, "Maybe back in the States it is" [1:21:54]. Todd calls Anil to get the car—they are going to find Todd's neighbor, the *dhobi* (laundryman), and have him rewire the office—"I'll be right back with a consultant," Todd explains. In the next scene, the neighbor is seen at the top of a light pole working with wires to get the office connected, and as he makes the final connection, sparks fly and the computers turn back on. The fact that Todd's technology "consultant" is a laundryman may be an organizational anomaly in American workspaces where the "selection, recruitment and promotion of employees [happens] on the basis of merit" (Ward et al., 2001, p. 170), but this is not the case in countries like

India where informal labor is widely available, communal, and job expertise is often not as compartmentalized.

As the night wears on, the MPI decreases. An angry customer demands to speak with a supervisor, and Asha takes the call. The man on the line is angry that he's buying an American eagle but the call center is in India. The man goes on talking about how his factory job was outsourced to Mexico and his brother had to move because there are no jobs in their town. Asha patiently listens to the man and offers a solution. She says, "See, we understand that many Americans are upset about outsourcing, so we have located American-made versions of all our products. If you have a pen, I will give you the website of an American company that makes an eagle statue very similar to ours, same size, same materials, only theirs is made 100% in America" [1:24:32]. As Todd and Dave watch and listen, Asha explains that the other company's eagle is much more expensive, and the customer reluctantly agrees to buy the Western Novelty eagle after all. The point here in the film is that outsourcing has both pros and cons—the major pro is lower-cost products and the major con is lost jobs, exacerbated by "educated American workers [who] are now facing intense competition from the offshore outsourcing of services to China and India" (Liu & Trefler, 2008, p. 1).

As their workday ends, and the MPI reaches 5:57, Todd congratulates the team and invites them all to celebrate at the Lotus Club—a local bar that caters to call center workers who end work at 6:00 a.m. Todd looks for Dave in the flooded office and finds him exiting the bathroom with an upset stomach (due to the *gola*). Dave reveals that there is another reason he came to Gharapuri—"I need to wipe our proprietary data off these hard drives before we pull out of India"—as they're going to China—"China's the new India—20 heads for the price of one. What're you gonna do?" [1:26:08]. In the relentless pursuit of profit, driven by cold capitalism, the outsourced jobs get outsourced to an even cheaper labor market. Research suggests that although Indian labor has many benefits for outsourcing, such as an English-speaking and low-cost educated workforce, the precarity of Indian call centers and labor can also be problematic, thus a gradual shifting of some services to locations like China and Philippines (Taylor, 2012; Cumbers et al., 2008).

As Todd enters the Lotus Club, and informs the staff that their jobs have been outsourced [1:27:32], the staff listen in astonishment but then turn to each other to smile, saying it's not so bad. However, Puro seems devastated [1:26:48]. He explains, "we've trained them to a point where they can get a job anywhere—Microsoft, Dell, Office Tiger. They will get a job in a week. And with severance pay, you can have some fun" [1:28:39]. However, management is different, Puro explains. It's harder to find those jobs and Puro is concerned since he is not a young man anymore. He is especially worried that Bhagyashree, his fiancé, will decide to marry someone else upon finding out about Puro's unemployment. Todd asks why there is a hurry for them to get married. "Astrology," Puro explains, "our moons are lined up. Auspicious time. She must marry this year" [1:29:03]. Puro's dilemma highlights how economic, familial, and astrological factors weigh equally on an individual's decision to get married, particularly in more traditionally primed cultures like India that fall somewhere along a *being* (places more value on relationships) and *growing* (value placed on spiritual aspects of life) cultural orientations (Kluckhohn & Strodtbeck, 1961; Martin & Nakayama, 2018).

In the next scene, as Dave tries to convince Todd to train the new manager in Shanghai, two men bring in and begin to install a glass window—the window that Todd had been asking for the supervisor's desk since the day he arrived in Gharapuri [1:34:33]. Visually, the glass that now separates Todd and Dave becomes symbolic of their ideological differences, particularly when Todd refuses to go to China. Dave brushes off his refusal and keeps listing all the benefits he'll get from taking on this new job, but it's no use this time. Todd has changed in ways that Dave cannot understand. Todd walks out and Dave follows him, offering even more financial benefits: "What do you want Todd? Just tell me what you want. You can't quit. Then you'll have worked your ass off here for nothing ... Who am I going to send to Shanghai?" [1:35:28]. Todd stands with his back to Dave, listening, and knows what he's going to do.

Next, a man is seen walking through the airport. As the camera pans up, we see a smiling Puro walking with his new wife, Bhagyashree. By now the audience knows that Puro is going to Shanghai, as arranged by Todd, to train the new call center employees. Puro says, "Todd, you saved my life," to which Todd says, "You saved mine. Don't worry about running the center, you'll be great. Break a leg" [1:36:09]. The men embrace and part ways to their separate flights. Todd has returned to wearing quintessential American-style jeans, ready to return to America—his sojourn in India is now over, but the impact it has had on his personal growth and cultural values can best be understood by his complex movement from culture shock to adjustment.

Sojourning the U-curve: From Culture Shock to Cultural Adjustment

One of the earliest scenes of the film shows a weary and disheveled Todd arriving in the Mumbai airport [3:44–8:36]. Todd exits the airport and nervously walks through a crowd of drivers with signs waiting to pick up travelers, but does not see his name or his driver anywhere, despite going past a man holding a sign that says, "Mr. Toad," which we later learn was his ride—locals pronounce the name Todd like "toad." Todd escapes a group of taxi drivers that have surrounded him, and asks the driver of a "Cool Cab" to take him to the train station. Todd is relieved, but then the driver puts Todd's suitcase in an auto-rickshaw behind the car. Todd realizes his error and tries to reclaim his suitcase, but the driver begins driving away as half of Todd's body is inside the vehicle. Todd stumbles inside and next thing he knows, he's being whisked off to the train station.

The scene that follows is a juxtaposition of images from Mumbai streets—a visual opportunity to set the stage for Todd's new, temporary home. As popular Indian music plays in the background, Todd nervously witnesses frantic, crowded, and dilapidated snippets of Indian urban life from his auto-rickshaw. This selective montage of Mumbai, put together using only dismal and congested images of an otherwise vibrant, global city, is an exaggerated cinematic choice to separate America and India. In this case, "ethnicity becomes a mode of action and representation" embodied in Todd and his perceptions of India thus far, and "refers to a decision people make to depict themselves or others symbolically as the bearers of a certain cultural identity" (Cohen, 1993, p. 197). Yet what the narrative accomplishes, and continues developing in its characters and their contexts, are complex symbols of mobility—of continuous urban, suburban, transportational, social, economic, and cultural movements.

At the Mumbai train station Todd faces another level of cultural uncertainty as he is asked to run after a train, and helped by strangers to jump on board a moving one that is overcrowded. Todd, who is now inside the train car looking uncomfortable and tired, slowly shuffles down the aisle, as a boy stands up to offer Todd his seat. Todd gratefully takes the seat, only to find that the boy has now seated himself on Todd's lap. Here, Todd's discomfort suggests we all have expectations for acceptable nonverbal behavior that when violated, as the boy on the train does by sitting on Todd's lap, are seen as "violations" that move along a positive–negative scale depending on the person, behavior, or context (Martin & Nakayama, 2018, p. 277). Yet, this scene also points out that our sense of proximity is culturally determined and that people from contact cultures like India "maintain closer interpersonal spacing" than those from noncontact cultures like America, for reasons as practical as overpopulation and urban congestion (Mazur, 1977, p. 53; Hall, 1966).

Todd's arrival in India thrusts him immediately into the culture shock stage of the U-curve model. Recall that culture shock refers to a relatively short-term feeling of disorientation, ambiguity, and helplessness as a result of being in unfamiliar cultural surroundings (Oberg, 1960). Todd's initial feelings seem that of anxiety and resentment at the position his employer has put him in, an experience common for work sojourners commencing their stay in foreign locations (Ward et al., 1998). From his first few minutes in India, Todd experiences culture shock, which is visually depicted through large crowds, stressful and crowded transportation experiences, and poverty, illustrated in the makeshift buildings that repeatedly appear in the montage.

Todd arrives in Gharapuri, weary and thirsty, and finds a vendor to purchase a sweet drink, called *gola*, similar to a shaved-ice snow cone [8:37–12:54]. Puro approaches Todd, asking "Are you Mr. Toad?". They struggle to pronounce each other's names correctly—Puro saying "Toad" and Todd saying "Poro." Once in Puro's car the scene changes to the streets of Gharapuri where his car inches through a road crowded with pedestrians, cows, bicycles, auto-rickshaws, and vendors. Puro insists that Mumbai is "terrible" and that Gharapuri is far cleaner, while the camera cuts to a man urinating on the street. Such culturally disorienting encounters for Todd, many nonverbal, seem to be a conscious and stereotypical call to separate American and Indian cultures. Yet, as is common in films depicting various symbols of cultural differences, these symbols are "invariably mundane items, drawn from everyday life" (Cohen, 1993, p. 197).

Differences in high- and low-power distance orientations appear once again during the car ride from the station, with Puro using a formal style of communication with Todd, and Todd insisting that Puro be less formal. Puro explains that he changed Todd's reservation to Auntie Ji's guest house, explaining how she "will take care of you better than your own real mother" [12:28]. Puro's assumption that Todd would be lonely in a hotel comes from his collectivist orientation, while for Todd, a hotel is preferable so he can be alone, and escape some of the intensity of this different culture.

In his room at the guest house, Todd admires the view and walks about checking out the accommodations. He pauses to look at an image of goddess Kali, who is holding a large blade, a bloody head, and dons a garland of severed heads. Todd finds the image troubling and looks for a way to remove the picture. Goddess Kali, here, is introduced as a cultural symbol that is steeped in Indian, mainly Hindu, mythology. Symbols are vehicles for culture, or "quite simply carriers of meaning" (Cohen, 1993, p. 196). In Hinduism, Ma Kali, a name derived from the Sanskrit root word 'kaal' or time, stands as an emblem of Mother Nature—"primordial, creative, nurturing and devouring in turn, but ultimately loving and benevolent" (Heaphy, 2017). The symbolism of Kali runs deeper, but for now it is an obvious, yet disturbing, symbol of Indian cultural identity. Todd, who claims an American cultural identity, finds himself disconnected from the cultural identity of his host nation (Cohen, 1993, p. 197).

After a long first day, Todd collapses on a chair at the guest house as Auntie Ji insists on bringing him food because he's all "skin and bones" [24:33-30:18]. She wants to introduce him to a "nice Indian girl" and when Todd refuses she asks if he is "homosexual." Todd excuses himself and walks to the courtyard where he examines a shrine. The statue there is of Hindu deity Lord Shiva, with a pink flower at the feet and blue powder rubbed on the forehead. This is the second time Todd is introduced to a cultural symbol, Shiva, the destroyer and one of the Hindu trinity alongside Brahma (creator) and Vishnu (preserver). Shiva is the husband and mythological counterpart of Kali, and the supine body on which she stands in religious iconography is Shiva's, who depicts "pure formless awareness *sat-chit-ananda* (being-consciousness-bliss) while she represents 'form' eternally supported by the substratum of pure awareness" (Temple Purohit, 2019). Such cultural symbols and Auntie Ji's maternal gestures function as constant reminders to Todd that he is now a sojourner in a collectivist, and spiritually primed country.

In a key scene, the staff ask Todd about the products they're selling. Manmeet asks about an item—a cheesehead hat, which Todd explains is something Americans like to wear to sporting events. Another employee asks about a burger brand—an iron device to burn a design on a beef burger. Todd explains, "You know, the thing you use to burn a symbol into a cow with? In America, that's how you keep track of your cows, it's branding" [28:17]. As Todd notices shocked expressions on his employees' faces, he realizes how this practice that seems normal to him is offensive to people from a culture where cows are largely revered. This is a moment when Todd begins his transition toward cultural adjustment. The haze of culture shock and the blinders of ethnocentrism are beginning to fade ever so slightly. To punctuate this moment, Asha raises her hand as Todd has grown uncomfortable and suggests that Todd needs to "learn about India" [28:54].

A sign that Todd has started his sojourning movement from culture shock to adjustment is seen in how cultural symbols and nonverbal codes specific to India are more naturally integrated into the next few scenes, as Todd starts finding meaning and purpose in them. In the office, Puro performs a *puja* (prayer ritual) to a statue of Lord Ganesh—who in Hindu mythology is revered as the remover of obstacles so that devotees can succeed, and is often worshipped when people are starting a new business or traveling (BBC, 2009). Later at the guest house Todd finishes a meal in the courtyard and climbs up and places the tray of leftover food, waiting nervously to see if anyone takes it, which someone does. Todd has picked up on some of the mundane nonverbal gestures displayed by locals (in this case, the domestic staff at Auntie Ji's house, who would often pass a tray full of leftovers over the courtyard wall), and he has started adapting to the collectivistic rhythm of Gharapuri. Some cultural symbols, however, still confound Todd, either for lack of significance or transference to his own cultural context. In the next scene as Todd crawls into bed, he takes a frightening look at the image of Kali. Once again, Kali is depicted through Todd's *othered* perspective, but the Indian music in the background suggests there is more to the story of Kali than the apparent imagery of death—a latent level of nuance that Todd is yet unable to grasp.

Despite small steps toward adjustment, Todd's experience of culture shock has not fully abated. An instance of this is seen in his experience at Mac Donnells, a fast-food restaurant in Gharapuri that resembles a McDonald's [34:59–37:17]. Todd orders two cheeseburgers, but the employee explains that they do not sell cheeseburgers there. A white man standing behind Todd watches knowingly and suggests he get the "maharaja veggie burger. It's as close as you're gonna get" [35:34]. As a cultural symbol, Mac Donnells serves a dual purpose—one, as a local copy of the global McDonald's chain whose "particular meaning [is] only recognized as such by those who share the culture," as seen in Todd's enthusiasm to eat there and feel less homesick; and second, as one of many "symbols from one cultural group [that] are regularly copied by others . . . [and] represent the outer, most superficial layer of culture," which Todd also realizes from how Mac Donnells caters to local tastes (Hofstede, 1998, p. 8).

As Todd and the American man enjoy their veggie burgers, the latter talks condescendingly of Indian culture and his experience in customer service. His ethnocentrism is apparent not only in his joke that 'India' stands for "I'll Never Do It Again," but also in the way he describes his employees as "accent neutrals." He then offers Todd some advice—"I remember feeling like you do. I was resisting India. Once I gave in, I did much better" [36:53]. Just then, a *sadhu* (wearing yellow robes and carrying a *danda*, or staff) knocks on the window and looks at the men. Sadhus are Hindu ascetics who have given up attachment to material, familial, and so on affections to devote themselves to religious practice. They rely on donations from people for food and other needs, a practice generally supported among India's collectivistic and pious communities. Although the sadhu here is used for comic relief, they are often revered for their religious devotion. The sadhu is yet another cultural symbol, as someone who has achieved that liberation from material attachments. He also stands in stark contrast with McDonald's, a cultural symbol of American consumerism, and even though both symbols "are visible to an outside observer; their cultural meaning, however, is invisible and lies precisely and only in the way these practices are interpreted by the insiders" (Hofstede, 1998, p. 8).

Todd is starting to adjust and bit by bit allows himself to recognize the talent and the kindness around him—in Asha's skill and intellect, in Puro's generosity and thoughtfulness. The recurrent visuals of Kali in Todd's room signal her power of rebirth and regeneration (Heaphy, 2017)—she is slowly devouring Todd's ego and helping him liberate himself, not from his physical body like the sadhu, but from his ethnocentric and egotistical frame of mind that is preventing him from embracing India, embracing the person he is becoming, and finding success in his career.

In a key scene, Todd leaves for work not realizing it is Holi, the Hindu springtime festival of colors [38:58–44:04]. Todd walks along an empty street, which is confusing to him because the streets are usually bustling with people, mopeds, cars, and more. He wonders at the splashes of colorful *gulal* (colored powder) that he sees on the ground and the buildings. Puro finds Todd on the street and rushes up to him saying, "You should not wear good clothes on this day!" [40:03]. Meanwhile, a shuttered window in the background has opened and a person there prepares to launch a colorful attack. Puro grabs Todd—"Watch out!!"—and they duck behind a tower in the square. As children from buildings throw balloons filled with *abeer* (colored water), Todd and Puro try to hide. Puro briefly explains that Holi is the "celebration of colors, changing of seasons" [40:24]. Puro says they can run down an alley up ahead as they hide from a group of boys looking for targets. As Puro runs up to the boys to throw his abeer-filled balloons and shoots a boy with an abeer-filled *pichakaree* (a plastic pipe used to suction water and shoot it out, like a water gun), he beckons Todd to make a run for it, as if they are in a gun battle with enemies. Todd gets hit with another large cloud of powder, this time blue, as two boys laugh from a building above. Todd, now donning American red, white and blue abeer, demands a water balloon so he can counterattack. As Oberg (1960) argued, one way to overcome culture shock and move toward adjustment is to get involved in the other culture as a participant observer, and this is just what Todd does as he partakes in the Holi revelry.

Todd finally yields and embraces Holi, and India by extension. Puro cheers, Happy Holi!, and they grab from piles of powder, throw handfuls into the crowd, as Todd grabs a pichakaree to shoot abeer, and joins in a dancing crowd. Later, Todd joins the revelers as they go to rinse in a nearby river. From a Christian perspective, this is like Todd's christening, as he immerses himself in the water and rises reborn and in a union—not with Christianity, but union with India at long last. While Holi in the film depicts Todd's "rebirth," for Western viewers unfamiliar with Holi, Todd's immersion in the water signals to them his symbolic baptism, or initiation ritual into a new culture. Todd and Puro sit on the *ghaat* (steps along the water's edge) drying off and enjoying samosas when the boy who stole Todd's phone earlier bounces down the stairs to return it. Symbolically, now that Todd has changed, he's being allowed to have back this link to his old life in America. He had to learn to fully let it go to find peace and balance in India, which positively impacts him both personally and professionally.

Later Asha discovers that the shipment of complementary products from Western Novelty has gone to the wrong Gharapuri, which is on an island several hours away, and the next few scenes detail Todd and Asha's experiences as they travel to the other location. Todd and Asha are walking around the second Gharapuri waiting for the next ferry, and they stop at a temple with a Shiva lingam. Todd asks what a lingam is, and Asha awkwardly avoids answering. A Shiva lingam is a symbol (often made of stone) built inside temples dedicated to honoring Lord Shiva—it consists of a rounded teapot-shaped bowl with a cylindrical shape at the top (Das, 2019). It is meant to be a symbol of creation with each section representing the "holy trinity" of Hindu Gods—Brahma as the rounded base, Vishnu as the elongation of the bowl where it resembles a teapot, and Shiva as the cylindrical portion. The cylindrical portion is also considered a phallic symbol, which is why Asha reluctantly explains, "Well you know . . . The male part" [1:01:05]. Inside the temple, Asha elaborates—"It's a symbol of creation." Todd asks about the base being the female part, and Asha awkwardly says:

> Yes, they go together. You see, Shiva was a very powerful god and he grew tired of the cycle of life and death and reincarnation, so he decided to give up the pleasures of life, and he smeared his body in ash . . . and he didn't eat or drink or indulge in any physical pleasure, and this created a terrible fire within him . . . and it transformed him into a blazing lingam which threatened to destroy all creation. And the other gods didn't know what to do, so a yoni appeared, the symbol of the goddess. And she absorbed this terrible heat, restoring balance to the world and saving the universe from destruction. [1:02:23]

This story of Shiva resembles Todd's sojourning journey—from arriving in India and resisting it, not giving in, and gradually through Asha and others, he is able to release and find balance, and all the while the future of the company in India also hangs in the balance. Of course, the sexual innuendo of the story is not lost on either Todd or Asha, as romantic feelings between them grow. This morphs into a series of comedic mishaps involving a blown-up ferry that results in an awkward, and somewhat unexpected, romantic tryst between Todd and Asha in the only available "Kamasutra" or honeymoon suite at a local hotel. Of course, the understanding is that their tryst must never be known, especially for Asha who hails from a traditionally conservative family [1:06:52–1:15:08].

Back in Gharapuri, Asha and Todd meet in the local market after work. Todd approaches from behind and flirtatiously grabs Asha, but she quickly directs him to "act normal" because she can't risk being seen in a romantic relationship with him. As they walk along the river, Todd mentions that he'll have to leave soon since the MPI is nearly at six, asking her if she's thought about going to the United States. Todd invites Asha into the guest house for tea, but she says she can't, since "people might talk" [1:11:58]. Todd is frustrated—"why do you worry so much what people think?," he asks. She explains that she's engaged, and Todd is startled. Asha has been engaged since she was four years old—the families are generations' old friends. "Do you love him?," Todd asks. Asha says she doesn't love him, *yet*. Todd is astonished. On asking if Asha will tell her fiancé about Todd, she says no, and Todd hurtfully questions, "So what do you call this, what you and I are doing?". Asha pauses and says, "Holiday in Goa"—she explains that a friend of hers snuck away to Goa (western Indian state known for beautiful beaches) with a young man she loved, a month before her wedding to another man. Todd is hurt, but Asha says he means more than that to her and begins to cry. Resigned to this reality, and in fear of being watched, they revert back to professional gestures, shake hands, and Asha slips him a note as they go their separate ways.

In this discussion with Asha, we can see how the U-curve does not consist of a single adjustment. Especially when someone is in another culture for an extended period of time, there are a series of U-curves that happen. Subsequent experiences of culture shock are not as severe as the first one, but even after adjusting, a person is likely to experience other moments of culture shock where they struggle to understand things about the new culture—especially as they get involved in things like romance, schooling, family responsibilities, and so on. Here, Todd has largely adjusted but when it comes to romance, he has trouble understanding Asha's situation and respecting the fact that she doesn't see her situation as settling. She views her pending marriage as a way to save face and show respect for her parents, her family, and her community.

Todd better grasps his cultural adaptation, when he gets to know his neighbors [1:15:09–1:18:59]. Later, in Auntie Ji's courtyard, the *dhobi* beckons Todd to his side of the wall. Todd climbs over and follows the man nervously through a maze of ramshackle homes. This part of the city is visually and socially impoverished, reminiscent of urban slums that house a large population of India's informal laborers. Ultimately, they come to the man's home on the seaside where two women and a girl are sitting on the ground with a meal. Todd greets them as the women return the greeting with a traditional *Namaste*. The elderly woman places rice, a hardboiled egg, and some gravy on Todd's plate, while the young woman connects two live wires hanging from above to turn on a makeshift hotplate that makes a roti. Todd eats with his hands, as is customary Indian practice, as others in the background watch on.

What we see here is Todd's appreciation of his host culture's generosity, and also the positive development of migrant–host relations as the *dhobi* returns Todd's favor by inviting him to lunch. On a latent level, what this scene also reveals, perhaps inadvertently, is the objectionable lack of dignity for informal labor/laborers among India's higher social classes and castes.

Had Todd been Indian, the *dhobi* would likely have not reached out, being aware of India's social and caste ladder where he is placed on rather a low rung. Todd being from a culture where low-power distance is the preferred value, being invited to a laundryman's slum dwelling is not considered a social affront.

After learning that their jobs have been outsourced, Todd and Asha head to their colleague's apartment so they can be alone. The two kiss and Todd asks Asha about the dot on her forehead. She explains that it's a *bindi*, a third eye—"It's the eye with which you see the most important things. Sometimes two eyes aren't enough and they need help" [1:31:06]. She goes to explain that Todd "has already been my third eye." Todd asks what she means, and she explains:

> Well, my father is an assistant manager in a phone company and my mother comes from a small village. A girl in my position has her whole life mapped out in front of her. Everything I've done, I've had to fight for. "Asha, you can't go to university." "Asha, you can't work in a call center." "What would people say?" What you said, it was the first time I'd ever heard anything like that . . . "Asha can do anything." I always wanted to believe that, but until you, I didn't believe it was true. [1:31:50]

Todd and Asha continue their sweet, tearful farewell, but Asha's confession to Todd is potently symbolic of India's patriarchal society where women often have to sacrifice their personal and professional goals to meet familial or social demands.

As the film ends, Todd is back in Seattle walking along the street with a bag of groceries as he calls his mother [1:36:49]. She asks how his time in India was and Todd says that he'll tell them about it when he comes to visit them—something which he'd told Puro that he rarely did. Back in his apartment, Todd makes himself tea and adds a lot of sugar, the way they did at Auntie Ji's. He walks over to a plate on display that has an image of George Washington on it, and sticks Asha's bindi on Washington's forehead. Meanwhile, in the background, we can hear music that is a blend of a Pearl Jam song (Long Road), and an Indian classical raga. Suddenly, Todd's phone rings with a discerning Bollywood ringtone that Asha had earlier put on it, for when she calls him. Todd smiles, knowing it is Asha calling, and answers the phone as the movie ends. The implication is that Todd and Asha, though countries apart, will remain in communication in some way.

Todd's transformation is now clear—he is no longer beholden to a job he hates and has found a way to free himself of it. In the process, he has learned the importance of relationships over money and is looking to improve his relationship with his parents—cultural values he learned from his time in India. Todd finds ways of incorporating his Indian experiences into his American life, with his change in tea preparation and the bindi on Washington's forehead. The imagery of George Washington donning a bindi captures Todd's internal adjustment along the U-curve. He is still decidedly American, but he has changed and can see the world and his personal and professional relationships through a new lens—a third eye, as it were—that is no longer so ethnocentric and blind to other ways of living, working, and communicating.

CONCLUSION

The story of *Outsourced* (2006) is a lighthearted critique of Western business practices, outsourcing, and American ethnocentrism. Todd's sojourn to India prompts a movement in his own identity as he learns to let go of his American ethnocentric mindset and strict corporate practices to embrace a more fluid cultural identity that translates into more mobile, adaptable, and, ultimately, successful business practices. The significance of this romantic comedy goes beyond classroom conversations about intercultural communication, as seen in how popular a selection it was at film festivals. *Outsourced* (2006) was selected at international film festivals in Dubai (2006), Mumbai (2007), Toronto (2006), and Vancouver (2007), among others. It also won several awards, including Best Picture at the Bend Film Festival (2007) and Seattle International Film Festival Golden Space Needle Awards. It received Audience Awards at both the Indian Film Festival of Los Angeles (2007) and the Bollywood and Beyond Film Festival (2007), as well as Best of the Fest and John Schlesinger Awards at the Palm Springs Film Festival (2007).

The cross-cultural film's depiction of outsourcing in the Indian context does provide some level of nuance to this business practice, at least for American viewers, but ultimately it is a shallow critique. On the one hand, the American viewer (for whom this film seems to be geared) can put faces to the voices at the call centers they've interacted with, and get to know a little bit about these fictional characters. On the other hand, there is little depth to the characters at the call center, and the film relies on American stereotypes of Indian culture for comic relief, including its tropical climate, poverty, unsanitary practices, exoticism of its people, customs, and religious rituals, as well as its outsourced call centers. Particularly, as Todd moves along the U-curve, the film turns complex cultural symbols into key symptoms of his culture shock in India, made worse by his experiences of physical discomfort, unfamiliar food, heavy traffic, large crowds, and limited personal space. Despite Todd's cultural transformation, the film seemingly suggests that the relentless push toward greater profits is a train no one can stop given how at the end the call center is suddenly moved from India to China.

In terms of cultural representation, the film is unapologetically critical of American culture being materialistic, in contrast with Indian culture that is supposedly spiritual, and better for the soul. A problem, however, with this depiction is that it perpetuates another set of popular stereotypes about India as a mystic place where Westerners can go to 'find' themselves—in the same way that it stereotypes American culture as a study in vapid consumerism, thus taking a myopic view of the actual diversity and richness of both cultures. One area where the film is successful is the visual theme of Goddess Kali that is woven throughout. While details about Kali are likely lost on the average American viewer, her presence throughout the film mirrors Todd's ultimate adjustment as his ego and ethnocentric mindset are finally destroyed allowing him to become a better version of himself. Kali appears in imagery and *murtis*, but her presence is also apparent with the sadhu and the Shiva lingam. Just as Todd offers concise explanations for complex aspects of American culture, Indian characters offer rather brief explanations of the complex deity Kali. Still the symbol of Kali is an interesting cultural thread the film offers, to track the protagonist's movement toward cultural adjustment.

What is clear in the end is that movement between cultures, especially in the context of business practices, needs to be done with respect for all cultures involved. Business success will either not be achieved, or not sustainably achieved, if corporations do not adapt to other cultures as they move and expand around the globe. At the micro-level, individuals doing the movement across borders and cultures need to embrace the opportunities for identity movement and growth not only for personal reasons, but also for professional success. As today's workplaces are more diverse than ever, even those who do not sojourn to distant locations will benefit from an open mind and a willingness to embrace different cultural perspectives and practices.

Chapter 7

Front Cover

Fashion and Fluid Sexualities in an Intra-Asian Relationship

Sorrells (2016) argues that "intercultural relationships are often sites where notions of sexuality and sexual identities intersect, collide and coalesce with ethnic, racial, religious, and national cultural differences" (p. 105). Issues of contested sexualities in Asian and Asian American cultures, ethnic stereotyping, and identity ascription and avowal are addressed in the 2015 Ray Yeung film *Front Cover*. Ryan is a gay, American-born Chinese fashion stylist who is confident in his sexual orientation, but rejects his ethnic heritage. Ning is a Chinese actor from Beijing sojourning in New York City and Ryan is assigned as his fashion advisor for a magazine cover. What begins as a fraught professional relationship grows into a romantic relationship as both men grapple with the relational complexities and taboo of same-sex relations, considered a social anathema in Chinese culture. Ryan is comfortable performing his sexuality in American urban and professional spaces that are openly inclusive of nonbinary genders and diverse sexual orientations. Standing in sharp contrast is Ning, who uses his Asian celebrity status and his girlfriend from China as foils for his closeted gay identity. Ning is also deeply proud of his Chinese heritage, which is a stark contrast to Ryan's rejection of it.

As Cheshire (2016) mentions, "this is not only a clash of personalities but of cultures as well," with both Ryan and Ning's sexual orientation (or denial of it) being rooted in the former's rejection and the latter's acceptance of their Chinese heritage. Starting with Ryan's self-admission that he is a "potato queen" (gay Asian male who likes white males), to Ning's labeling of same-sex relations as "abnormal" and something that when publicly displayed amounts to "no shame" (*Front Cover*, 2015), the film portrays how cultural dynamics around "sexual orientation in society and in interpersonal relationships are often experienced as either completely invisible or hypervisible" (Sorrells, 2016, p. 105). As a Chinese celebrity touring New York City in an effort to expand his global appeal, Ning struggles to understand American culture. While he gets a brief respite from homophobia in NYC as he grows closer to Ryan, he ultimately returns to China and to his career where being gay is perceived as shameful and would destroy his lucrative profession—a reality that influences his decision to remain closeted. For Ryan, in becoming close with Ning, he learns to embrace and be proud of his ethnic heritage. The men's intra-ethnic friendship and romance is presented as complex and emotionally fraught, but also a turning point for both, as they reject and reinforce the cultural othering, sexism, and racism encountered from cultural insiders and outsiders.

We begin this chapter by reviewing literature that discusses how nonbinary sexualities and same-sex relationships are perceived in Asian cultures. This is followed by a brief overview of how cultural identities are negotiated through processes of ascription or avowal, and impacted by the circulation of ethnic stereotypes, after which we take up our case study of the film using these intercultural communication concepts in the context of sojourning and mobile sexualities.

SEXUALITIES IN ASIAN AND ASIAN AMERICAN CULTURES

Cultures and cultural identities are fluid and mobile, especially in a postglobalized world. Sexuality and sexual identities are no different, as we find in the film *Front Cover* (2015), where protagonists Ning and Ryan are constantly moving through stages of denial and acceptance of who they are in terms of their ethnicity, cultural location, and sexual orientation. Research on culture, communication, and sexual identity suggests that dominant attitudes toward same-sex relations are largely shaped by a society's "gender belief system" (Bem, 1993) and related cultural prescriptions (Lim, 2002; Kyes & Tumbelaka, 1994). Lim's (2002) study on public attitude toward same-sex relations in Singapore reveals its youth culture's disdain for the LGBTQI+[1] community, where most respondents stated that "they would feel upset if they discover that their child, brother or sister was gay" (p. 12). Bem (1993) has defined the *gender belief system* as a set of cultural "beliefs and opinions about males and females and about the purported qualities of masculinity and femininity" (p. 23). Stereotypes, prescriptions, and perceptions about what comprises socially 'acceptable' masculine and feminine roles populate this system (Bem, 1993; Lim, 2002). Sexual minorities seen as a "threat" are exiled beyond the margins (Lim, 2002, p. 3). Lim's (2002) research also supported the finding that violating gender role expectations in Asian countries has more severe consequences for men compared to women in same-sex relations. The same was found to be true for intra-ethnic attitudes toward LGBTQI+ Asians in America (Chan, 1989, 1995).

In Asian countries like China, being gay is a cultural affront. Men and women, in Asian cultures, are seen as members of a collectivist community that requires them to eventually become wives/mothers and husbands/fathers. The rejection of same-sex relationships has been traced back to Confucianism and the collectivist culture of China that values family loyalty over individual interests (Neillands et al., 2008; Liu et al., 2011). Heterosexuality is the cultural norm and anyone who doesn't conform to it is "not considered to be conforming to a group value" (Liu et al., 2011, p. 2; Lin & Lin, 1981; Hui & Triandis, 1986). It is not only the person rejecting heteronormativity who is culturally stigmatized, so too is their family. To keep up social appearances many Chinese gay men marry straight women, but same-sex infidelity is common (Neillands et al., 2008; Liu et al., 2011).

Chan (1989) believes that "homosexuality may be even more restricted by Asian-American cultural norms" compared to its disapproval within Asian families and American society, stressing that it is often regarded by the former group as a "White, Western phenomenon" (p. 19).[2] It is fair to say that family expectations weigh heavily on gay men in the Asian American community who often choose to not "come out," fearing their community's "rejection and stigmatization" (Chan, 1989, p. 19; Liu et al., 2011). Given the negative perception and familial rejection of lesbian and gay Asian Americans, Chan (1989) surmises that LGBTQI+ individuals from this ethnic group look for support in other communities where their gender identity and sexual orientation would not be questioned. Gender differences also surfaced as a marker of discrimination among gay and lesbian Asian Americans in Chan's (1989) study where gay male participants experienced greater gender discrimination than racial. Most lesbians, however, reported higher discrimination based on race than for sexual orientation.

Although being gay was tolerated in ancient China, Wu (2003) argues that it wasn't until the 1950s that it became seriously persecuted. In 1978, the first edition of the *Chinese Classification of Mental Disorders* was published and being gay was listed as a "disorder," leading healthcare systems to treat it as such (Wu, 2003). It was not until 2001 that this designation was removed (Wu, 2003). The resulting stigma made gay men reluctant to express their sexuality for fear of being rejected not only by family and friends but also face "discrimination in employment, health care, education, housing, and other basic rights" (Neilands et al., 2008, p. 839; Gill, 2002). Moreover, China's one-child policy and male-heir bias added cultural pressure on gay men to follow traditional gender role prescriptions (Neilands et al., 2008).

As part of their research on cultural integration among Asian and Pacific Islander (API) sexual minorities in the United States, Hahm and Adkins

(2009) explore how in addition to family pressures, "personal sacrifice," and intergenerational conflicts, external factors like "racism, sexism, and acculturation" have had a negative impact on this ethnic group's development of "positive sexual identity" (Hahm & Adkins, 2009, p. 156; Dong-Jin, 2001; Berry, 2001). The API sexual minorities are attempting two layers of acculturation at the same time. As a reminder, acculturation is the process of cultural adaptation that migrants, sojourners, and/or co-cultural groups go through in a foreign society "to adopt the language, values, beliefs, and behaviors of new socio-cultural environments" (Hahm & Adkins, 2009, p. 157). The process, at least in the case of an API migrant's move to a Western society, also involves the movement of an individual's value system from a community-focused one to one that emphasizes an individual-focused one. As Asians try to integrate their ethnicity and collectivist orientations within individualistic American culture, Asian gay men are additionally struggling to "establish an authentic sexual identity that may be incongruent with the norms of both mainstream North American culture and their parents' culture of origin" (Hahm & Adkins, 2009, p. 156; Chan, 1995). Stereotypes of gay Asians as "asexual and passive" within the white LGBTQI+ community in America have led many Asian American sexual minorities to feel isolated from their sexual identity groups (Hahm & Adkins, 2009, p. 157; Choi et al., 1999). Also, homophobic attitudes from co-ethnic members impact the "self-worth and health" of Asian gay men in the United States (Chan, 1992).

Luu (2009) puts a face on an acculturative dilemma that many Asians commonly face in their host and home spaces—that of being gay in rather unforgiving cultural and social contexts. She cites an example of an Asian university student, who is openly gay and living in the United States, and is constantly asked by Taiwanese relatives if he has a 'girlfriend.' Many who are coming to terms with their minority sexual identity in a foreign, if less conservative, space, are still afraid of disclosing their sexual orientation in case they are disowned or disinherited by their families (Luu, 2009). A 19-year-old Asian American interviewee of Luu (2009) ascribes this heteronormative conservatism to "core Asian values" founded on Confucian teachings that "heavily stress patriarchy, [and] tear families apart" under the guise of cultural collectivism.

There has, however, been slow growth toward recognizing LGBTQI+ relationships, and ratification of some laws in favor of minority sexual identity and gender expression in China ("International Lesbian, Gay, Bisexual, Trans and Intersex Association," 2016, p. 35, 159). Chinese media have played a part in advocating LGBTQI+ issues of late, including distribution of films/shows in Chinese theaters and online media that celebrate same-sex relationships and family dynamics. These include the French-Chinese film *Seek McCartney* (2014), a 2016 web drama called *Addiction*, Fan Popo's docu-drama *Mama Rainbow* (2014) ("International Lesbian, Gay, Bisexual, Trans and Intersex Association," 2016), as well as *Front Cover* (2015)—the film we are exploring in this chapter.

Hahm and Adkins (2009) ascribe this gradual social change in China and its media to capitalism, global consumer trends, and its growing "influence on the emergence of homosexuality as a public identity" (p. 169). That said, China's globalized move toward consumerist individualism is still new, and still errs on the side of collectivism and Confucian values (Hahm & Adkins, 2009; Leung, 2008; Hofstede, 2001). It is this protean and structural nature of China and its diaspora's cultural and social attitudes toward sexual minorities that must be kept in mind by researchers, educators, and interventionists alike, when addressing "API sexual minorities' desire to remain closeted" (Hahm & Adkins, 2009, p. 169). It is also imperative for us to be sensitive and strategic when using labels to understand how Asians and Asian Americans (in this case Chinese migrants, and Chinese Americans) navigate through the complexity of their minority sexual and ethnic identities (Hahm & Adkins, 2009). The tensions around sexual orientation and ethnicity described here are illustrated in the challenges that Ryan and Ning face in the film—in embracing his sexual orientation, Ryan initially rejects his ethnicity and in embracing his ethnicity and nationality, Ning feels pressure to reject his sexual orientation.

CULTURAL IDENTITIES

We all have multiple cultural identities and which aspects of those cultural identities we prioritize in an interaction depends on various factors such as context, people involved, and more. The term cultural identities refers to "identifications with and perceived acceptance into a group which has shared systems of symbols and meanings as well as norms/rules for conduct" (Collier, 1989, p. 296). It also relates to "contextual structures and public discourses that produce representations and subjectivities" (Chen & Collier, 2012, p. 45). When someone is able to know what behavior is appropriate for a particular situation and for a particular cultural identity, they are said to have cultural competence (Collier, 1989). Salience is an important dimension of cultural identities because it addresses how people negotiate their various identities in different communication interactions, determining which ones are more prominent within a given context. As Collier (1989) explains, "salience refers to the relative importance of the identity in a particular situation relative to other identities" (p. 296). For example, two identities that are part of Ryan are being gay and being Chinese American. In many situations throughout the film, Ryan's gay identity seems to be most salient for him, but not his Chinese American identity, which he tries to downplay until the end of the film.

When communication is intercultural—that is, the people involved identify themselves as being from different cultural groups—people need to have intercultural communication competence in order for their communication to be successful. Intercultural communication competence is "conduct perceived to be appropriate and effective for both cultural identities being advanced" (Collier, 1989, pp. 296–97). Avowal and ascription of identities is especially relevant in intercultural communication because the terms help capture the way that identities are negotiated in communication with culturally different others, and the challenges therein (Martin & Nakayama, 2018).

Avowal refers to how a person tries to present themselves to others (Chen & Collier, 2012)—it provides a glimpse into what a person wants others to think of them and what that person thinks of themselves. Ascription is how people assign certain identities to others (Martin & Nakayama, 2018). For communication between people to be successful, there needs to be harmony between the avowed and ascribed identities. In other words, the people we communicate with ought to ascribe an identity to us that is consistent with our avowed identity, and vice versa, for an intercultural interaction to be successful. If there is incongruity—that is, if an individual's avowed identity is not recognized by the person they're talking to—then conflict is likely to occur. Effective intercultural communicators affirm the most prominent or relevant identity of the other person they are communicating with during an interaction (Collier & Thomas, 1988).

Conflict between avowed and ascribed identities, as well as misunderstandings of cultural identity salience, occurs all too often because these processes "involve different status levels, histories, and degrees of agency" (Chen & Collier, 2012, p. 45). For example, in one study researchers investigate ascription of American national identity and its ties to whiteness (Devos & Ma, 2008). The authors found that study participants implicitly ascribed American national identity to the white, British actress Kate Winslet more than they did to the Asian American actress Lucy Liu (Devos & Ma, 2008). Their findings reveal a bias toward whiteness when measuring explicit versus implicit ascription of American national identity, such that the actual American actress was regarded as less American when measured at the implicit level (Devos & Ma, 2008). The consequences of incongruity (and sometimes congruity) between avowed and ascribed identities can have significant impacts on people. In their study of two nonprofit organizations (NPOs), Chen and Collier (2012) show how divergent avowal and ascription among organization members "acted to subjugate already marginalized clients" (p. 43). The two NPOs' missions are to support underserved Asian and Asian American women. Sometimes, however, congruity between avowed and ascribed identities can be problematic, especially when they involve stereotypes. Chen and Collier (2012) discuss how some of the subjugation came from the clients' own avowed identities, which was matched by employee ascriptions on clients, constructing "clients as needing to be protected, thus removing their capability for independence" (p. 59).

Stereotypes of Asians and Asian Americans were a contributing factor to the results that Chen and Collier (2012) found in their analysis of two NPOs. A stereotype is a "judgment made about another solely on the basis of ethnic or other group membership" (Jandt, 2016, p. G-6). These judgments can be positive, but are mostly used in ways that are negative or othering, and can come from both outside and inside a community (Neuliep, 2015). A common stereotype that is ascribed to Asians and Asian Americans in the United States is that of "forever immigrant" (Ng, Lee & Pak, 2007)—people who can/will never assimilate into American society, and even whose loyalty to the United States is questioned (Lee, 1996).

We encounter stereotypes in many contexts and media representations are an often studied context where stereotypes of Asians and Asian Americans are sustained. Heavy media consumers are more likely to adopt and internalize such stereotypes (Ramasubramanian, 2011) and exposure may start from a very young age. For example, Williams and Korn (2017) show how the children's series, Thomas and Friends, others and promotes fear and misunderstanding of the Asian character, Hiro, in one of the films. Thomas and Friends is a preschool age media empire that teaches children about friendship, but the authors reveal the problematic latent messages about cultural differences that promote fear and perpetuate Asian stereotypes such as "forever immigrant" (Ng, Lee & Pak, 2007) and the model minority stereotype[3] (Williams & Korn, 2017).

One of the negative consequences of stereotyping is that people will adopt these judgments of the targets of stereotyping (external stereotypes), and another negative outcome may be that the targets internalize stereotypes of themselves (internal stereotypes). External stereotypes impacting Asians and Asian and Pacific Islander American communities are frequently based on ethnicity, race, and the model minority myth. Internal stereotypes that disadvantage people are often related to cultural values and gender roles, including face-saving and traditional views of masculinity. Chang and Subramaniam (2008) found stress caused by Western ideals of masculinity that Asian men are expected to emulate was a leading impediment to help-seeking behaviors for Asian men. The stereotype responsible for this cultural othering equates masculinity with whiteness and Asian American men are feminized (Chang & Subramaniam, 2008; Eng 2001). To fight such stereotypes, cisgender Chinese males use adaptation strategies to fit-in with ideals of white masculinity or to turn the dominant groups' focus away from their ascribed feminization by "overcompensating in other areas" (Chang & Subramaniam, 2008, p. 125; Chen, 1999). Ultimately, gender stereotyping has negatively affected Asian males' ascribed and avowed identities. The in-group stereotype that hurts LGBTQI+ Asians the most is the larger Asian American community's conflation of heterosexuality with "real" masculinity, the deviance from which would also mean deviating from "'traditional Asian values' of getting married, having children, and passing down the family name" (Kumashiro, 1999, p. 492).

FILM ANALYSIS

We structure our analysis of the film along three major themes—*buried identities*, *movement to embrace*, and *embracing and reburial*. This structure mirrors the main intercultural conflicts of the film as the two characters who share so much wrestle with parts of themselves that they see in the other.

Buried Identities

Both of the main characters has a part of their identity that they seek to bury. Recall that salience is an aspect of cultural identities that captures how people negotiate different identities in different contexts (Collier, 1989), for example, highlighting a sexual identity in certain contexts over an ethnic identity. At the beginning of the film, the two main characters each have an identity that they not only try to make less salient, they seem to wish it was nonexistent.

From the opening scenes of the film, as the viewer is introduced to Ryan, it becomes clear that he embraces his gay identity but buries and seeks to make less salient his Chinese ethnic identity. The film opens with Ryan in an iconic Yellow Cab riding through New York City when an Asian-presenting man rides up on a bike with a food delivery bag. Their eyes meet and Ryan is visibly uncomfortable, even a little disgusted [1:40]. As Ryan struggles to get the car window up he then turns to the cab driver saying politely, but firmly, "Driver, step on it." In the scenes that follow, Ryan is depicted as a confident stylist eager to move up in the industry. Unfortunately he is informed by his boss, Francesca, that he has not been assigned to style a coveted magazine photo shoot, and instead has been assigned to style Ning Qi, an up-and-coming, wealthy Chinese celebrity, whom Francesca and her firm are anxious to please. Ning wants to work with a Chinese stylist and so Francesca concedes, without a care that her decision hurts Ryan.

When Francesca ascribes Chinese ethnic identity to Ryan, it conflicts with his avowed identity, which is a source of his anger and frustration. Ryan lost out on a coveted styling opportunity that he was counting on and the incongruity between the ascribed identity and his avowed identity is what is so hurtful. Had Francesca handled the interaction differently, *asking* Ryan if he would do this assignment rather than *ordering* him, it may not have felt so demeaning and disrespectful for Ryan.

Following the news about the new assignment, Ryan and his makeup artist friend, Janet, watch one of Ning's movies in her apartment. She tries to reassure him that Ning could become a global celebrity, but Ryan is doubtful. Ryan says, "I can't believe she gave the cover to Eddie. And I didn't get it because I'm Asian." Janet tries again to reassure him but Ryan says, "You know, maybe my parents were right. In America, Chinese people should only be doctors . . . at least they'd be proud" [7:20]. Janet pushes back, "Stop feeling sorry for yourself! You're hard-working, you're talented, and bitchy. Perfect for the fashion world" [7:54]. In his comment about how Chinese people should be doctors in America, Ryan reveals how he has internalized the model minority stereotype of Asian Americans. Despite his success in the fashion industry, his heritage as Chinese American is something that he sees as a burden weighing him down in pursuit of his dreams—after all, he didn't get the assignment he wanted and was given another less desirable one specifically because of his Chinese background.

Ryan's Chinese and familial immigrant background are also tied in with socioeconomic status. Two scenes in the film particularly reveal Ryan's shame in his ethnicity that is wrapped up in the salience of class identity, leading him to lie about his parents' careers. The first scene has Ryan meet Ning for dinner in an effort to get to know each other better [24:30]. In the process, each character's attempt to bury part of their identity becomes apparent. Ning asks what Ryan's parents do for work, and Ryan says that his father is a lawyer and his mother a teacher of art history at New York University. Puzzled, Ning asks if they want Ryan to be a lawyer or doctor and Ryan casually responds, "No, they're not Chinese in that way, no."

In the second scene, later in the film when the two have become close, Ning asks why Ryan hasn't told his parents that they aren't dating [52:00]. Ryan says that he doesn't want to disappoint his parents since it would make them happy to see him with a Chinese man. Ryan also admits that he lied about his parents' professions when in fact his parents comes from humble roots and are nail salon owners. Ryan seems to be ashamed of his lower-class upbringing, as he admits to Ning later in the conversation. He explains, "I remember seeing them work on people's feet all day long, and I told myself when I grow up I'd never do that." Ning reassures Ryan that it is an honest job, but Ryan says, "I know. I'm a snob. I bite the hand that feeds me." Seemingly, his shame in his family's social standing is also wrapped up in his ethnic heritage. Nail salons, specifically being a nail technician, is a common job for low-income Asian immigrants, especially in the Vietnamese and

Chinese diasporas (Chen, 2018; Sharma et al., 2018). For Ryan, his parents are stereotypically Chinese, from their behavior to their jobs, so lying about their profession is part of his attempt to disavow his ethnicity. Yet he ascribes professions to his parents that fit into the model minority stereotype of Asian Americans being high-wage earning, peace-loving, family-oriented people who are invariably doctors, lawyers, and/or engineers.

Ascription of Ning and Ryan's ethnic identity to racist Asian stereotypes is something we find in an important scene where Ning is being photographed by a white American photographer, Gus, with Ryan there to style him during the photo shoot. The shoot starts and Ning sits on a chair with the New York City skyline in the background. As he crosses his legs, Gus declares, "This is not gonna work." Ning's underwear line is visible through the silk pants. As Ryan asks Ning to remove his underwear, Gus rudely interjects, "Talk to him in Chinese. Tell him we can't shoot with his underpants on." Ning responds, "Well, you tell him in English I won't do what he wants" [36:22]. In this instance Gus' racist and condescending remark is indicative of his ascription of Chinese identity on Ryan, as well as Ning. Ryan begs Ning to do as Gus wants since this photo shoot is important for both their careers.

Also, the assumption here, as Ryan's reaction suggests, is that Gus' supposed photographic talent means that people tolerate his abusive behavior. Ning reluctantly agrees, provided everyone else leaves the set, and despite Ryan's objection declares, "If he can shout, he can move lights around. We can't let white devil win all . . . tooth for tooth. He should respect people more" [36:47]. On hearing Ning's demand, Gus looks indignantly at Ning and then bows, but does so in a sarcastic way. In fact, the bow gesture that Gus does is reminiscent of the *wai* in Thai culture. Gus' mocking gesture illustrates how he essentializes Asian cultures as being all the same, while adding another layer of offensive discrimination to his behavior toward Ning that plays into the 'forever immigrant' or 'perpetual foreigner' stereotypes (Ng, Lee & Pak, 2007; Williams and Korn, 2017; Ramasubramanian, 2011).

As the scene continues, Gus takes some photos of Ning, but stops again when Ning crosses his ankle over his knee, revealing the sole of his foot that has dirt on it (he's been walking around the rooftop and studio barefoot, after all). Ryan offers to call Dex (whose job we presume it is to take care of such issues on set), but Gus insists that Ryan wash Ning's feet. As Ryan cleans Ning's feet, Gus loudly grumbles in the background, "I hate working with fucking amateurs." Ning leans in to Ryan, who is now kneeling at Ning's feet washing them, and tenderly says, "You don't have to do this" [38:30]. Ryan doesn't respond, but he is clearly upset, as is Ning, whose jaw muscles we see tensing up from the overhead shot. Ryan, here, begins to embrace his Chinese side, because he has Ning's support in response to Gus' racist ranting, in that he knows he doesn't deserve such discriminatory treatment.

A few shots in, the camera cuts to Ryan's face, with Gus in the background who now shouts, "What the fuck are you doing, giving him a pedicure?" Then an assistant (who also presents as a white male) further insults them by adding, "I thought you people were supposed to be good at that sort of thing." Ryan stands up, turns to the two men and shouts back, "Shut the fuck up!" as he throws the towel at Gus. It is not just the ascription of Chinese identity that the white assistant feels entitled to give the protagonists, but he resorts to drawing on stereotypes like 'low-wage, immigrant identity' and 'manual labor,' identities that we already know Ryan is ashamed of when he lies to Ning about his parents' jobs earlier [39:02]. As the scene ends, Ning gets up and says, "Come on, let's go!" and the two run out onto the street. We've mostly seen Ryan communicate shame, reluctance, even disdain for his Chinese heritage, but here in the face of such aggressive and racist insults, he stands up for his ethnic identity. It pushes him to stand up for that aspect of his cultural self that he has mostly buried and assert that he doesn't deserve this othering treatment.

Back at the earlier dinner scene when Ryan and Ning are trying to get to know each other [26:20], Ning asks an awkwardly phrased question about Ryan's parents' knowledge of his sexual identity: "And they know that you are . . . you know, abnormal?" Ryan fights his anger and asserts, "I'm not abnormal." Ning tries to correct by offering "unusual" instead, but Ryan cuts back in, saying "They're ok with it." Ning says, "I can't imagine any parent being ok their son's—". Ryan cuts him off and says incredulously, "I can't imagine that you've never worked with someone gay. We must exist in China." Ning says there are gay people in China that he's worked with, but never "someone like you, so . . . no shame." Ryan is confused and says, "You know, it's not all that hard being gay nowadays." Ning asks Ryan if he ever experienced any problems or taunting for being gay. Ryan recalls, uncomfortably, that some of the other children in his Sunday school where he learned Chinese made fun of him and called him names. He recollects the children tried to make him cry, but he never cried in front of them, and now he's "so happy to be in this industry where being gay is not just accepted, but celebrated." Ning awkwardly clears his throat as he realizes Ryan's anger about Ning's questions and homophobia. This is where we find Ryan simultaneously embracing his gay identity and downplaying his ethnic identity, while Ning is seen burying his gay identity under his apparent homophobic facade.

As Ning's character develops, it is clear that he fully embraces his Chinese national and ethnic identity, and eventually we learn that he is burying his gay identity. In the beginning, Ning's avowal of his ethnic pride is equally met with Ryan's ascription of Ning's Chinese-ness. When Ryan first goes to meet Ning, the scene opens with a shot of a cab driving along a cobblestone street with someone inside it speaking in a different language, presumably Mandarin [7:57]. The man is James, Ning's PR representative, who tells Ryan in Mandarin, "He's waiting for you," assuming Ryan knows this Chinese language. Ryan presents as Asian, so often others like James ascribe Chinese or generally Asian identity to him, much to Ryan's displeasure. Ryan, who by now is exasperated asks, "And why does he not want to go to the Moxy Club?" to which James, also frustrated, says, "Well, it's his first time in America. I guess he feels a bit homesick." Ryan, sounding a bit snooty, enquires "Does he even speak English?" and James affirms, adding that Ning's mother is a government translator. Ryan's linguistic snobbery is a result of his ascription of Ning as a cultural outsider, who by virtue of his Chinese nationality and choice of venue (a Chinese restaurant in Chinatown), *must not know* English.

This interaction, and others to follow, set the stage for potential incongruity (even frequent agreement) between the avowed and ascribed identities of Ryan, Ning, and some others they interact with, creating intercultural communication barriers at times. Ryan's ascription of Ning's co-ethnic othering is reinforced when later in the conversation with James he gets to know that he is the replacement stylist, because Ning believed the first stylist "didn't know anything about Chinese culture." At this point Ryan feels insulted and even scared to meet Ning alone, retorting through gritted teeth, "It's a styling job, not a history lesson."

The ascription-avowal intercultural dynamic is seen at play in Ning's ascription of Ryan's Asian American identity as well. As Ryan enters the restaurant to meet Ning, he finds him sitting with four other Asian presenting (presumably, Chinese) people at a circular table [9:22]. Of the four, two are women sitting on either side of Ning, fussing over him and massaging his neck. Ryan reluctantly says, "Hi, Mr. Qi?" in his American accent. Ning looks up and inquires, "Ryan?" but he says it with an accent so the R sounds like an L to an American ear. Ryan corrects him, "Ryan, with an R," and Ning responds, "I said the same thing, Ryan," again with the R sounding like an L. As Ryan stiffly and uncomfortably sits with them, Ning says, "You don't look Chinese," and Ryan cheerfully responds, "Oh, why thank you! Yeah, some people think I'm half Caucasian." Here, Ning's ascription of Ryan burying his Chinese ethnicity complements the latter's avowed identity, thus making Ryan happy to be perceived as mixed race in appearance. To continue his ascription of Ryan's Americanness, Ning tells his friends, "He's ABC. American borrow Chinese," as his friends laugh. The term ABC is used to refer to American-born Chinese individuals, or American citizens of Chinese descent. In this case, Ning appears to be making light of Ryan and American–Chinese relations by changing it to *American-borrow-Chinese*, reflecting American economic dependence on China.

Ryan's rejection contrasted with Ning's embrace of Chinese ethnicity is a source of conflict in their work styles. Culturally more individualistic and American, Ryan feels at home when he is alone with his image board, planning Ning's style, and is uncomfortable when faced with the more collectivist and high-context nature of Ning's work and social life. Ning explains his work preference to Ryan, declaring that playing mahjong, drinking wine, and becoming friends or "pengyou" first will help their work communication. After all, they "are both Chinese so should help each other," which is incongruous with Ryan's culturally low-context sensibility, leading him to admit to Ning that he's "not a very social person" (Martin & Nakayama, 2018). Their intercultural clash here is quite apparent, as it is throughout the film. Ryan, who makes American identity more salient in work situations, is accustomed to working meals where business is done while eating. Ning, who makes his Chinese identity more salient, uses meals as a time to build relationships and specifically *not* to conduct business. Beyond this American versus Chinese approach to business is the added layer of Ryan's ethnicity and Ning's assumptions that Ryan embraces his Chinese heritage, which he does not at first—in fact, he is proud when people, Ning included, don't see him as Chinese, or at least not fully Chinese.

Ning's ascription of Chinese identity on Ryan is balanced by his own avowed identity that leads him to proudly embrace Chinese culture, heritage, and history. During an initial meeting, Ning makes plain his sense of patriotism and love for China and its culture, which he wants Ryan to understand when styling him. Ning explains, "I think my style should be very Chinese because China not poor anymore. We are much stronger, so I don't want to wear those Western-style clothes. I want to represent a new China" [16:15]. But Ryan is not the only character with part of his identity being buried. While Ning is the opposite of Ryan in terms of embracing Chinese ethnicity, Ning is also the contradiction to Ryan in terms of embracing gay identity.

We find Ning burying his gay identity in a scene where Ryan wants to know why Ning always travels in a group [17:27]. Ning asserts his avowed, heterosexual identity, explaining "Oh, my fans are more women. They're very important. I need women to tell me what to think." Ning's avowed heterosexuality is also indicative of his attempt to ascribe his sexual identity to Chinese values of masculinity (Liu et al., 2011). We see this when Ning and the entourage push back, when Ryan gives him the pajama jacket he bought in Chinatown. Ning explains he wants to look "strong and manly." Ryan insists that with the right material and tailoring, Ning will look "strong and manly," even "sexy." Ryan explains that "Asian men are rarely seen as sex symbols in this country, okay? So we're trying something new and refreshing here." Ignoring his entourage's advice, Ning finally decides to try it, and puts the shirt on right there. Ryan glances over and finds himself admiring Ning's body. Ning catches his eye, they subtly exchange glances, but then Ning turns around angrily, and insists he must ask his girlfriend for advice on the outfit.

At the time of this scene, the audience has only seen Ryan as the one who is trying to bury part of his identity—his ethnic identity. Here is the first moment where we see Ning trying to bury part of his identity—his gay identity. Ning's emotional reaction and the way he quickly mentions having a girlfriend suggest that he does not want to be associated in any way with being gay. In other words, Ning is fearful of a gay identity being ascribed to him, and pushes back by boldly asserting a heteronormative relationship. In fact, Ning is so worried about being perceived as gay that shortly after he fires Ryan and his firm, but Ryan persuades him to continue working together.

In a related scene, Ryan is socializing at a club when he receives an angry call from Francesca, his boss, telling him that Ning has dropped the firm [19:17]. Ryan is aghast and angry: "That fucking homophobe." He insists that he'll fix it and goes to Ning's apartment. Ryan quickly gets to the point of asking why Ning fired the firm—"Is it because I'm gay?" Ning insists that it is not. Ryan goes on—"Well, let me tell you something, okay? All the good stylists are gay. All right, listen, you have an interview next week, so let's just please try and work together." Now Ning pushes back, "We are fire and water. We do not mix . . . Unless . . . you don't show your 'homo' side so openly." Ryan is shocked, "My 'homo' side? Are you serious right now? You must . . . wait, what do you mean by my 'homo' side?" Ryan realizes that Ning is worried that Ryan is romantically interested in him and he explains that he is not. He goes on to explain, "I'm what they call a 'potato queen.' I'm only interested in White men. I've never slept with a Chinese man before, and I never will, so don't worry. You're safe. Deal?" Ning, a little flustered, agrees to keep working together. Ryan leaves, furious, and Ning stares longingly out the window as Ryan walks onto the street.

Movement to Embrace

As the men get to know each other and form a friendship, they each begin to let down their guards and embrace, even if temporarily, the identity that they work so hard to hide. This movement to embrace becomes most apparent for both characters when Ryan's parents visit and they spend the day with Ryan's grandmother, Mama. After Ryan is fired, he and Ning spend a night drinking and smoking marijuana in Ryan's apartment, and the next morning Ryan's parents, Mr. and Mrs. Fu, arrive for a preplanned day with Mama [43:27]. The four sit in Ryan's living room having an awkward conversation. Mrs. Fu nags about Ryan's dating preference for white men and chides him for not dating Chinese men. It seems she is trying to encourage a romance between

Ryan and Ning. Ryan is squirming in his seat, mortified. Mrs. Fu asserts, "Gay people ok. White people no ok" [47:45]. Mr. Fu agrees, explaining, "It's true. Chinese like water, take long time to boil, but once hot, lifetime to cool down. White man like sand: fast hot, fast cold, do not last" [48:08]. Ning looks at Mr. Fu, we can assume in amazement at this father's acceptance of his son's sexual orientation—something which he implied earlier is not his own experience with his parents.

Here again we see how each man struggles to accept a part of their identity that the other embraces—Ning with his sexual orientation and Ryan with his Chinese ethnicity. Ryan's parents are relatively at ease with their son being gay (although they were not accepting at first). But they resent, or at least struggle to understand his attempts to deny his own (and thereby their) ethnicity. It may be hurtful for Mr. and Mrs. Fu to see their son rejecting, even acting disgusted, embarrassed, or ashamed of his ethnicity, which they are proud of. Ryan is uncomfortable with his parents because their presence and their Chinese-ness make the ascribed ethnic identity that he seeks to reject hard to deny. We learn later from Mrs. Fu that they have not always been close, nor have they always been accepting of Ryan being gay. Ning, meanwhile, is proud to be Chinese, and he is especially proud to help represent the "new China," as he discussed with Ryan earlier. Chinese identity ascribed to him is a source of gratification and aligns with his avowed identity. But to have a gay identity ascribed to him makes him deeply uncomfortable because it is something that he tries to reject and suppress. Earlier in the film Ning had been quick to make plain his heterosexual relationship and supposed heterosexual identity at any hint of him being gay. In this interaction, however, with Ryan's parents appearing to ascribe a gay identity to Ning, he does not push back. Seeing Chinese parents being supportive of their gay son—chiding him not for being gay, but rather for not dating Chinese men—seems to be a bridge that helps Ning begin moving toward embrace.

Later that afternoon while visiting Mama, Mrs. Fu and Ning have a private conversation in the park [48:55]. Ning tries to politely correct her in the assumption that he is gay, but Mrs. Fu interrupts—"I know, I no say. Your parents know you are . . .?" and she trails off, looking tenderly at Ning. Ning faces her and says, "No." This is the first moment that we see Ning acknowledging his sexual orientation. Mrs. Fu sees Ning's reluctance and discomfort, and she offers, "Give them time." She goes on:

> When Ryan little, we no time for him. After school, he go to community center all day. The boys there beat him. He come home, one cut here, one black eye there. We scold him, think it will make him stronger, more like a man. He hate us. Chinese people very old-fashioned, take long, long time changing. When Ryan tell us he no like girl, we no talking one whole year. Then Mama sick. He

know life is short. We talking again. Now, no problem. You good Chinese son. You no want tell your parent because you no want hurt their feeling. You want to give them hope.

Ning asks, "What about grandkids?" Mrs. Fu smiles, shrugs, and says, "It's fate. Some things . . . are never meant to be." Mrs. Fu's tender, honest approach with Ning helps him move further toward embrace—enough that he actually verbalizes an acknowledgment of his gay identity. Mrs. Fu being Chinese understands Ning's culture and communicates with him in a culturally relevant way to help guide him toward coming to terms with his sexual orientation.

Later during the afternoon in the park, Ryan and Ning find a vendor where they purchase refreshments for the group. Ning asks why Ryan hasn't told his parents that they are not dating. Ryan says he didn't want to disappoint them—they are so happy to see him with a Chinese man. The family then watch a traditional Chinese musical performance in the park. Ryan and Ning stand in the back enjoying the performance and exchange an affectionate look. In these scenes Ryan shows his own initial movements toward embracing his ethnic identity in the way he shows respect for his parents and does not want to disappoint them by explaining that he and Ning are just friends, and the way that he affectionately looks at them during the performance. In getting away from the hustle of Manhattan, to the park with his family and to the performance, Ryan opens up to the identity he usually works so hard to bury.

After the day with Ryan's family, Ryan and Ning go to a club together [55:06]. Ryan and Ning dance, but soon Ryan and a white presenting man at the club catch each other's eyes while Ryan is dancing across from Ning. As the man tries to move in to dance with Ryan, Ning starts to walk away. Ryan grabs him to come back to the dance floor. Suddenly, Ning grabs Ryan's face, giving him a passionate kiss, which Ryan returns with lust. In the next scene, they are in Ryan's apartment having passionate sex. As they cuddle in bed later in the night, Ning asks, "Am I your first Chinese?" Ryan says that Ning is his "first Asian ever." Ning wonders, "Is it different?" Ryan doesn't respond verbally, but just continues stroking Ning's arm and hand and perhaps nods ever so slightly. Ning asks, "How do you feel?" Ryan laughs, "Like a virgin." Ryan asks Ning, "This isn't your first time, huh?" As Ning looks at him, Ryan says, "Oh please, I could tell the difference." Ryan then asks how long Ning has been closeted—"too many" he replies and then snuggles his face in Ryan's neck, saying, "I don't want to go."

In this pivotal scene both men move past their own hurdles to embrace the identity they usually bury. Ning leans into his gay identity and attraction to Ryan, kissing him in public, followed by passionate love-making. Ryan, who usually chooses white partners in an attempt to whitewash his Chinese ethnicity, chooses a Chinese man instead. Not only do they both lean in to these identities, but they also seem happy about it—at least in the context of this new romance. In the morning when Ryan remembers that he was fired the day before, Ning urges him to come to Beijing, implying that they could continue their romance in China. Ryan begins to consider it, but dreams of a romance are quickly shattered when Chinese media publish photos of Ning and Ryan suggesting that Ning is gay.

Embracing and Reburial

The characters have moved toward embracing their previously buried identities, but as one comes to embrace it more openly, the other eventually returns to rejection, illustrating that an effort to embrace a buried identity doesn't always result in full acceptance. We can make sense of Ryan's acceptance of his Chinese ethnicity and Ning's rejection of his gay identity by paying attention to the cultural salience of their situation, that is, the cultural contexts for their different struggles and communication choices (Collier, 1989). Given the sociocultural stigma toward same-sex relationships in China (Liu et al., 2011; Neilands et al., 2008), it could be argued that Ning had a harder identity hurdle to overcome (i.e., coming out), than Ryan coming to terms with his ethnic heritage.

Ning's reburial of his gay identity is evident when Ning confronts Ryan about the photo of them sharing a drink at the park published in a Chinese magazine [1:06:30]. Ryan is confused at Ning's accusation that he leaked the photo, and responds, "What the fuck? Why would I do that? I don't even know what this stupid magazine is." In his angry rejection of Chinese media, Ryan reverts to disavowing his ethnic heritage, mainly because it has led to Ning mistrusting Ryan. When Ryan asks what is written in the magazine, Ning explains that it says, "'Ning is in love.'" Ryan reassures him that it doesn't technically say Ning is gay, but Ning explains that the Chinese press have previously written about Ning possibly being gay, and worries that his parents will be ashamed of him and that his career will be destroyed. Ryan is not able to grasp the cultural values that bind Ning, and affectionately offers Ning a home with him in America, in case he can't go back. Ning looks at Ryan angrily and says, "I will never act again. My dream is over." Ryan says he was planning to go to China, but Ning responds while holding back tears, "Don't you understand anything? I have to carry on my family name." Ryan asks, "So, what are you going to do, just stay in the closet forever?" Ning then storms out.

The predicament that Ning finds himself in is all too real for many Chinese individuals who come out as gay or lesbian, or think about coming out. Not only are they treated as social pariahs for rejecting traditional gender roles but their parents/families are blamed for failing to inculcate values about the importance of heterosexuality and reproduction in Asian society (Chan, 1989). To save face, for their families and themselves, many Asian gay men marry women and eventually produce heirs (Neilands et al., 2008). We imagine Ning would chart a similar future for himself, and we see a preview of that in a scene where his girlfriend arrives from China and meets Ning in his apartment [1:08:09]. She has presumably seen the magazine article and is upset, yet tries to be romantic with Ning who is smoking on his balcony. Later they kiss, seemingly attempting to have an intimate night together, but the interaction lacks passion. They both know it does not work and they both look melancholic at their predicament—needing to be in a relationship for their respective careers, but knowing that their love is rooted in platonic friendship and lacks sexual attraction.

In the next scene, while Ryan is visiting his mother, Ning calls and invites him to his apartment [1:10:20]. Ning seems to be in better spirits, and after offering Ryan a glass of his favorite petite sirah wine, apologizes for his earlier outburst. He reluctantly explains: "There are many directors who want me in their next film, but they are afraid of the magazine. I need to clear my name before they use me. So . . . can you please help me? Say something on my—." Ryan realizes Ning is asking him to publicly confirm that he is not gay. Offended and angry, Ryan starts to leave, with Ning chasing after him begging for help, but Ryan continues to storm out. Here we see a desperate attempt to make Ryan a part of Ning's effort to bury his gay identity, and perhaps also Ning's assumption that Ryan's shared ethnic heritage would make him understand why Ning's sexual orientation has to be closeted.

The reburial of Ning's gay identity is complete when Ning attends the press conference with his female fiancé and his PR agent, James, taking questions from journalists who are interested to hear about his engagement and Ning's next projects [1:15:43]. Ryan is in the audience reviewing his public statement, and Ning's fiancé flaunts her engagement ring, when a journalist asks if Ning will comment on the photos from the magazine that "stirred up rumors." Ning explains, "You know, the press has a very big imagination. It was a normal photograph and the photographer use angle to make me and my friend look abnormal. The other person in the photo is actually good friend of us, and he is here now so I ask him to come up and tell you the truth." Later, Ning thanks Ryan for making the public statement and Ryan says that he hopes Ning is happy. Ning says, "We Chinese have a saying—you have to plow in order to harvest. You have to give up something in order to achieve your dream" [1:20:47]. Ning seems to be saying that he has chosen to give up on embracing his true sexual orientation (and a fulfilling romantic partnership) in order to achieve his dream of professional success and making his parents and nation proud. The men embrace in one final farewell, and Ryan leaves. Ning, in these two scenes, does his bit to fully rebury his gay identity using his ethnic pride, Ryan's public statement, James' PR skills, and his fiancé's flashy diamond ring as symbols of his faux, heterosexual identity ascription.

Ryan, has many times in the past, buried his ethnic identity, especially when negotiating his complex relationship with Ning, but has now learned to embrace his Chinese identity more openly. After Ning asks Ryan to clear his name for the suggestive magazine photographs and to provide Ning a false identity ascription, Ryan is heartbroken and visits his parents to seek comfort. His mother gives him a hand massage, and affectionately chides him for dry hands [1:10:20]. She knows he is brokenhearted over Ning, and uses nonverbal gestures and affectionate reprimands to comfort and support her son—these are cultural nuances that Ryan now understands and appreciates. The powerful scene at Ning's press conference tells us that Ryan has found a way to negotiate his ethnic and sexual identities with greater communicative competence. As Ning introduces Ryan, and the journalists applaud as he gets up to take questions, Ryan is asked to describe their relationship. Ryan seems uncomfortable, and struggles with the paper which has his prepared statement. He puts it down, declaring, "I am gay," and the crowd murmurs. Ryan continues:

> I told Mr. Qi this the first day we met. But Ning doesn't mind me being gay. He's a type of person that treats everyone equally, despite race, class or sexuality. And I think it takes someone who is very happy and confident with himself to be so kind and accepting. Yeah, very proud to call Ning my friend. No, actually, he's like a brother to me.

As Ning and Ryan both fight back tears and heartbreak, James steps in to escort Ning to his flight back to Beijing. Ryan has done what Ning asked him to do, that is, he doesn't out Ning. But, he also doesn't directly confirm that Ning is not gay. Ryan, in this scene, seems to find a balance of his American and Chinese identities by confidently stating that he himself is gay, and more fluidly connects his avowed gay identity with his (now accepted) ascribed Chinese identity.

Ryan has moved from burying his ethnic identity to embracing it, and we see that clearly in the last scene of the film. Ryan walks through the city and returns to Chinatown, but this time with a different relationship with his ethnicity. This time as he walks through the neighborhood, he is at ease and interacts with Asian-presenting tourists there, now that he has learned to embrace his Chinese heritage. Yet, Ning remains where he was at the beginning—proud of his Chinese identity, but closeted about his sexual orientation. Ryan, on the other hand, has changed. He was always open and comfortable with being gay, but he was ashamed of being Chinese, finding it hard to connect his two identities. In the end, he has learned acceptance and pride in his ethnicity, and his identity movement has come full circle.

CONCLUSION

The characters' identity movements from burying, to eventually embracing, and/or reburying are determined by the cultural values and social spaces they inhabit. Ning's sojourn to New York City opened his eyes to the possibility of coming out and falling in love, but ultimately it was his career and fear of being shamed for being gay that held him back. Ryan gradually comes to accept and integrate the avowal and acceptance of his identity as both gay and Chinese American. This moving film has earned many accolades, including winner of Best Screenplay at the 2016 FilmOut San Diego Film Festival, winner of the Best Domestic Feature at the 2016 Outflix Film Festival in Memphis, the winner for Audience Award and Best Narrative Film at the 2016 Boston Asian American Film Festival, and winner of Best Actor at the 2017 Golden Koala Chinese Film Festival.

This national and international recognition for the film's nuanced depiction of ethnic and sexual identity movement in the context of an intra- and intercultural relationship reinforces the value and power of film to tell stories about diverse and evolving identities. The conclusion illustrates that there are not always happy outcomes with identities that challenge cultural norms. The film ends positively for Ryan's Chinese American identity balance, despite the heartbreak he endures. Through his relationship with Ning, Ryan moves from burying to embracing his Chinese heritage. The film ends sadly for Ning in that he wasn't able to find a balance with his profession (and the cultural expectations therein) and his sexual orientation, resulting in him having to give up on living openly as a gay man. Ning's sojourn to New York City prompted Ryan's identity movement and growth, and the story of their relationship illustrates how real life sojourning and travel can change both those who move, and those from the host culture interacting with migrants. The experience of visiting a different culture and seeing another way of living was eye opening for Ning, but didn't change him long term. Knowing the culture he was returning to led him to revert back to burying his gay identity, albeit brokenhearted. *Front Cover* (2015) teaches audiences that context and cultural norms are important determining factors in how people prioritize and negotiate their various identities such that a person may minimize or fully reject a part of themselves that is too much in conflict with a given context or set of cultural norms.

NOTES

1. In this chapter, we use the acronym LGBTQI+. Although there are several variations of the acronym, our goal is to be sensitive and inclusive of the community/people who identify with it.

2. We are aware that the term "homosexual" is derogatory, but we use it in this chapter only in the context of direct quotations, per GLAAD's recommendation.

3. The model minority myth is a white-constructed stereotype that positions Asians and Asian Americans as hardworking, serious, successful, and passive (Chou & Feagin, 2016). It is damaging because it fosters unrealistic and often inaccurate expectations of people. It also perpetuates rifts between racial groups, such as those between Asian Americans and Black Americans, and allows "white America to avoid any responsibility for addressing racism or the damage it continues to inflict" (Chow, 2017).

Chapter 8
Afterword

The stories depicted in these six films shed light on the variety of relationships, life circumstances, movements, and histories where intercultural communication can aid in understanding. While some of the films have weaknesses when they rely on stereotypes for storytelling, all of them teach audiences something about how to navigate the varying ways that they may encounter intercultural interactions and global movement—perhaps by moving themselves or by meeting an immigrant who is different from them.

Beginning with a focus on migration, we analyzed two films where immigration is central to their stories. In chapter 2's *The African Doctor* (2016), immigration, racism, othering, and cultural adaptation take center stage. We show how cultural adaptation is a complex, multilayered process whereby both the migrant and the host culture must be open to change. We argue that as hard as it is to culturally adapt (especially when one has never had to before, as with the Marly-Gomont villagers) and learn to accept people who seem different, this film illustrates that it can ultimately be a rewarding and fulfilling experience for everyone—migrants and hosts alike.

The story of the Galindo family in chapter 3's *A Better Life* (2011) takes a different perspective of immigration—depicting how cruel, formidable, and othering immigration experiences can be, at least for unauthorized migrants in the United States. In this chapter we focus on the immigration industrial complex, as well as differing cultural values, conflict styles, and facework. We argue that that film cleverly depicts La Migra as a third character that haunts everyone, helping audiences to sense the weight that unauthorized status has on families and communities in the United States. Moreover, in blended families like the Galindos, where parents are immigrants and children are citizens who grew up in the United States, culturally different approaches to conflict and facework can make navigating the tensions, complications, and challenges of dealing with immigration authorities especially difficult. However, familial love can override all of the seemingly intractable cultural differences, as it does for Carlos and Luis. While the film tragically ends with Carlos' deportation, there is hope that he, like so many others, will return to his home and be reunited with his son—personifying for audiences how tragic and cruel immigration systems in the United States can be, but also how family bonds are no match for La Migra because these bonds drive people to always return home no matter the risks.

In the second part of the book, we focus on movement in more of an historical sense when looking at cultural conflicts depicted in the films *Rabbit Proof Fence* (2002) and *A Borrowed Identity* (2014). In chapter 4, for analyzing *Rabbit Proof Fence* (2002), we take an intercultural communication spin on racial othering and spatial mobilities, and argue that the film's symbolic use of the fence highlights cruelty of colonialism and white savior mindsets. The fence also symbolically illustrates the way familial bonds, similar to Carlos and Luis in *A Better Life* (2011), transcend state attempts to separate families. The yearning and drive for a parent and child to be reunited, no matter the risk, is more powerful than any fence, wall, or border that a state can erect.

Restrictions on movement appear again in chapter 5 when analyzing *A Borrowed Identity* (2014). In this film, movement emerges in terms of cultural identities along interreligious and interethnic lines with Eyad's growth along the minority identity development model, his eventual adoption of Yonatan's identity, and how his communication and opportunities change as he enters different social spaces as either Arab Eyad or Jewish Yonatan. Restrictions on movement depicted in the story serve to illustrate to audiences how states can limit or halt movement (socioeconomic, physical, etc.) for citizens that it deems risky, likely to the detriment of those marginalized groups. The film is sympathetic to the Arab perspective in the long-standing ethnic and religious conflict between Israel and Palestine, and that is something audiences ought to understand. In the relationship between Eyad and Edna, the film mimics others analyzed in this book that show audiences how enriching and powerful intercultural relations can be. But this film also does well with introducing audiences to how complex and painful building intercultural relationships can be and in acknowledging that sometimes certain intercultural barriers are impossible to overcome, as is depicted in the breakup between Eyad and Naomi.

In the final section of the book, we turned our attention to a particular type of movement—sojourning—and the kinds of (non)verbal communication challenges and barriers to intercultural communication that people spending time abroad for a specific purpose may encounter. We looked at two films that tell stories of sojourners and the hardships they faced—*Outsourced* (2006) and *Front Cover* (2015). In chapter 6's *Outsourced* (2006), we return to cultural adaptation, focusing on the U-curve model, and examine the protagonist's movement along that model in light of global capitalism and interethnic stereotypes. This lighthearted film has weaknesses in the way it relies on stereotypes of both Indian and American cultures to tell the story of Todd's sojourn in India. The film is especially problematic in the way it perpetuates American stereotypes of India as being impoverished, dirty, excessively spiritual, and a destination for those yearning for spiritual renewal. Still, a surprising strength that is likely lost on the average American viewer is the way Goddess Kali and related imagery is woven into the story to signal Todd's transformation. The film is also critical of American-style corporate practices and global capitalism. In that sense, the film is useful for Western audience members to see Todd's personification of moving along the U-curve and how important it is to adapt business practices to local cultures in order to achieve overall success.

Sojourning for professional reasons is also what drives the story in *Front Cover* (2015). Ning is in the United States for a specific business purpose—to expand his celebrity to the American market—and Ryan is assigned to work with him for the specific purpose of styling him to appeal to an American audience. In analyzing this film, we used intercultural communication lenses on identity avowal/ascription, contested sexualities, and intra-ethnic stereotyping. Both Ryan and Ning are gay and ethnically Chinese; however, each one desires to downplay one of those identities. Ryan is openly gay but minimizes his Chinese heritage, while Ning is proud of his Chinese heritage but tries to hide his sexual orientation. The other's embrace of that identity which each man seeks to hide is a source of conflict as they build a relationship. This film illustrates to the audience the value of intercultural relationships to help us know and understand ourselves better, which can help us in all aspects of our lives. At the end of the film Ning chooses to remain sexually closeted for sake of his career and returns to China intending to marry his girlfriend. Ryan, however, has learned to embrace his Chinese ethnicity with pride and appears happy having reached a fuller and more balanced sense of self-identity.

The films featured in this book illustrate the variety of ways and contexts that intercultural communication and relationships impact our lives—from professional settings, to schools, to families, to romance, to friendships, and across historical contexts. The films also reveal the variety of types of identities that can be considered intercultural—national, racial, ethnic, religious, sexual, and more. And in examining the films through an intercultural lens we can also see how movement and mobility structure so many aspects of our intercultural lives—from physical movement to a new place or to return home, to symbolic movement and growth of an identity or identities, to movement in our knowledge and understanding of histories, to incremental sociopolitical movements toward peace.

Film is a powerful medium to tell compelling stories of movement and intercultural encounters that can give audiences an idea about what to expect when they inevitably face their own intercultural encounters. The films selected here and our analyses provide in-depth readings on the movement and intercultural aspects of each film text—calling attention to both strengths and weaknesses in them. All in all, these films and our analyses are valuable tools that can open discussions of complex, divisive, and difficult topics using relatable narratives and visual storytelling to unpack experiences of movement, mobility, and intercultural communication.

While we selected films from a variety of cultural contexts, we encourage future research that analyzes popular cross-cultural films from more and different places. Recent films also worthy of scholarly attention include *Parasite* (2019), which explores intercultural relationships across socioeconomic lines in the South Korean cultural context, and *Lionheart* (2018), which explores patriarchy and feminism in a Nigerian business and familial context. Moreover, film is hardly the only artistic medium suitable for analysis of intercultural communication and mobility. Certainly, popular music, theater, fashion, and street art, among others, would also be welcome venues for future scholarly research on how audiences learn to navigate movement and intercultural encounters. Our teaching experiences and our passions align with cinema, and we hope you have found new ways to engage with these six films as well as learned ways that you can engage with other cross-cultural films.

References

Aborigines Act 1905. (2016). History and information about Australian orphanages, children's homes and other institutions. *Find & Connect* (online). https://www.fin dandconnect.gov.au/ref/wa/biogs/WE00406b.htm

Adler, P. (1987). Culture shock and the cross-cultural learning experience. In: L. F. Luce & E. C. Smith (Eds.), *Toward Internationalism: Readings in Cross-Cultural Communication* (pp. 24–35). Cambridge, MA: Newbury.

Al-Saji, A. (2010). The racialization of Muslim veils: A philosophical analysis. *Philosophy and Social Criticism, 36*(8), 875–902. doi: 10.1177/0191453710375589

Antraás, P. & Helpman, E. (2004). Global Sourcing. *Journal of Political Economy, 112*(3), 552–580. doi: 10.1086/383099

Atkinson, D. E. (2004). *Counseling American minorities: A cross-cultural perspective* (6th edition). New York: McGraw-Hill.

Australian Human Rights Commission. (2014). *Bringing them home: Separation of Aboriginal and Torres Strait Islander children from their families* [Video]. YouTube. https://www.youtube.com/watch?v=Sl82VMuuKI0

Balser, B. B., Foxman, A. H., Stern, C. M., Jacobson, K., Levin, M., Glovsky, R. D., Alster, E. S. & Levin, G. (2006). Confronting anti-semitism: Myths, facts. *Anti-Defamation League*. https://www.adl.org/media/2133/download

Batt, R. & Moynihan, L. (2002). The viability of alternative call centre production models. *Human Resource Management Journal, 12*(4), 14–34. doi: 10.1111/j.1748-8583.2002.tb00075.x

BBC. (2009). Ganesh Chaturthi. *BBC: Religions*.https://www.bbc.co.uk/religion/reli gions/hinduism/holydays/ganesh.shtml

Bem, S. L. (1993). *The lenses of gender: Transforming the debate on sexual inequality*. New Haven, CT: Yale University Press.

Berry, C. (2001). Asian values, family values: Film, video and lesbian and gay identities. *Journal of Homosexuality, 40*(3/4), 211–231. doi: 10.1300/J082v40n03_11

Berry, J. W. (1992). Psychology of acculturation: Understanding individuals moving between two cultures. In: R. W. Brislin (Ed.), *Applied Cross-Cultural Psychology* (pp. 232–253). Newbury Park, CA: Sage.

Berry, J. W. (1997). Immigration, acculturation, and adaptation. *Applied Psychology, 46*(1), 5–34. doi: 10.1111/j.1464-0597.1997.tb01087.x

Berry, J. W., Kim, U. & Boski, P. (1987). Psychological acculturation of immigrants. In: Y. Y. Kim & W. B. Gundykunst (Eds.), *International and Intercultural Communication Annual* (Vol. 11, pp. 62–89). Newbury Park, CA: Sage.

Bhattacharyya, G. (2005). *Traffick: The illicit movement of people and things*. Ann Arbor, MI: Pluto Books.

Brenner, N. & Stuart E. (2009). Introduction. In: N. Brenner & S. Eldin (Eds.), *State, space, world: Lefebvre and the survival of capitalism* (pp. 1–48). Minneapolis, MN: University of Minnesota Press.

Brew, F. & Cairns, D. (2004). Do culture or situational constraints determine choice of direct or indirect styles in intercultural workplace conflicts? *International Journal of Intercultural Relations, 28*(5), 331–352. doi: 10.1016/j.ijintrel.2004.09.001

Bringing them home - Community guide - 2007 update. (2007). *Australian Human Rights Commission*. https://www.humanrights.gov.au/bringing-them-home-community-guide-2007-update

Brown, P. & Levinson, S. (1987). *Politeness: Some universals in language usage*. Cambridge, England: Cambridge University Press.

Cairncross, F. (1997). *The death of distance*. Boston, MA: Harvard Business School Press.

Campbell, A. F. (2016). Many Americans want work, but they don't want to mow lawns. *The Atlantic*. https://www.theatlantic.com/business/archive/2016/07/why-the-guys-mowing-your-lawn-are-probably-foreign/490595/

Cannadine, D. (2013). *The Undivided Past: Humanity beyond our differences*. New York: Alfred A. Knopf.

Casey, E. S. (2001). Between geography and philosophy: What does it mean to be in the place-world? *Annals of the Association of American Geographers, 91*(4), 683–693. doi: 10.1111/0004-5608.00266

Chalabi, M. (2018). How many migrant children are detained in U.S. custody? *The Guardian* (online). https://www.theguardian.com/news/datablog/2018/dec/22/migrant-children-us-custody

Chan, C. S. (1989). Issues of identity development among Asian-American lesbians and gay men. *Journal of Counseling and Development, 68*(1), 16–20. doi: 10.1002/j.1556-6676.1989.tb02485.x

Chan, C. S. (1992). Cultural considerations in counseling Asian American lesbians and gay men. In: S. Dworkin & F. Gutierrez (Eds.), *Counseling Gay Men and lesbians* (pp. 115–124). Alexandria, VA: American Association for Counseling and Development.

Chan, C. S. (1995). Issues of sexual identity in an ethnic minority: The case of Chinese American lesbians, gay men, and bisexual people. In: A. R. D'Augelli & C. J. Patterson (Eds.), *Lesbian, gay, and Bisexual Identities over the lifespan: Psychological perspectives* (pp. 87–101). New York: Oxford University Press. doi: 10.1093/acprof:oso/9780195082319.003.0004

Chang, T. & Subramaniam, P. R. (2008). Asian and Pacific Islander American men's help-seeking: Cultural values and beliefs, gender roles, and racial stereotypes. *International Journal of Men's Health, 7*(2), 121–136. doi: 10.3149/jmh.0702.121

Chavez, K. R. (2013). Pushing boundaries: Queer intercultural communication. *Journal of International and Intercultural Communication, 6*(2), 83–95.

Chen, A. S. (1999). Lives at the center of the periphery, lives at the periphery of the center: Chinese American masculinities and bargaining with hegemony. *Gender and Society, 13*, 584–607. doi: 10.1177/089124399013005002

Chen, M. (2018). Is the nail salon industry any better for workers now? *The Nation.* https://www.thenation.com/article/nail-salon-worker-safety/

Chen, Y. W. & Collier, M. J. (2012). Intercultural identity positioning: Interview discourses from two identity-based nonprofit organizations. *Journal of International and Intercultural Communication, 5*(1), 43–63. doi: 10.1080/17513057.2011.631215

Cheshire, G. (2016). Front cover. [Review of the movie *Front Cover*]. *Rogerebert.com* Retrieved from: https://www.rogerebert.com/reviews/front-cover-2016

Choi, K.-H., Kumekawa, E., Dang, Q., Kegeles, S. M., Hays, R. B. & Stall, R. (1999). Risk and protective factors affecting sexual behavior among young asian and pacific islander men who have sex with men: Implications for HIV prevention. *Journal of Sex Education and Therapy, 24*(1–2), 47–55. doi: 10.1080/01614576.1999.11074282

Chou, R. S. & Feagin, J. R. (2016). *The myth of the Model Minority: Asian Americans facing racism*. New York: Routledge.

Chow, K (2017). 'Model minority' myth used again as a racial wedge between Asians and Blacks. *NPR: Code Switch* (online). https://www.npr.org/sections/codeswitch/2017/04/19/524571669/model-minority-myth-again-used-as-a-racial-wedge-between-asians-and-blacks

Cocroft, B. K. & Ting-Toomey, S. (1994). Facework in Japan and the United States. *International Journal of Intercultural Relations, 18*(4), 469–506. doi: 10.1016/0147-1767(94)90018-3

Cohen, A. P. (1993). Culture as identity: An anthropologist's view. *New Literary History, 24*(1), 195–209. doi: 10.2307/469278

Colby, S. L. & Ortman, J. M. (2015, March). Projections of the size and composition of the U.S. population: 2014 to 2060. *United States Census Bureau.* https://www.census.gov/content/dam/Census/library/publications/2015/demo/p25-1143.pdf

Cole, T. (2012). The white-savior industrial complex. *The Atlantic: Global.* https://www.theatlantic.com/international/archive/2012/03/the-white-savior-industrial-complex/254843/

Coleman, H. L. K. (1995). Strategies for coping with cultural diversity. *The Counseling Psychologist, 23*(4), 722–740. doi: 10.1177/0011000095234011

Collier, M. J. (1989). Cultural and intercultural communication competence: Current approaches and directions for future research. *International Journal of Intercultural Relations, 13*, 287–301. doi: 10.1016/0147-1767(89)90014-X

Collier, M. J. & Thomas, M. (1988). Cultural identity: An interpretive perspective. In: Young Yun Kim & William B. Gudykunst (Eds.), *Theories in Intercultural Communication,* International and Intercultural Communication Annual, Volume XII (pp. 99–120). Newbury Park, CA: Sage.

Connor, W. (1994). *Ethnonationalism: The quest for understanding*. Princeton, NJ: Princeton University Press.

Cresswell, T. (1997). Imagining the nomad: Mobility and the postmodern primitive. In: G. Benko & U. Strohmayer (Eds.), *Space and Social Theory: Interpreting modernity and postmodernity* (pp. 360–382). Oxford: Blackwell Publishers, Ltd.

Cumbers, A., Nativel, C. & Routledge, P. (2008). Labour agency and union positionalities in global production networks. *Journal of Economic Geography, 8*(3), 369–387. doi: 10.1093/jeg/lbn008

D'Acosta, K. (2018). What are the jobs that immigrants do? *Scientific American.* https://blogs.scientificamerican.com/anthropology-in-practice/what-are-the-jobs-that-immigrants-do/

Das, S. (2019). The real meaning of the Shiva's linga symbol: The often misunderstood icon. *Learn Religions. Indian Arts and Culture: Hinduism.* https://www.learnreligions.com/what-is-shiva-linga-1770455

de Certeau, M. (1984). *The practice of Everyday Life.* (S. Rendall, Trans.). Berkeley, CA: University of California Press.

Devos, T. & Ma, D. S. (2008). Is Kate Winslet more American than Lucy Liu? The impact of construal processes on the implicit ascription of a national identity. *British Journal of Social Psychology, 47*, 191–215. doi: 10.1348/014466607X224521

Dickerson, C. (2018). Detention of migrant children has skyrocketed to highest levels ever. *New York Times* (online). https://www.nytimes.com/2018/09/12/us/migrant-children-detention.html

Dong-Jin, S. (2001). Mapping the vicissitudes of homosexual identities in South Korea. *Journal of Homosexuality, 40*(3/4), 65–79. doi: 10.1300/J082v40n03_04

Dossani, R. & Kenney, M. (2006). The Next Wave of Globalization: Relocating Service Provision to India. *Berkeley Roundtable on the International Economy, Industry Studies Association Working Paper* Series. http://isapapers.pitt.edu/

Eng, D. L. (2001). *Racial castration: Managing masculinity in Asian America.* London: Duke University Press.

Feinstein, H. (2015). A matter of semitics: A borrowed identity. *Filmmaker Magazine.* https://filmmakermagazine.com/94670-matter-of-semitics-a-borrowed-identity/#.XoM1zC3MzOR

Fernie, S. & Metcalf, D. (1998). (Not) hanging on the telephone: Payment systems in the new sweatshops. CEPDP (390). *Centre for Economic Performance, London School of Economics and Political Science*, London, UK. ISBN 0753012170. http://eprints.lse.ac.uk/20275/1/%28Not%29Hanging_on_the_Telephone_Payment_systems_in_the_New_Sweatshops.pdf

Foucault, M. (1980). *Power/knowledge: Selected interviews and other writings 1972–1977* (C. Gordon, Ed.). New York: Harvester Press.

Foucault, M. (2012). The history of sexuality. In: W. Longhofer & D. Winchester (Eds.), *Social theory re-wired: New connections to classical and contemporary perspectives* (pp. 464–470). New York: Routledge.

Gandhi, P. P. (2002). India-U.S. economic relations: A perspective. In: A. Kapur, Y. K. Malik, H. A. Gould & A. G. Rubinoff (Eds.), *India and the United States in a Changing World* (pp. 328–348). New Delhi: Sage.

Garson, B. (1988). *The Electronic Sweatshop: How computers are transforming the office of the future into the factory of the past.* New York: Simon & Schuster.

Gerber, M. (2013). For Latinos, a Spanish word loaded with meaning. *Los Angeles Times*. https://www.latimes.com/local/la-xpm-2013-apr-01-la-me-latino-labels-2 0130402-story.html

Gibbs, D. N. (1991). *The Political Economy of Third World Intervention: Mines, money, and U.S. policy in the Congo Crisis*. Chicago, IL: University of Chicago Press.

Gill, B. (2002). China's HIV/AIDS crisis: Implications for human rights, the Rule of Law and U.S.–China relations. *Testimony before the Congressional-Executive Commission on China, Roundtable on HIV/AIDS*. https://pdfs.semanticscholar.org/51c3/3e3417881d4e65a4b03612914a2f43dae9ab.pdf

Goffman, E. (1967). *Interaction ritual*. New York: Doubleday.

Golash-Boza, T. (2009). The immigration industrial complex: Why we enforce immigration policies destined to fail. *Sociology Compass, 3*(2), 295–309. doi: 10.1111/j.1751-9020.2008.00193.x

Gomez, C. & Taylor, K. A. (2018). Cultural differences in conflict resolution strategies: A US–Mexico comparison. *International Journal of Cross Cultural Management, 18*(1), 33–51. doi: 10.1177/1470595817747638

Guiraudon, V. (2001). Immigration policy in France. *Brookings*. https://www.brookings.edu/articles/immigration-policy-in-france/

Hall, E. T. (1966). *The Hidden Dimension*. Garden City, NY: Doubleday.

Hall, E. T. (1976). *Beyond culture*. New York: Doubleday.

Hahm, H. C. & Adkins, C. (2009) A Model of Asian and Pacific Islander sexual minority acculturation. *Journal of LGBT Youth, 6*(2–3), 155–173. doi: 10.1080/19361650903013501

Hamilton, K., Simon, P. & Veniard, C. (2004). The challenge of French diversity. *Migration Information Source, Migration Policy Institute*. https://www.migrationpolicy.org/article/challenge-french-diversity

Harvey, D. (1989). *The condition of postmodernity: An enquiry into the origins of cultural change*. Cambridge, MA: Blackwell.

Heaphy, L. (2017). Kali – A most misunderstood goddess. *Kashgar*. https://kashgar.com.au/blogs/gods-goddesses/kali-a-most-misunderstood-goddess

Helms, J. E. (1995). An update of Helm's White and people of color racial identity models. In: J. G. Ponterotto, J. M. Casas, L. A. Suzuki, & C. M. Alexander (Eds.), *Handbook of multicultural counseling* (pp. 181–198). Sage Publications, Inc.

Hiltner, S. (2017). Illegal, undocumented, unauthorized: The terms of immigration reporting. *The New York Times*. https://www.nytimes.com/2017/03/10/insider/illegal-undocumented-unauthorized-the-terms-of-immigration-reporting.html

Hofstede, G. (1980). *Culture's consequences: International differences in work-related values*. Beverly Hills, CA: Sage.

Hofstede, G. (1991). *Cultures and organizations: Software of the mind*. London: McGraw-Hill.

Hofstede, G. (1998). Think globally, act locally: Cultural constraints in personnel management. *MIR: Management International Review, 38*, 7–26.

Hofstede, G. (2001). *Culture's consequences: Comparing values, behaviors, institutions, and organizations across nations* (2nd edition). Thousand Oaks, CA: Sage.

Hofstede Insights. (2009). *Country Comparison*. https://www.hofstede-insights.com/country-comparison/mexico/

Hui, C. H. & Triandis, H. C. (1986). Individualism-collectivism: A study of cross-cultural researchers. *Journal of Cross-Cultural Psychology, 17*(2), 225–248. doi: 10.1177/0022002186017002006

Human Rights and Equal Opportunity Commission. (1997). *Bringing them home: National inquiry into the separation of Aboriginal and Torres Strait Islander children from their families*. [Report]. Sydney, NSW: Commonwealth of Australia.

Huselid, M. (1995). The impact of human resources management practices on turnover, productivity, and corporate financial performance. *Academy of Management Journal, 38*(3), 635–672. doi: 10.5465/256741

Hussain, M. (2019). Liberté for whom: French Muslims grapple with a republic that codified their marginalization. *The Intercept*. https://theintercept.com/2019/02/23/france-islamophobia-islam-french-muslims-terrorism

Indigenous Australia Timeline - 1901 to 1969. (2018). *Australian Museum* [online]. https://australianmuseum.net.au/indigenous-australia-timeline-1901-to-1969

International Lesbian, Gay, Bisexual, Trans and Intersex Association. (2016). *Carroll, A., State Sponsored Homophobia 2016: A World Survey of Sexual Orientation Laws: Criminalisation, Protection and Recognition*. Geneva: ILGA. https://ilga.org/downloads/02_ILGA_State_Sponsored_Homophobia_2016_ENG_WEB_150516.pdf

Jandt, F. E. (2016). *An Introduction to Intercultural Communication: Identities in a Global Community* (8th edition). Thousand Oaks, CA: SAGE.

Jeffcoat, J. (Director). (2006). *Outsourced* [Film]. ShadowCatcher Entertainment.

Johnson, J. L., Bottorff, J. L., Browne, A. J., Grewal, S., Hilton, B. A. & Clarke, H. (2004). Othering and being othered in the context of health care services. *Health Communication, 16*(2), 255–271. doi: 10.1207/S15327027HC1602_7

Judy, R. W. & D'Amico, C. (1997). *Workforce 2020: Work and workers for the 21st century*. Indianapolis, IN: Hudson Institute.

Kamarck, E. & Stenglein, C. (2019). How many undocumented immigrants are in the United States and who are they? *Policy 2020, The Brookings Institution*. https://www.brookings.edu/policy2020/votervital/how-many-undocumented-immigrants-are-in-the-united-states-and-who-are-they/

Kammer, J. (2015). The Hart-Celler Immigration Act of 1965. *Center for Immigration Studies*. https://cis.org/Report/HartCeller-Immigration-Act-1965

Kashua, S. (2002). *Dancing Arabs*. New York: Grove/Atlantic, Inc.

Kaufman, D. (2014). Israeli's Jerusalem bagels make their way to NYC. *New York Post*. https://nypost.com/2014/04/22/israels-jerusalem-bagels-make-their-way-to-nyc/

Keesey, D. (1998). Weir(d) Australia: Picnic at hanging rock and the last wave. *Literature Interpretation Theory, 8*(3–4), 331–346. doi: 10.1080/10436929808580207

Kim, Y. Y. (2001). *Becoming intercultural: An Integrative Theory of communication and cross-Cultural Adaptation*. Thousand Oaks, CA: Sage.

Kipling, R. (1929). The white man's burden: The United States and the Philippine Islands, 1899. In: *Rudyard Kipling's Verse: Definitive Edition*. Garden City, NY: Doubleday.

Kisangani, E. F. & Scott Bobb, F. (2010). *Historical dictionary of the Democratic Republic of the Congo* (3rd edition). *Historical Dictionaries of Africa, No. 112*. Lanham, MD: The Scarecrow Press.

Kluckhohn, F. & Strodtbeck, F. (1961). *Variations in Value Orientations*. Evanston, IL: Row, Peterson.

Kopan, T. (2018). DHS: 2,000 children separated at border. *CNN*. https://www.cnn.com/2018/06/15/politics/dhs-family-separation-numbers/index.html

Kumashiro, K. K. (1999). Supplementing normalcy and otherness: Queer Asian American men reflect on stereotypes, identity, and oppression. *International Journal of Qualitative Studies in Education, 12*(5), 491–508. doi: 10.1080/095183999235917

Kyes, K. B. & Tumbelaka, L. (1994). Comparison of Indonesian and American college students' attitudes toward homosexuality. *Psychological Reports, 74*, 227–237. doi: 10.2466/pr0.1994.74.1.227

Le, T. N. & Stockdale, G. D. (2005). Individualism, collectivism, and delinquency in Asian American adolescents. *Journal of Clinical Child and Adolescent Psychology, 34*(4), 681–691. doi: 10.1207/s15374424jccp3404_10

Lee, S. J. (1996). *Unraveling the 'Model Minority' stereotype: Listening to Asian American youth*. New York: Teachers College, Columbia University.

Lefebvre, H. (2009a). Reflections on the politics of space. In: N. Brenner & S. Eldin (Eds.), *State, space, world: Lefebvre and the survival of capitalism* (pp. 167–184). Minneapolis, MN: University of Minnesota Press.

Lefebvre, H. (2009b). Space: Social produce and use value. In N. Brenner & S. Eldin (Eds.), *State, space, world: Lefebvre and the survival of capitalism* (pp. 185–195). Minneapolis, MN: University of Minnesota Press.

Leung, K. (2008). Chinese culture, modernization, and international business. *International Business Review, 17*(2), 184–187. doi: 10.1016/j.ibusrev.2008.02.009

Lim, V. K. (2002). Gender differences and attitudes towards homosexuality. *Journal of Homosexuality, 43*(1), 85–97.

Lin, T. Y. & Lin, M. C. (1981). Love, denial and rejection: Responses of Chinese families to mental illness. In: A. Klienman & T.-Y. Lin (Eds.), *Normal and Abnormal Behavior in Chinese Culture* (pp. 387–401). Dordrecht, Holland: D. Reidel Publishing Company.

Lipsey, R. E. (2004). Home and host country effects of foreign direct investments. In: R.E. Baldwin & L.A. Winters (Eds.) Challenges to globalization: Analyzing the economics (pp. 333-382). Cambridge, MA National Bureau of Economic Research .https://www.nber.org/chapters/c9543.pdf

Liu, H., Feng, T., Ha, T., Liu, H., Cai, Y., Liu, X. & Li, J. (2011). Chinese culture, homosexuality stigma, social support and condom use: A path analytic model. *Stigma research and action, 1*(1), 27–35. doi: 10.5463/sra.v1i1.16

Liu, R. & Trefler, D. (2008). Much ado about nothing: American jobs and the rise of service outsourcing to China and India (NBER Working Paper No. 14061). *NBER Program(s): International Trade and Investment, Labor Studies*.

Lock, S. (2018). Global business travel industry: Statistics and facts. *Statista*. https://www.statista.com/topics/2439/global-business-travel-industry/

Low, S. M. (1996). Spatializing culture: The social production and social construction of public space in Costa Rica. *American Ethnologist, 23*(4), 861–879. doi: 10.1525/ae.1996.23.4.02a00100

Low, S. M. & Lawrence-Zuniga, D. (2003). Locating culture. In: S. M. Low & D. Lawrence-Zuniga (Eds.), *The anthropology of space and place: Locating culture* (pp. 1–47). Malden, MA: Blackwell Publishing.

Luu, V. (2009). When it's stifling to be out: Gay Asian American men say cultural values keep them from coming out. *Northwest Asian Weekly.* http://nwasianweekly.com/2009/07/when-it%E2%80%99s-stifling-to-be-out/

Lynch, M. (2013). Sojourners. In: I. Ness (Ed.), *The Encyclopedia of Global Human Migration.* Hoboken, NJ: Blackwell Publishing, Ltd.

Lysgaard, S. (1955). Adjustment in a foreign society: Norwegian Fulbright grantees visiting the United States. *International Social Science Bulletin, 7,* 45–41.

MacGaffey, J. (2005). Congolese traders: Unofficial immigrants in France. In: M. Ember, C. R. Ember & I. Skoggard (Eds.), *Encyclopedia of Diasporas: Immigrant and Refugee Cultures around the World* (pp. 551–558). New York: Springer.

Map. (2018). *Bringing Them Home.* https://bth.humanrights.gov.au/our-stories/map

Marantz, A. (2011). My summer at an Indian call center. Lessons learned: Americans are hotheads, Australians are drunks — and never say where you're calling from. *Mother Jones: Politics.* https://www.motherjones.com/politics/2011/07/indian-call-center-americanization/

Martin, C. (2012). Desperate mobilities: Logistics, security and the extralogistical knowledge of 'appropriation'. *Geopolitics, 17*(2), 355–376. doi: 10.1080/14650045.2011.562941

Martin, J. N. & Davis, O. I. (2001). Conceptual foundations for teaching about whiteness in intercultural communication courses. *Communication Education, 50*(4), 298–313. doi: 10.1080/03634520109379257

Martin, J. N. & Nakayama, T. K. (2010). *Intercultural Communication in Contexts* (5th edition). New York: McGraw-Hill.

Martin, J. N. & Nakayama, T. K. (2013). *Intercultural Communication in Contexts* (6th edition). New York: McGraw-Hill.

Martin, J. N. & Nakayama, T. K. (2018). *Intercultural communication in contexts* (7th edition). New York: McGraw-Hill.

Martinez, D. & Slack, J. (2013). What part of "illegal" don't you understand? The social consequences of criminalizing unauthorized Mexican migrants in the United States. *Social and Legal Studies, 22*(4), 535–551. doi: 10.1177/0964663913484638

Martinez, E. (1998). What is white supremacy?" *SOA Watch.* http://soaw.org/resources/anti-opp-resources/108-race/482-what-is-white-supremacy

Maruca, J. (2019). College students watch more streaming services than ever. *The Daily Free Press.* https://dailyfreepress.com/2019/01/22/college-students-watch-more-streaming-services-than-ever/

Massey, D., Arango, J., Hugo, G., Kouaouci, A., Pellegrino, A. & Taylor, J. E. (1993). Theories of international migration: A review and appraisal. *Population Development Review, 19*(3), 431–466. doi: 10.2307/2938462

Mazur, A. (1977). Interpersonal spacing on public benches in "contact" vs. "noncontact" cultures. *The Journal of Social Psychology, 101*(1), 53–58. doi: 10.1080/00224545.1977.9923983

Merkin, R. S. (2006). Uncertainty avoidance and facework: A test of the Hofstede model. *International Journal of Intercultural Relations, 30*(2), 213–228. doi: 10.1016/j.ijintrel.2005.08.001

Moreton-Robinson, A. M. (2003). I still call Australia home: Indigenous belonging and place in a White postcolonising society. In: S. Ahmed (Ed.), *Uprootings/regroundings: Questions of home and migration* (pp. 23–40). London: Berg Publishing.

Moser, P. (2010). Israeli village stirs up hummus war. *The Telegraph*. https://www.telegraph.co.uk/expat/expatnews/6935306/Israeli-village-stirs-up-hummus-war.html

Muslim Arab Bedouins serve as Jewish state's gatekeepers. (2013). *Al Arabiya*. https://english.alarabiya.net/en/perspective/profiles/2013/04/24/Bedouin-army-trackers-scale-Israel-social-ladder-.html

Neal, D. (1995). Industry-specific human capital: Evidence from displaced workers. *Journal of Labor Economics, 13*(4): 653–677. doi: 10.1086/298388

Neilands, T. B., Steward, W. T. & Choi, K. H. (2008). Assessment of stigma towards homosexuality in China: A study of men who have sex with men. *Archives of Sexual Behavior, 37*(5), 838–844. doi: 10.1007/s10508-007-9305-x

Neuliep, J. W. (2015). *Intercultural communication: A contextual approach* (6th edition). Thousand Oaks, CA: Sage.

Ng, J. C., Lee, S. S. & Pak, Y. K. (2007). Contesting the model minority and perpetual foreigner stereotypes: A critical review of literature on Asian Americans in education. *Review of Research in Education, 31*(1), 95–130. doi: 10.3102/0091732X06298015

Noyce, P. (Director). (2002). *Rabbit-proof fence*. [Film]. Showtime Australia. www.amazon.com/Prime-Video/

NPR Staff (2011). Ike's warning of military expansion, 50 years later. *NPR Morning Edition*. https://www.npr.org/2011/01/17/132942244/ikes-warning-of-military-expansion-50-years-later

Oberg, K. (1954). *Culture shock*. Bobbs-Merrill Series in Social Science. Indianapolis, IN: Bobbs-Merrill.

Oberg, K. (1960). Culture shock: Adjustment to new cultural environments. *Practical Anthropology, 4*, 177–182. doi: 10.1177/009182966000700405

Oetzel, J., Ting-Toomey, S., Chew-Sanchez, M. I., Harris, R., Wilcox, R. & Stumpf, S. (2003). Face and facework in conflicts with parents and siblings: A cross-cultural comparison of Germans, Japanese, Mexicans, and U.S. Americans. *Journal of Family Communication, 3*(2), 67–93. doi: 10.1207/S15327698JFC0302_01

Oetzel, J. G., Ting-Toomey, S., Yokochi, Y., Masumoto, T. & Takai, J. (2000). A typology of facework behaviors in conflicts with best friends and relative strangers. *Communication Quarterly, 48*(4), 397–419. doi: 10.1080/01463370009385606

Ogden, P. E. (1991). Immigration to France since 1945: Myth and reality. *Ethnic and Racial Studies, 14*(3), 294–318. doi: 10.1080/01419870.1991.9993713

Onasch, E. A. (2017). Lessons on the boundaries of belonging: Racialization and symbolic boundary drawing in the French civic integration program. *Social Problems, 64*, 577–593. doi: 10.1093/socpro/spw037

Our History. (2020). *Healing Foundation.* https://healingfoundation.org.au/about-us/our-history/

Pappé, I. (2011). *The forgotten Palestinians: A history of Palestinians in Israel.* New Haven, CT: Yale University Press.

Parameswaran, R. (1996). Coverage of 'bride burning' in the 'Dallas Observer': A cultural analysis of the 'Other.' *Frontiers: A Journal of Women's Studies, 16*(2/3), 69–100. doi: 10.2307/3346804

Park, H. & Finch, A. (2016). Promoting intercultural sensitivity through New Korean Cinema films. *East Asia Journal of Popular Culture, 2*(2), 169–191. doi: 10.1386/eapc.2.2.169_1

Parry, S. (1995). Identifying the process: The removal of 'half-caste' children from Aboriginal mothers. *Aboriginal History, 19*, 141–153.

Passi, C. (2013). National Sorry Day: An important part of healing. *Reconciliation Australia.* https://www.reconciliation.org.au/national-sorry-day-an-important-part-of-healing/

Pedersen, P. (1995). *The Five Stages of Culture Shock: Critical incidents around the world.* Westport, CT: Greenwood.

Phinney, J. S. (1989). Stages of ethnic identity development in minority group adolescents. *The Journal of Early Adolescence, 9*(1–2), 34–49. doi: 10.1177/0272431689091004

Pilkington, D. (1996). *Follow the rabbit-Proof Fence.* St Lucia, Qld: University of Queensland Press.

Posthuma, R., White, G., Dworkin, J., Yánez, O. & Stella Swift, M. (2006). Conflict resolution styles between co-workers in US and Mexican cultures. *International Journal of Conflict Management, 17*(3), 242–260. doi: 10.1108/10444060610742344

Rabinow, P. (2003). Ordonnance, discipline, regulation: Some reflections on urbanism. In: S. M. Low & D. Lawrence-Zuniga (Eds.), *The anthropology of space and place: Locating culture* (pp. 353–362). Malden, MA: Blackwell Publishing.

Radford, J. (2019). Key findings about U.S. immigrants. *Pew Research Center.* https://www.pewresearch.org/fact-tank/2019/06/17/key-findings-about-u-s-immigrants/

Rainnie, A. Barrett, R., Burgess, J. & Connell, J. (2008) Call centres, the networked economy and the value chain. *Journal of Industrial Relations, 50*(2), 195–208.

Ramasubramanian, S. (2011). Television exposure, model minority portrayals, and Asian-American stereotypes: An exploratory study. *Journal of Intercultural Communication, 26*(1), 1–17.

Reich, R. (1990, January-February). Who is us? *Harvard Business Review,* 1–3. https://hbr.org/1990/01/who-is-us

Rieder, J. (2008). *Colonialism and the emergence of Science Fiction.* Middleton, CT: Wesleyan University Press.

Riklis, E. (Director). (2014). *A Borrowed Identity* [Film]. Strand Releasing.

Ritzer, G. & Lair, C. (2008). The globalisation of nothing and the outsourcing of service work. in: L. MacDonald & M. Korczynski (Eds.), *Service Work: Critical Perspectives* (pp. 31–51). London: Routledge.

Rogers, J. (2014). The national curriculum – knowing the truth about Australia's history. *Reconciliation Australia*. https://www.reconciliation.org.au/the-national-curriculum-knowing-the-truth-about-australias-history/

Rothstein, R. (2017). America is still segregated. We need to be honest about why. *The Guardian*. https://www.theguardian.com/commentisfree/2017/may/16/segregation-us-neighborhoods-reasons

Rouhana, N. N. (1997). *Palestinian citizens in an ethnic Jewish state: Identities in conflict*. New Haven, CT: Yale University Press.

Rouhana, N. N. & Bar-Tal, Dl. (1998). Psychological dynamics of intractable ethnonational conflicts: The Israeli- Palestinian case. *American Psychologist* 53(7), 761–770. doi: 10.1037/0003-066X.53.7.761

Sadri, G. & Rahmatian, M. (2003). Resolving conflict: Examining ethnic-racial and gender differences. *Equal Opportunities International, 22*(2), 25–39. doi: 10.1108/02610150310787342

Said, E. W. (1978). *Orientalism: Western conceptions of the Orient*. New York: Vintage.

Sharma, P., Waheed, S., Nguyen, V., Stepick L., Orellana, R., Katz, L., Kim, S. & Lapira, K. (2018). *Nail file: A study of Nail Salon Workers an industry in the United States*. UCLA Labor Center and California Healthy Nail Salon Collaborative. https://www.labor.ucla.edu/wp-content/uploads/2018/11/NAILFILES_FINAL.pdf

Sherman, C., Mendoza, M. & Burke, G. (2019). U.S. held record number of migrant children in custody in 2019. *AP News* (online). https://apnews.com/015702afdb4d4fbf85cf5070cd2c6824

Sorrells, K. (2016). *Intercultural communication: Globalization and social justice* (2nd edition). Thousand Oaks, CA: SAGE.

Sprigg, C. A., Smith, P. R. & Jackson, P. R. (2003). Psychological risk factors in call centers: An evaluation of work design and well being (Research Report 169). Prepared by the *University of Sheffield, Health and Safety Laboratory and UMIST for the Health and Safety Executive*, pp. I-81. https://www.hse.gov.uk/research/rrpdf/rr169.pdf

Taylor, P. (2012). *Governance, Labour and the global Call Centre Value Chain*. https://pdfs.semanticscholar.org/ff00/1ae395f5f0182c82ce40d530fd7e3fbe3c15.pdf?_ga=2.207484560.2038101287.1584746479-407342213.1584746479

Taylor, P. & Bain, P. (2005). 'India calling to the far away towns': The call centre labour process and globalization. *Work, Employment and Society, 19*(2), 261–282. doi: 10.1177/0950017005053170

Temple Purohit. (2019). Goddess Kali-The dark mother. *Temple Purohit: Destination for all your spiritual needs*. https://www.templepurohit.com/goddess-kali-the-dark-mother/

Thayer, S. M., Updegraff, K. A. & Delgado, M. Y. (2008). Conflict resolution in Mexican American adolescents' friendships: Links with culture, gender and friendship quality. *Journal of Youth and Adolescence, 37*(7), 783–797. doi: 10.1007/s10964-007-9253-8

The Islamic veil across Europe. (2018). *BBC News*. https://www.bbc.com/news/world-europe-13038095

Tilbrook, L. (2007). Nyungar tradition: Glimpses of Aborigines of south-western Australia 1829-1914. *Australian Institute of Aboriginal and Torres Strait Islander Studies* (AIATSIS). (original published by University of Western Australia Press, 1983). http://aiatsis.gov.au/sites/default/files/catalogue_resources/m0022954.pdf.

Ting-Toomey, S. (1994). Managing intercultural conflicts effectively. In: L. Samovar & R. Porter (Eds.), *Intercultural Communication: A Reader* (7th edition, pp. 360–372). Belmont, CA: Wadsworth.

Ting-Toomey, S. (1999). *Communicating Across Cultures*. New York: Guilford.

Ting-Toomey, S. (2005). The matrix of face: An updated face-negotiation theory. In: W. B. Gudykunst (Ed.), *Theorizing about Intercultural Communication* (pp. 211–234). Thousand Oaks, CA: Sage.

Ting-Toomey, S. & Kurogi, A. (1998). Facework competence in intercultural conflict: An updated face-negotiation theory. *International Journal of Intercultural Relations, 22*, 187–225. doi: 10.1016/S0147-1767(98)00004-2

Ting-Toomey, S. & Oetzel, J. G. (2001). *Managing Intercultural Conflict Effectively*. Thousand Oaks, CA: Sage.

Triandis, H. (1995). *Individualism and collectivism*. Boulder, CO: Westview.

Tulloch, J. (1982). *Australian cinema: Industry, narrative and meaning*. Sydney: George Allen & Unwin.

Turan, K. (2015). Review: 'A Borrowed Identity' shows life in Israel from an Arab's point of view. *Los Angeles Times*. https://www.latimes.com/entertainment/movies/la-et-mn-a-borrowed-identity-review-20150702-column.html

Urios-Aparisi, E. (2016). Stormy weather: An intercultural approach to the water metaphor in cinema. In: K. Fahlenbrach (Ed.), *Embodied Metaphors in Film, Television, and Video Games: Cognitive Approaches* (1st edition, pp. 67–81). New York: Routledge.

Varela, J. R. (2018). Trump's border wall was never just about security. It's meant to remind all Latinos that we're unwelcome. *NBC News*. https://www.nbcnews.com/think/opinion/trump-s-border-wall-was-never-just-about-security-it-ncna952011

Ward, C., Bochner, S. & Furnham, A. (2001). *The psychology of Culture Shock*. New York: Routledge.

Ward, C., Okura, Y., Kennedy, A. & Kojima, T. (1998). The U-curve on trial: A longitudinal study of psychological adjustment and sociocultural adjustment during cross-cultural transition. *International Journal of Intercultural Relations, 22*(3), 277–291. doi: 10.1016/S0147-1767(98)00008-X

Warren, R. (2019). U.S. undocumented population continued to fall from 2016 to 2017, and visa overstays significantly exceeded illegal crossings for the seventh consecutive year. *Center for Migration Studies*. https://cmsny.org/publications/essay-2017-undocumented-and-overstays/

Weissberg, J. (2014). Film review: 'Dancing Arabs.' *Variety*. https://variety.com/2014/film/festivals/film-review-dancing-arabs-1201277842/

Weitz, C. (Director). (2011). *A Better Life* [Film]. Lime Orchard Productions.

Williams, M. G. & Korn, J. U. (2017). Othering and fear: Cultural values and Hiro's race in Thomas & Friends' Hero of the Rails. *Journal of Communication Inquiry, 41*(1), 22–41. doi: 10.1177/0196859916656836

Winant, H. (2001). *The world is a ghetto: Race and Democracy Since World War II.* New York: Basic Books.

Winkelman, M. (1994). Cultural shock and adaptation. *Journal of Counseling and Development, 73,* 121–127. doi: 10.1002/j.1556-6676.1994.tb01723.x

Wooden, W. S., Kawasaki, H. & Mayeda, R. (1983). Lifestyles and identity maintenance among gay Japanese-American males. *Alternative Lifestyles, 5,* 236–243. doi: 10.1007/BF01082992

World Migration Report 2020 (2019). *International Organization for Migration.* https://publications.iom.int/system/files/pdf/wmr_2020.pdf

"World's population is increasingly urban with more than half living in urban areas." (2014). *United Nations.* http://www.un.org/en/development/desa/news/population/world-urbanization-prospects-2014.html

Wu, J. (2003). From "long yang" and "dui shi" to tongzhi: Homosexuality in China. *Journal of Gay and Lesbian Psychotherapy, 7*(1–2), 117–143. doi: 10.1300/J236v07n01_08

Yeung, R. (2015). *Front cover* [Motion picture]. United States: NewVoice Production.

Yiftachel, O. (2009). Critical theory and 'gray space': Mobilization of the colonized. *City, 13*(2–3), 240–256. doi: 10.1080/13604810902982227

Zauzmer, J. & McMillan, K. (2018). Sessions cites Bible passage used to defend slavery in defense of separating immigrant families. *Washington Post.* https://www.washingtonpost.com/news/acts-of-faith/wp/2018/06/14/jeff-sessions-points-to-the-bible-in-defense-of-separating-immigrant-families/?noredirect=on&utm_term=.31858184205c

Index

Aboriginal and Torres Strait Islander children, 61
The Aboriginal and Torres Strait Islander Healing Foundation, 70
aboriginal motherhood, 66
Aboriginal Protection Act, 60
acculturation, 14–15. *See* intercultural adaptation
acculturative marginalization. *See* marginalization
acculturative stress, 23–24, 99
adjustment, 14, 99
The African Doctor, 3, 141; Anne's adoption of separation, 22; change in France's economic system, depiction of, 12; construction of the 'Other,' 10; culture shock and cultural adjustment, 3; depiction of migration, 10; intercultural adaptation, 10, 13–16; issues of racialization of migrants, 3, 9–10, 25–27; migrant network, 27–28; mode of mitigating migrant-host tensions, 22; race-based isolation, 19; Seyolo's attempts at assimilation, 21; story of Kamini's family, 3, 9, 12–16; U-curve of cultural adaptation, analysis of, 12–16
Afro-Belgian identity, 10

Amazon Prime, 6
American identity, 131
American pop-culture symbols, 96
American work-family ethic, 96
anticipation, 14, 17
Asian American identity, 130
assimilation, 15, 21
assimilationist policies for Aboriginal people, 60
attitudes toward self, 79
Australia, 58
Australian Curriculum, 70
Australian national identity, 62–63

Berry, J. W., 99
A Better Life, 3, 141–42; boundaries between immigration and criminalization, 42–43; conflict-managing communication, 38–39; conversation between Carlos and Blasco, 39–40; depiction of intercultural conflict, 45–52; father-son relationship, 3, 31, 40–41; Galindo family's migration challenges, 3, 44, 141–42; Luis' daily life, 41; Luis' movement to collectivistic conflict-resolution strategies, 51; Luis' perceptions of work, 41; migration-related issues,

3, 31; negotiation of culturally different conflict styles, 3; realities of unauthorized immigration, 44; story, 3, 21; unauthorized border crossings, 39–45. *See also* United States, immigration in
biculturalism, 14–15
Blumenbach, 59
borders, 1–2, 15–16, 32, 35, 44–45, 52–53, 63–64, 67–69, 81, 96–98, 117, 142
A Borrowed Identity, 3–4, 73, 142; Arab neighborhood of Jerusalem, 82; depiction of hummus, 82; ethnic conflicts and interpersonal relationships, 86–89; Eyad's identity development, 82–84; Eyad's relationship with Edna, 88–89, 142; fluid movement between Muslim Arab and Jewish cultures, 86; gray spaces, 86; intercultural challenges, 4; minority identity, 85; Naomi and Eyad's relationship, 87–88; Salah's experiences of religious othering, 87; spatial shifts and identity movements, 80–86; story, 4; Yonatan's identity, 81, 84–85, 142
Bracero program, 34
Bringing Them Home report, 70

call center offshoring, 97–98
Cheshire, G., 119
Children for Peace, 75
Chinese American, 4, 123–24, 127, 138
Chinese culture, 119
Chinese ethnic identity, 126–32
Chinese Exclusion Act, 34
Christian missionaries, 59
cinema, 1, 5, 65, 144
collectivism, 35–36
collectivist cultures, 36–37
colonial and postcolonial spaces, 62
conflict-managing communication, 38–39
conformity, 78

Congo Crisis, 10
corporeal movement, 35
COVID-19 global pandemic, 1, 6
criminalization, 34–35, 43, 53
cross-cultural films, 2–5, 116, 144. *See also The African Doctor; A Better Life; A Borrowed Identity; Front Cover; Outsourced; Rabbit-Proof Fence*
cultural adaptations, 2
cultural assimilation, 2
cultural disorientation, 14
cultural hostility, 18
cultural identities, 2, 4, 10–11, 14–15, 21, 24, 39, 49, 51, 58, 64, 74, 108–109, 116, 120, 123–26, 142
cultural integration, 20, 23–24, 121. *See also* Integration
cultural nationalism and nativism, 11
cultural recovery, 19
culture shock, 2, 14, 17–18, 99–100; acculturation phase of, 14–15, 19–20; acculturative stress over, 99; coping stage of, 14–15, 19; elation stage of, 18; four-step process, 14–15; recovery phase of, 14–15, 19

Dancing Arabs, 73, 90
deculturation, 16
Democratic Republic of Congo. *See* Zaire (Republic of Zaire)
deportation of immigrants, 32
depression, 18
diverse value orientations, 2
diversity, 1

economic globalization, 96–98
Eisenhower, 33
electronic sweatshop, 98
ethnic conflicts and interpersonal relationships, 86–89
ethnic discrimination, 76
ethnic identity, 15, 74, 78, 86, 123, 126, 128–29, 132–34, 137; development model, 78

ethnicity, 74
ethnicity-based organizations, 34
ethnonational conflicts, 75
ethnoreligious identity, 73

face negotiation theory, 38
facework, 3, 31–32, 35–38, 48–51, 141
familial communication, 36–37
Follow the Rabbit-Proof Fence, 57
Foucault, Michel, 61
France, 11–13, 17; civic integration program, 12–13; discriminatory laws, 12; economy, 12; integration of migrants in, 12
French immigration policy, 12
Front Cover, 4, 119, 139, 142–43; embracing and reburial of identity, 135–38; Gus' mocking gestures, 128–29; movement to embrace, 132–35; negotiation of different identities, 126–32, 143; Ning's ascription of Chinese identity on Ryan, 131–32; Ning's character, 129–31; Ryan meeting with Ning, 127; Ryan's identity, 126–27; Ryan's reaction to racist remarks, 128; story, 4, 119–20
frustration, 18

Garimara, Doris Pilkington, 3; *Follow the Rabbit-Proof Fence*, 3
gay identity, 126, 131–32
Genocide Convention, 65
global capitalism, 4, 143
globalization, 1–2, 4, 15, 35–36, 39, 74, 95–98, 102
global movements, in films, 2
gray space, 77–78
Green Line, 75, 91n1

Hart-Cellar Act, 1965, 34
hierarchy of difference, 59
Hindu cultural symbols, 96, 109–13, 117
Hofstede, Geert, 36–37
Holi, 96, 104, 112, 114

hostility, 18

illegal border crossings, 32
Immigration and Naturalization Service, 34
immigration industrial complex, 3, 31–35, 141; definition, 33; others, 34
India-US trade relations, 97
individualism, 35–36
individualist cultures, 36–37
integration, 2, 10–15, 20–24, 121
intercultural adaptation, 10, 99; interpersonal and individual dimensions of, 14; in migrant movements, 13–16
intercultural awareness, 4
intercultural communication, 2, 5–6, 58–59, 69, 71, 74, 90, 96, 116, 120, 124, 130, 141–44
intercultural communication competence, 124
intercultural conflict, 131; definition, 35; migrant families and, 39; relationship between communication and culture, 36. *See also A Better Life*
intercultural transformation, 16
interdependent cultures, 36
international migration, 99
interpersonal relationships, 53, 74, 86–90, 119
intractable ethnonational conflict, 75
Israel-Palestine conflict, 4, 74–76, 86, 142

Jeffcoat, John, 4
Johnson-Reed Act, 34

Kali, Goddess, 96, 109–10, 117
Kannyo, Edward, 11
Kanopy, 6
Kashua, Sayed, 4; *Dancing Arabs*, 4
Kipling, Rudyard, 59

Lefebvre, H., 77
Lionheart, 144

Lysgaard, Sverre, 14, 99

marginalization, 22–23
marginalized migrant, 15
marginalized people, 78
Marly-Gomont, 9–10, 12, 16–20, 23–24
Mexican culture, 38
migrant adaptation process, 99
migrant–host relationships, 15–16; acculturative marginalization, 22–23; cross-cultural communication in, 16; cultural integration, 23–24; in-group identity and maintenance, 21
migrant network, 16, 27–28
migration, 10; culture shock and cultural adjustment, 3, 10; international, 99; issues of racialization of migrants, 3, 9–10; sojourning, 98–101
military industrial complex (MIC), 33
minority identity, 78
minority identity development (MID), 78–80
mobile-based streaming services, 6
Mobutu, Joseph Désiré, 10–11
Moore River settlement, 61
mutual-face, 38. See also facework

National Sorry Day, 70
Netflix, 6
Noyce, Phillip, 3, 57

Oberg, Kalvero, 14, 17–18, 99–100
Occidental, 59
offshoring, 97; call center, 97–98; limitations, 97
Oslo Agreements, 1993, 76
other-face, 38, 48. See also facework
others/othering, 10, 13, 31, 34, 88; coethnic othering, 130; racial, 18, 57, 142
Outsourced, 4, 99, 142; cultural adjustments in, 107–16; cultural representation, 111–15, 143; depiction of Mumbai streets, 107–8; story, 95; Todd Anderson's movements, 95, 101–7; Todd's experience of culture shock, 108–11; Todd's transformation, 115–16, 143; U-curve model of adaptation, 20, 98–100, 114, 116, 143
outsourcing of services, 4, 96–98

Palestine Liberation Organization, 74
Palestinian *Intifada* (insurrection against Israeli occupation), 73, 76
Palestinian nationalism, 76
Parasite, 144
patriarchy, 66
Picnic at Hanging Rock, 65
Pilkington, Doris, 57. See also Garimara, Doris Pilkington
politeness theory, 37
Popular Movement of the Revolution party (*Mouvement Populaire de la Révolution*), 10
postcolonizing, 62
prejudice, 25–27
prison industrial complex (PIC), 33

Rabbit-Proof Fence, 3–4, 57, 142; assimilation, 3, 59–60; cultural breach and countermobility, 3; depiction of space, 61–63; girls and girls' movements, 67–69, 71; movements in, 58; race and racial hierarchy, 58–60; racial superiority in, 65; references to othering and captivity, 64; restrictions on movement within spaces, 61; role of patriarchy, 66–67; separating families, 60–61; story, 3; symbolic use of fence, 3, 58, 67–69, 142; Whiteness and half-castes, 64–67
race, 13, 18, 58–60, 125
race and racial hierarchy, 58–60; Eurocentric racist mindsets, 66
racialization, 25–27; of migrants, 3, 9–10, 13; racist sense of social hierarchy, 25
racialized social hierarchy, 62–63

racial othering, 18, 57, 142; colonization and, 58–60
racial purity, 59
racial segregation, 3
Rambaldi, Julien, 3, 9
Riklis, Eran, 4, 73

segregation, 15
Seko, Mobutu Sésé, 9, 11. *See also* Mobutu, Joseph Désiré
self-face, 38. *See also* facework
separation mode of acculturation, 15, 22
sexuality and sexual identities, in Asian And Asian American cultures, 4–5, 120–23, 143. *See also Front Cover*
Simon, Roger L., 3
social construction, 63
social mobility and movements, 2, 52–53
social production of space, 63
sojourner, 99–100
sojourning, 4, 98–101, 142–43
Sorrells, Kathryn, 14, 58–59, 95–96
South Korean culture, 144
space: colonial and postcolonial, 62; gray, 77–78; as political, 77–78; position/history/value, 77; social production of, 63; and social relations, 63; strategic uses of, 63; in terms of land and land rights, 62
spatial and identity movements, 76–80
spatial elasticity, 98
Stolen Generation, 3, 64, 66, 69–70
strategic space, 63

transnational companies, 97

U-curve model of adaptation, 14, 16–20, 96, 99, 114, 116, 143
unauthorized immigrant labor, 32–33
UN declaration of 1947, 75
United States, 2044, 1
United States, immigration in, 32–33; deportation of immigrants, 32; illegal border crossings, 32; immigrant labor, 32; link with criminalization, 34; national origins quota system, 34; policies, 34. *See also A Better Life*

Weitz, Chris, 3
West Australian Aborigines Act of 1905, 60–61
The White Man's Burden, 59
white savior (s), 59–60, 65–66
White supremacy, 59
Wilson, Sir Ronald, 65

Yeung, Ray, 4
YouTube, 6

Zaire (Republic of Zaire), 3, 9, 11, 17, 19–20, 27; Africanization of names, 11; civil unrest and ethnic wars, 10; industrialization and modernization, 11; Mobutu era, 10–11; in 1970s, 10–11; race-based hierarchies in, 10–11
Zairian-French identity, 24
Zairianization, 11
Zairian nationalism, 11
Zantoko, Anne, 12
Zantoko, Kamini, 3, 9
Zantoko, Seyolo, 9

About the Authors

The authors of this book come from very different cultural backgrounds yet share similar research interests, and have frequently collaborated on projects involving popular media and intercultural communication, visual cultures, mobility, and social change. Based on their experiences and shared interests studying, researching, and teaching intercultural communication and media in different cultural spaces, the authors are delighted to share their critical-cultural scholarship with readers.

Ishani Mukherjee grew up in Kolkata, India, in a Bengali-Hindu household. She is lucky to have had experiences living, studying, and working in India and the United States, and travelling to several European and Asian countries. Her doctoral degree is in Communication from the University of Illinois at Chicago, and she is a social science and critical-cultural scholar. Presently, Ishani is a faculty member at the University of Illinois at Chicago, and has previously taught at Northern Illinois University. Her work has been published in edited volumes and academic journals like *Studies in South Asian Film and Media, Convergence, Connexions*, and *Ada: A Journal of Gender, New Media, and Technology*. Ishani lives in Chicagoland, with her partner, son, and their dog. Ishani likes singing and playing music, watching movies, yoga, trying cuisines from different parts of the world, and interior designing.

Maggie Griffith Williams grew up in Pennsylvania, United States, in a Protestant, Irish American family. She has had the privilege of living, studying, working, and traveling in the United States, the Caribbean, and Europe. She received her doctorate in Communication from the University of Illinois at Chicago and is an interpretive and critical-cultural scholar. Currently, Maggie is a faculty member at Northeastern University in Boston and a visiting scholar at Fordham University in New York City. She has also served as a faculty member at the University of Illinois at Chicago and at Ramapo College of New Jersey. Her research has been published in academic journals such as *Mobile Media & Communication*, *Journal of Communication Inquiry*, *Convergence*, and *First Monday*. Maggie lives in New York with her husband and their two boys. She enjoys traveling, going to the movies, fitness, eating food from different cultures, and walking in cities around the world.

The authors were inspired to write this book based on their love of cinema and their shared experiences of teaching intercultural communication and media studies. Both authors have found success in using film as a pedagogical and practical tool to explain complex communication and media concepts, to advance student comprehension, and to achieve learning outcomes.

www.ingramcontent.com/pod-product-compliance
Lightning Source LLC
Chambersburg PA
CBHW032150010526
44111CB00035B/1432